THE SPECIAL OPERATIONS EXECUTIVE IN BURMA

CW01500748

Jungle Warfare and Intelligence Gathering in World War II

RICHARD DUCKETT

BLOOMSBURY ACADEMIC
LONDON • NEW YORK • OXFORD • NEW DELHI • SYDNEY

BLOOMSBURY ACADEMIC
Bloomsbury Publishing Plc
50 Bedford Square, London, WC1B 3DP, UK
1385 Broadway, New York, NY 10018, USA

BLOOMSBURY, BLOOMSBURY ACADEMIC and the Diana logo
are trademarks of Bloomsbury Publishing Plc

First published 2017 by I.B. Tauris & Co. Ltd.
Paperback edition published 2019 by Bloomsbury Academic

ISBN: HB: 978-1-7845-3912-2
PB: 978-1-7883-1988-1
ePDF: 978-1-7867-3272-9
eBook: 978-1-7867-2272-0

Series: International Library of Twentieth Century History, volume 106

Typeset by OKS Prepress Services, Chennai, India

To find out more about our authors and books visit
www.bloomsbury.com and sign up for our newsletters.

Richard Duckett is a lecturer in History at Reading College and a specialist on the Burma Campaign. He holds a BA from the University of Essex, an MA from the University of Reading and a PhD from the Open University. This is his first book.

'Drawing on declassified files, Richard Duckett finally lifts the lid on the exploits in Japanese-occupied Burma of Britain's Special Operations Executive. This is an excellent account of an important but long-hidden chapter of SOE's history, and essential reading for anyone wishing to fully understand Britain's involvement in Burma during World War II and SOE's global contribution to the Allied war effort.'

Roderick Bailey, University of Oxford, SOE Historian

'Long neglected by the prevailing narratives and histories, the experience of guerilla fighters and their officers in Burma in WWII comes alive in Duckett's outstanding new book. No one has previously devoted the necessary days and nights amidst dusty files in the archives, or uncovered the links between the official record and the private memoirs/memories of the key actors. His unique work establishes a new standard for research in this complex field.

It is all here – the suspicious attitude in 1941 of the British military establishment in Asia toward irregular warcraft as planned by SOE, the tension between the American, British, Indian, and Chinese armies, the complicated mobilisation of Kachin, Karen, and Chin fighters (and many others) in small stealth units to fight in 1942–3 against much better-equipped Japanese forces, the total dependence on uncertain air supply, and the gradual development of deep loyalties between foreign and local soldiers, through the deadly risks of combat. They gathered valuable intelligence, as originally intended, but also became ambush-hardened combat units. Thus, they became a model for the future.

Equally important, Duckett skilfully uncovers the complex 1945–50 landscape in which the SOE had to disentangle from the new Burmese state, while many SOE officers, now well-informed, remained alert against a "high policy" in which their former comrades on the "ethnic" frontiers were marginalised (some said "abandoned") by their leaders in London. The stage was thus set for the emergence of more fighting in an indigenous Burmese "cold war" on the Chinese frontier. In some senses that is where we are today, thus giving Duckett's book a disturbing but brilliant contemporary relevance.'

Robert Anderson, Professor at Simon Fraser University, Vancouver

'Although long considered the "forgotten" front, the war in Burma has been receiving increasing attention of late as archival discoveries have raised new questions and required attention to be given to actors at work behind the scenes. The present study of the Special Operations Executive in Burma from 1941 until 1945, drawing upon under-examined archival sources, will change how historians will view the place of the SOE in this campaign, as well as its supposed connections to postwar Burmese ethnic insurgents.

This very important book offers new insights into how the SOE helped to shift the campaign from a miserable defeat in May 1942 to a victorious drive to Rangoon just three years later. Well-written and steady in its analysis, the book will appeal to both the general reader and the military historian. It is certainly a welcome and significant addition to the literature on the Burma Campaign.'

Michael W. Charney, SOAS The University of London

For Kara and Emily, my two wonderful girls

and

In loving memory of my uncle, Sapper Arthur Clifford Wilson,
208 Field Company, 2 Division
21 December 1919–4 October 2002

And the grandfather I never knew, Staff Sergeant Victor Lloyd
Cruttenden, also 208 Field Company, Royal Engineers
29 July 1902–13 March 1952

CONTENTS

NOTE ON TRANSLATION AND TRANSLITERATION

For the sake of clarity, names of places and countries have been spelt as they were used at the time, and how they appear in the documents. For example, Rangoon is used instead of Yangon, and Siam for Thailand. Where Chinese names have been used, the Wade Giles transliteration has been employed rather than the more modern Hanyu Pinyin; hence readers will find Kuomintang as opposed to Guomindang. In addition, soldiers' ranks have been given for the time discussed, rather than their final rank.

ABBREVIATIONS

ABDA Command	American, British, Dutch, Australian Command
AFO	Anti-Fascist Organisation
AFPFL	Anti-Fascist People's Freedom League
ALFSEA	Allied Land Forces, South East Asia
AVG	American Volunteer Group
BCS	Burma Country Section
BCMS	Bible Churchman's Missionary Society
BDA	Burma Defence Army
BFF	Burma Frontier Force
BIA	Burma Independence Army
BNA	Burma National Army
Burif	Burma rifles
CAS(B)	Civil Affairs Service (Burma)
CBI	China, Burma, India
CCAO	Chief Civil Affairs Officer
CEF	Chinese Expeditionary Force
C-in-C	Commander in Chief
COS	Chief of Staff
Det. 101	Detachment 101, the American OSS unit in Burma
DMI	Directorate Military Intelligence
DSO	Distinguished Service Order
EWS(B)	Eastern Warfare School (Bengal)
EWS(C)	Eastern Warfare School (Ceylon)
EWS(I)	Eastern Warfare School (India)
FEM	Far Eastern Mission

FIC	French Indochina
FO	Foreign Office
Force 136	The cover name for SOE's India Mission from March 1944
GOC	General Officer Commanding
GSI	General Service Intelligence
GSI(K)	The cover name for SOE's India Mission until March 1944
HMG	His Majesty's Government
IM	India Mission, the SOE office set up in India in 1941
INA	Indian National Army
ISLD	Inter-Services Liaison Department, cover name for the Secret Intelligence Service
KDF	Kokang Defence Force
KNDO	Karen National Defence Organisation
KNLA	Karen National Liberation Army
MPAJA	Malayan People's Anti-Japanese Army
NCO	Non-Commissioned Officer
OM	Oriental Mission
OSS	Office of Strategic Services
PBF	Patriotic Burmese Forces
P-Division	Priorities Division
P Force	Peacock Force
PVO	People's Volunteer Organisation
Q	Quartermaster and therefore stores
SAC	Supreme Allied Commander
SACSEA	Supreme Allied Commander, South East Asia
SEAC	South East Asia Command
SEI	School of Eastern Interpreters
SIS	Secret Intelligence Service, MI6
SOE	Special Operations Executive
STS	Special Training School
VJ Day	Victory over Japan Day
WO	War Office
W/T	Wireless Transmitter

LIST OF ILLUSTRATIONS

Maps

Tables

Plates

who never swears', and sometimes 'Pa Bren Gun' because of his 'complete mastery over this favourite weapon of his'. Photograph courtesy of Simon Leney.

Plate 14 Lots of Bren Guns on display at the *Mongoose* Victory Parade, October 1945. Photograph courtesy of Simon Leney.

Plate 15 Lysander over the Burmese jungle. Like in Europe, the Lysander did sterling work for SOE in Burma. Photograph courtesy of Simon Leney.

Plate 16 *The Daily Worker*, Wednesday 22 December 1948 'Britons in Burma Rising Plot'. Headlines about the two former Force 136 officers, Tulloch and Campbell, and their alleged postwar support for the Karen against the government of the Union of Burma. Source: The National Archives, FO 371/69513.

ACKNOWLEDGEMENTS

There have been many people who have helped make the completion of this book possible, but none more so than my wife Kara and my daughter Emily; losing a husband and a daddy to the study was tough at times. Thank you for your support and love. My thanks must go next to my PhD supervisor, Dr Karl Hack. I know I must have had you pulling your hair out on occasion, but when I did, you never let on. Your professionalism throughout was exemplary and very much appreciated. You taught me such a lot. Thanks also to Dr Annika Mombauer, my second supervisor, who was always there to steady the boat and provide welcome commentary, support and encouragement. Many thanks must go to Steven Kippax for invaluable assistance; a man always ready and able to help. Through the Special Operations Executive group he created, many opportunities were made possible which have contributed a great deal to this work, so my thanks must also go to the members of our SOE community who have helped with queries over the years, providing such a wealth of specialist knowledge. Special thanks to Dr Rod Bailey for agreeing to be my external examiner, and whose studies of SOE in Albania and Italy have been such a source of guidance. Acknowledgements would not be complete without recognising the time and assistance given by the following, whose fathers served with SOE in Burma: Patricia Anderson and her husband Rodney, Sarah Houston, Priscilla Church and her mother Margaret Bennett, Simon Leney, Fliss Shaw, Duncan Gilmour and Simon Battersby. Thanks also to my interviewees, some of whom have, sadly, since passed away. Thanks to Tomasz Hoskins at I.B.Tauris. Lastly, to my mum and dad, whose love and support is always there.

TIMELINE OF THE WAR IN BURMA

1941

7 December: The Japanese attacked Pearl Harbor and Southeast Asia.
11 December: Victoria Point in southern Burma occupied by the Japanese.
23 December: Rangoon bombed.
25 December: Rangoon bombed.

1942

15 January: Main Japanese invasion of Burma.
15 February: Singapore surrendered.
23 February: Disaster at the Sittang Bridge.
8 March: Japanese occupied Rangoon.
1 May: Japanese occupied Mandalay.
10 May: British forces crossed the Chindwin heading for India.
17 December: First Arakan campaign began.

1943

8 February: First Chindit operation (Operation *Longcloth*) launched from Imphal.
11 May: Close of first Arakan campaign.

25 August: South East Asia Command (SEAC) formed.

7 October: Mountbatten, Supreme Allied Commander SEAC, arrived in New Delhi.

30 November: Second Arakan campaign began.

1944

5 February: Japanese feint in the Arakan.

5 March: Second Chindit campaign (Operation *Thursday*).

6 March: Japanese offensive against India began.

4 April: Japanese attacked Kohima.

22 June: Road between Kohima and Imphal re-opened.

Early July: Japanese began retreat from Imphal and Kohima.

8 November: Mountbatten ordered a third offensive in the Arakan.

2 December: XIV Army advanced to the Chindwin River.

1945

12 February: XIV Army crossed the Irrawaddy.

3 March: XIV Army recaptured Meiktila.

20 March: XIV Army recaptured Mandalay.

2 May: Landings in Rangoon (Operation *Dracula*).

July and August: Japanese attempted to break out of central Burma.

6 and 9 August: Atomic bombs dropped on Japan.

14 August: Japanese surrendered.

15 August: Victory over Japan (VJ) Day.

Map 1 Burma, 1942. Source: Clayton Newell, *Burma 1942*, US Army Center of Military History, January 1995.

Map 2 Ethnicity in Burma. Source: The Rohingya League for Democracy, Burma.

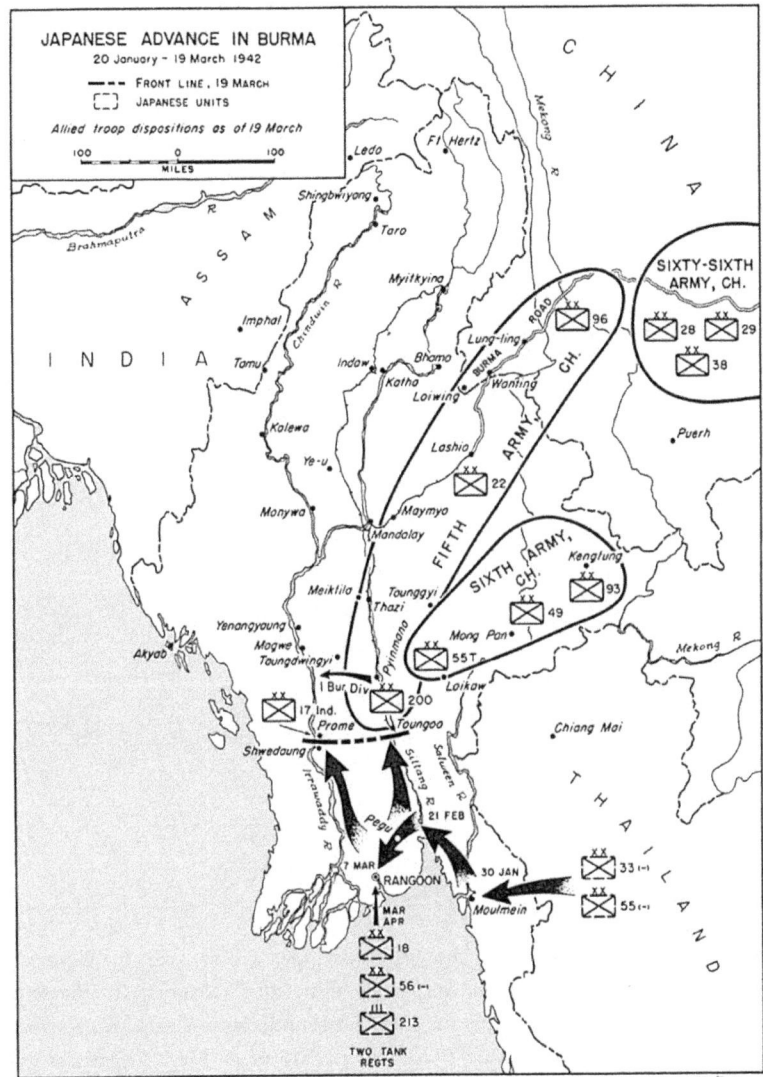

Map 3   The Japanese Advance through Burma, January – May 1942, with hook via Mawchi to Lashio highlighted. Source: Adapted from Dennis Richards and Hilary St George Saunders, *The Royal Air Force 1939–1945: Vol. II, The Fight Avails* (London: HMSO, 1954).

Map 4 Northern Burma, showing Fort Hertz and area of Japanese occupation. Source: Adapted from map entitled 'Transportation System 1942–1943', in Charles Romanus and Riley Sunderland, *United States Army in World War II: China-Burma-India Theater* (Location: Dept. of the Army, Office of the Chief of Military History, 1953).

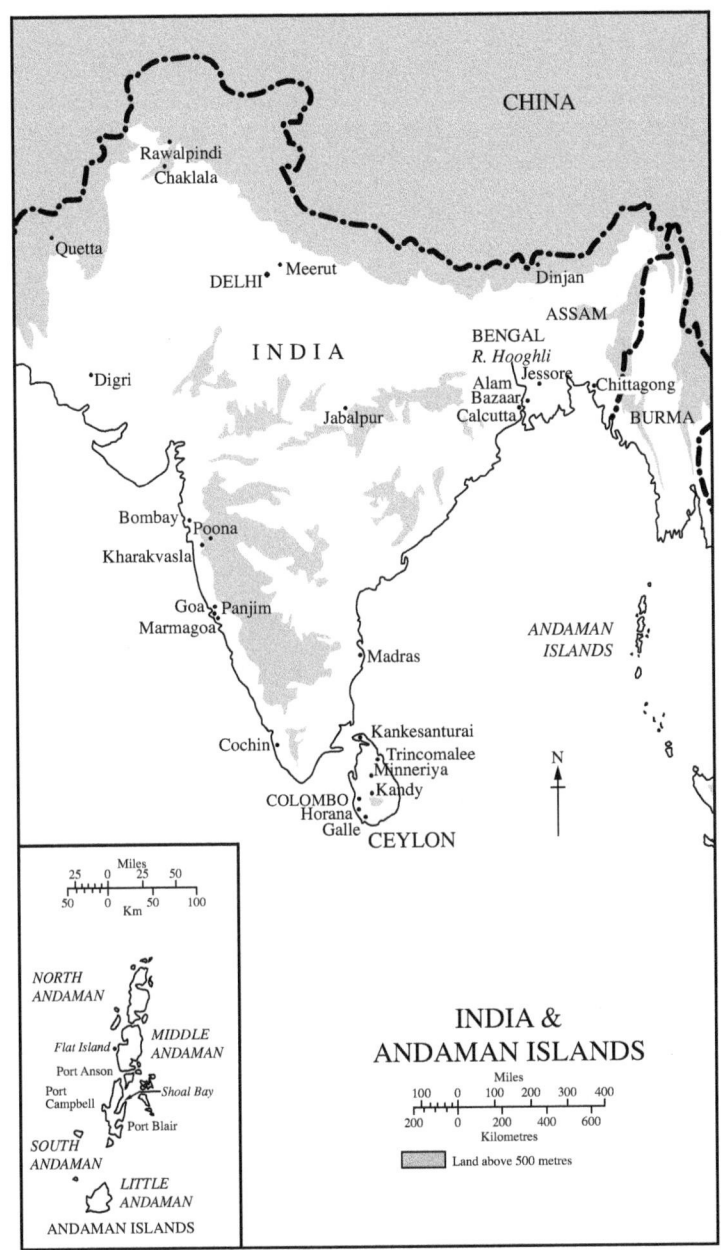

Map 5 India Mission training locations.

Map 6 Kokang territory, Operation *Spiers*.

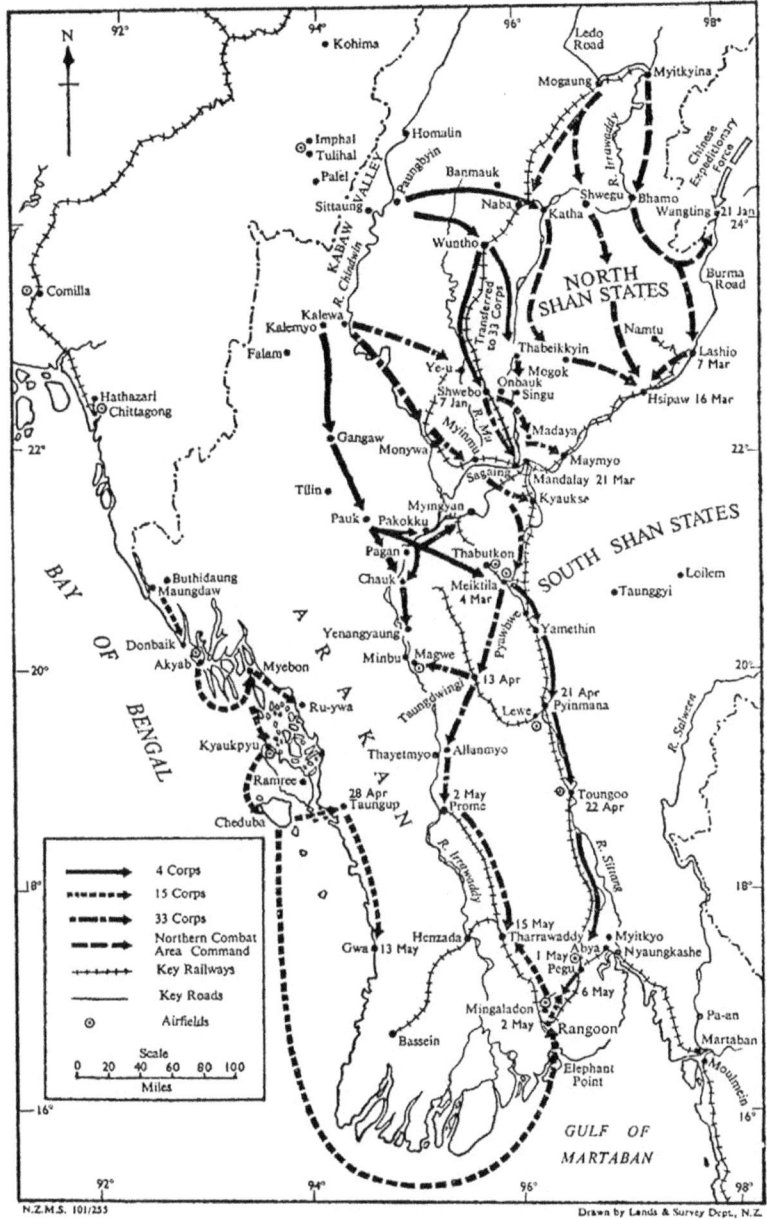

Map 7 The Reconquest of Burma, November 1944–May 1945. Source: Wing Commander H.L. Thompson, *New Zealanders with the Royal Air Force.*

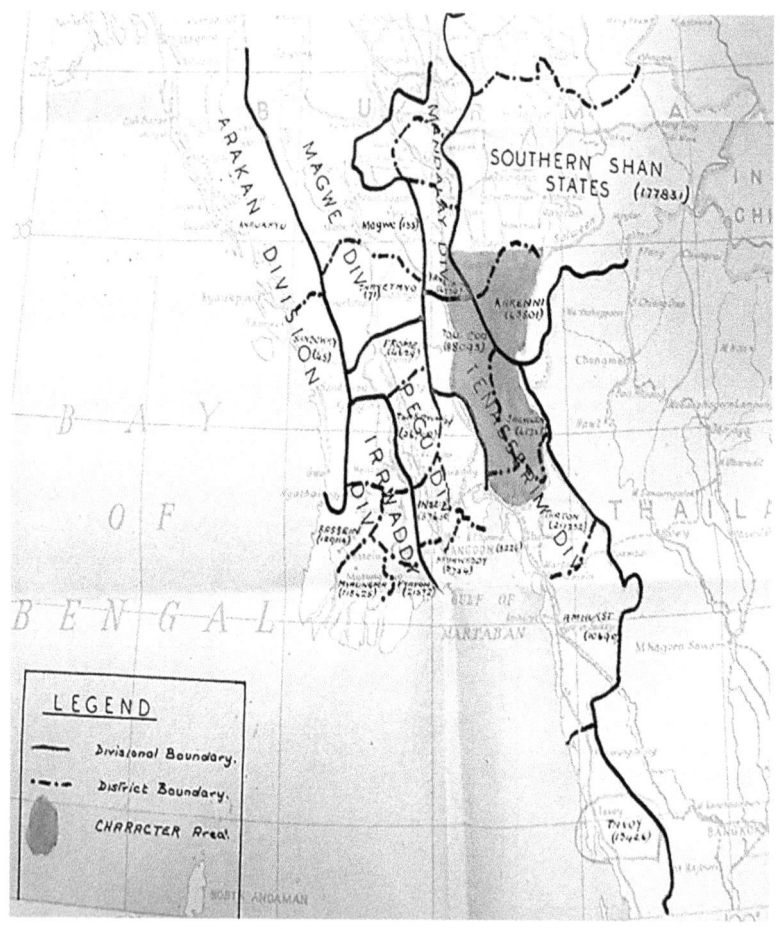

Map 8 The *Character* area of operations, 1945. Source: Adapted from The National Archives, HS 1/12.

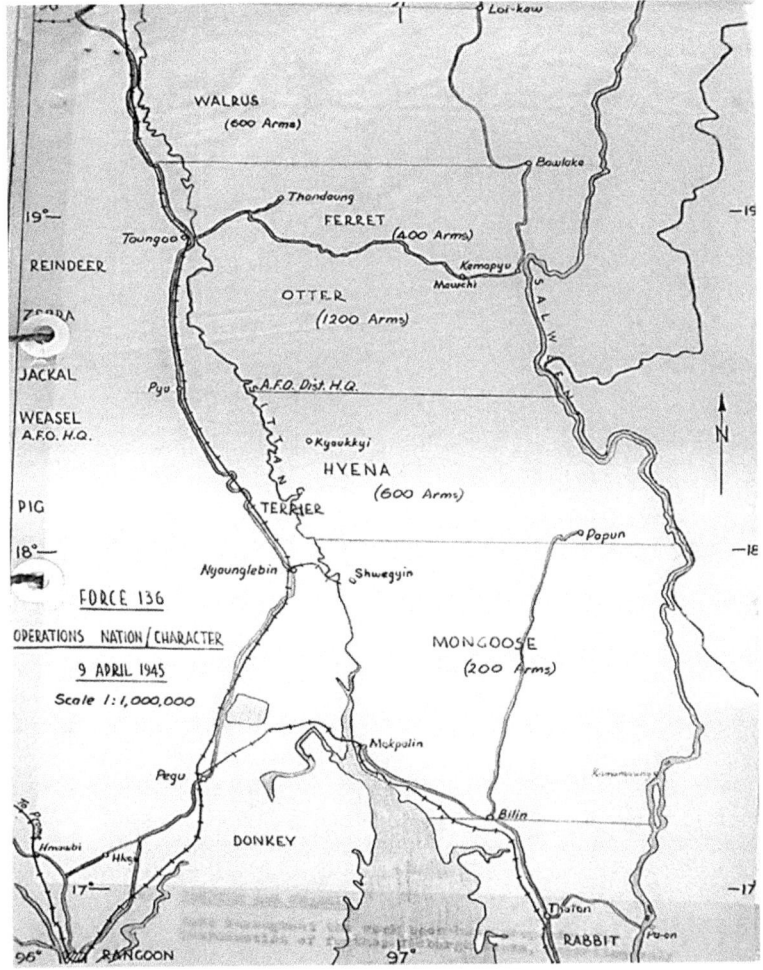

Map 9 Force 136 Operations *Nation/Character* 9 April 1945, showing arms distributed to Karens. Source: Adapted from The National Archives, HS 1/213.

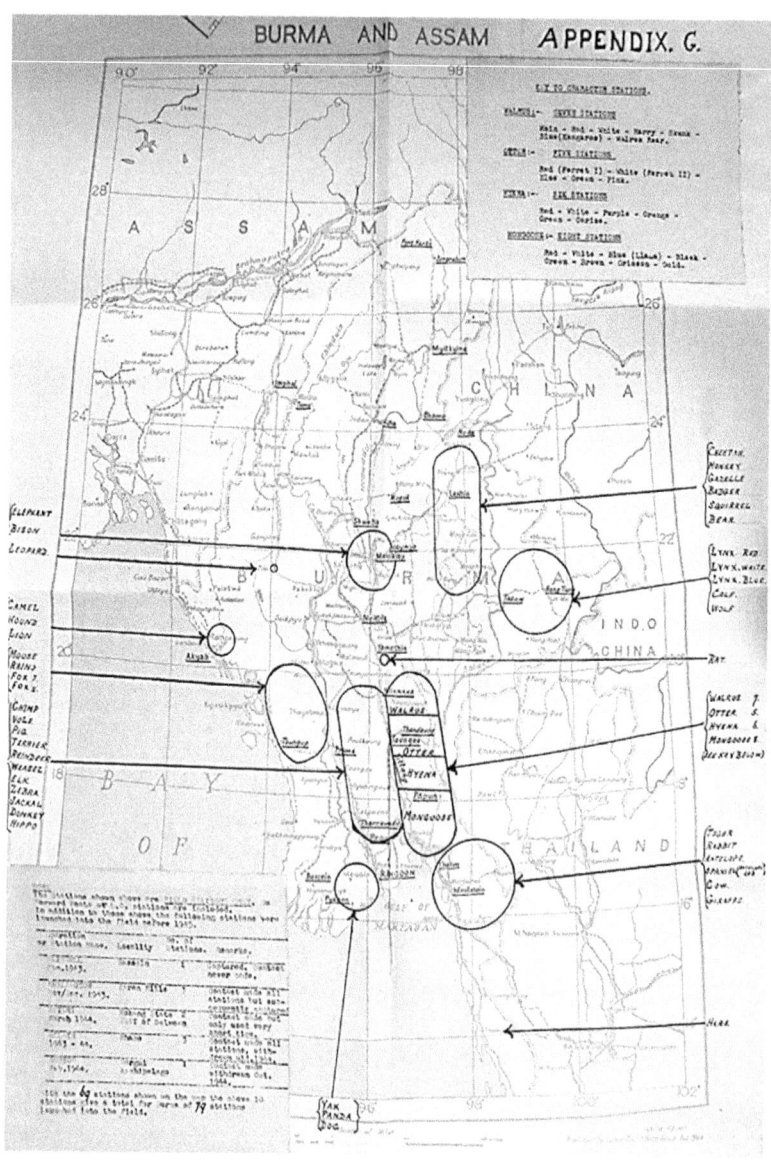

Map 10   SOE operations in Burma, 1945. Source: adapted from The
National Archives, HS 7/104.

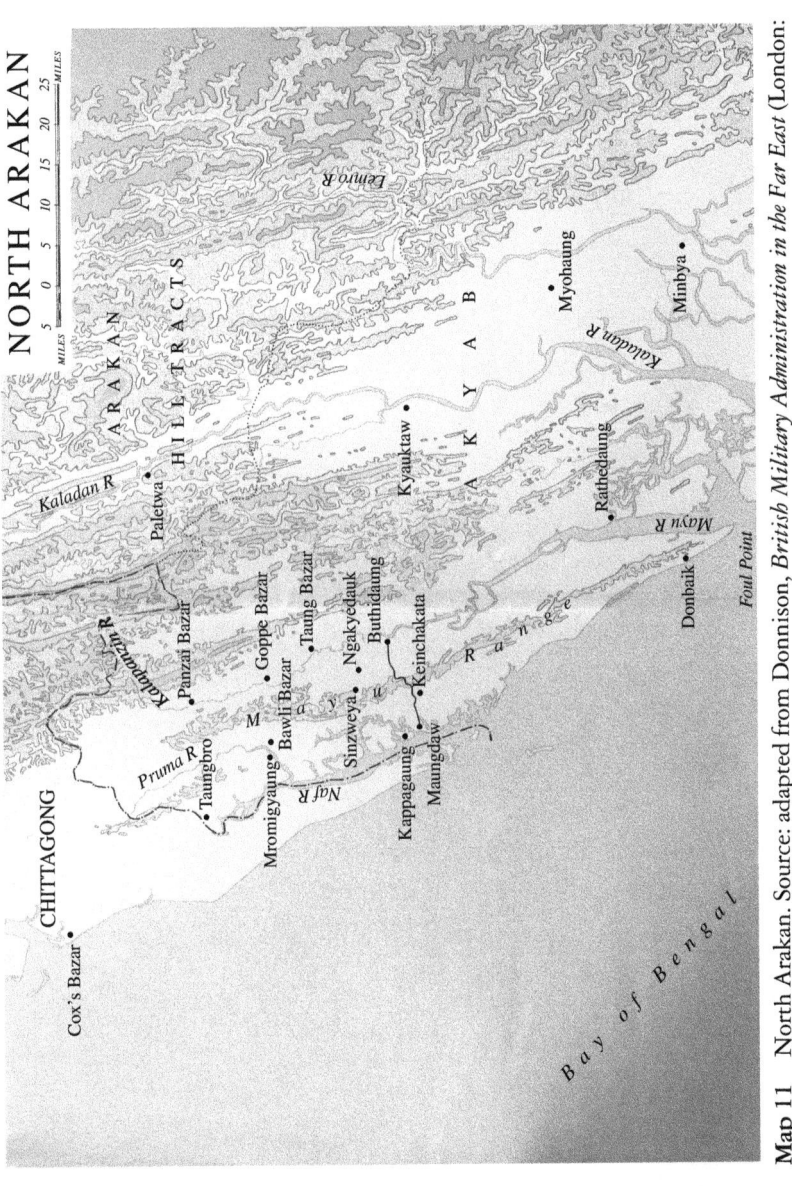

Map 11 North Arakan. Source: adapted from Donnison, *British Military Administration in the Far East* (London: HMSO, 1956), p. 17.

INTRODUCTION

THE SPECIAL OPERATIONS EXECUTIVE IN BURMA, 1941–5

The Special Operations Executive (SOE) was formed by the British Government during the early years of World War II with a mandate to strike back at Germany using unconventional means. The organisation existed from 1940 until 1946 and was global in its operations. The focus of this book is SOE in Burma (modern-day Myanmar). It covers a period of approximately five years from October 1940 when a decision was taken to send an SOE mission to Singapore, until October 1945, when the last of SOE missions were withdrawn from the Burmese jungle. In addition, an epilogue explores the period from the end of World War II in 1945 until just after Burma achieved independence in 1948.[1]

The SOE was created in July 1940 after the British and French armies had been rescued by the Royal Navy from the fjords of Norway and beaches of Dunkirk.[2] Britain 'stood alone' and faced a seemingly imminent Nazi invasion of the British Isles. Using the Home Guard as a cover, clandestine left-behind parties were hurriedly formed and trained. Their job, should the Nazis invade, was to allow German forces to advance over them. From secret hide-outs, these 'Auxiliary Units' would then attack German lines of communication.[3] While the Army was re-equipped and reorganised during the remainder of 1940 and the RAF fought the Battle of Britain, British planners also worked to conceive a means of striking back at the Nazis in occupied Europe. In the words of Hugh Dalton, the first politician in charge of SOE as Minister for Economic Warfare:

We have got to organise movements in enemy-occupied territory comparable to the Sinn Fein movement in Ireland, to the Chinese guerrillas now operating against Japan, to the Spanish irregulars who played a notable part in Wellington's campaign or – one might as well admit it – to the organisations which the Nazis themselves have developed so remarkably in almost every country in the world. This 'democratic international' must use many different methods, including industrial and military sabotage, labour agitation and strikes, continuous propaganda, terrorist acts against traitors and German leaders, boycotts and riots.

It is clear to me that an organisation of this character is not something which can be handled by the ordinary departmental machinery of either the British Civil Service or the British Military Machine. What is needed is a new organisation to co-ordinate, inspire, control and assist the nationals of the oppressed countries who must themselves be the direct participants. We need absolute secrecy.[4]

Only three months after Dalton wrote this and SOE was established, a decision was taken to deploy SOE to the Far East. The aim of SOE's Far Eastern Mission (FEM), also known as the Oriental Mission (OM), was to prepare for a possible war against Japan, applying the methods set out above by Dalton, and to raise secret left-behind parties modelled on the Auxiliary Units. A civilian called Valentine St John Killery was chosen to lead the FEM. Killery had extensive experience of the Far East in his capacity as a businessman working for Imperial Chemical Industries. Killery set up the Oriental Mission's headquarters in Singapore after he arrived on 7 May 1941. A Special Training School (STS) was established on some of Singapore's more rural coastline, at Tanjong Balai, numbered STS 101.[5] Captain Jim Gavin was selected as commanding officer for STS 101, which he opened on 26 June 1941.[6] It was intended that, in the event of a Japanese offensive, teams of men trained in Singapore would become left-behind parties to operate on the Japanese lines of communication.[7]

The beginning of the war in the Far East is usually associated with the Japanese attack on the American naval base at Pearl Harbor on the morning of 7 December 1941. However, half an hour before the attack on Pearl Harbor began, Japanese troops assaulted the eastern coast of

Malaya at Kota Bharu.[8] Agreement was reached between the Siamese Government and the Japanese ambassador on 8 December that allowed Japanese troops to cross Siamese territory into Burma. The RAF landing strip at Victoria Point, on the southernmost tip of Burma, was in Japanese possession by 11 December 1941.[9] Rangoon was bombed on 23 December, and again on Christmas day 1941, the same day that Hong Kong was captured. In Malaya, meanwhile, Japanese troops were in Kuantan, approximately half way to Singapore from their beach-head at Kota Bharu.[10]

The collapse of the Western colonial armies was rapid. Singapore was surrendered to the Japanese on 15 February 1942. By May 1942, the Dutch East Indies, the American colony of the Philippines, French Indochina, and the British possessions of Hong Kong, Malaya, Borneo, Singapore and Burma were all under Japanese control. The Japanese had conquered their so-called 'Greater Asian Co-Prosperity Sphere' with such speed, and with such a lack of effective opposition, that colonial Southeast Asia was never to be the same again.

Prior to the collapse described above, Killery had faced much obstruction from both the colonial and military authorities in the Far East. In particular, the idea of left-behind parties had been vetoed, first by the Commander in Chief (C-in-C) Far East, Air Marshal Sir Robert Brooke-Popham, and then the General Officer Commanding (GOC) Malaya, Lieutenant General Arthur Percival, followed by the Governor of Singapore, Sir Shenton Thomas. Shenton Thomas objected to recruiting Asians for left-behind parties on the grounds that this might be interpreted by colonial peoples as an admission of weakness, and that such a defeatist attitude could damage morale. In addition, he felt that arming Malayan Chinese might exacerbate existing political problems, especially since there were strong anti-colonial organisations in existence within both the communist and nationalist Kuomintang Chinese communities.[11] Killery commented on 24 October 1941 that Thomas and Percival 'appear to be scared stiff of Asiatic reactions [unless] they are merely using it as a strong weapon to defeat all arguments for an Oriental Mission organisation'.[12]

Imperial and political concerns were not the only cause of obstruction. The objection from the military, in particular General Percival, appears to have been due, at least in part, to Percival's affront when he accidently uncovered the plans for secret left-behind parties in his area of command.[13] Percival was probably just as significantly influenced by his fear of losing scarce resources, including officers.[14] This obstructionism meant that when the Japanese attack came in December 1941, the Oriental Mission was not as prepared to fulfil its objectives as it could have been.

Despite this official opposition to Killery's plans, in Burma as in Malaya, the Oriental Mission had hastily formed some left-behind parties, and was able to provide some cover for retreating Allied forces. Consequently, like the regular army, the SOE fought a continuous war against the Japanese in Burma from December 1941 until August 1945. It was also only in Burma that SOE was in action from before the Japanese invaded, remained committed throughout the subsequent occupation, and then participated in the defeat of enemy forces until surrender and beyond.[15] Despite the length of SOE's commitment to Burma, and its unique position in SOE history, no study has been produced that examines SOE in Burma in its entirety. This book aims to fill that gap.

For the purposes of this book, the Burma campaign will be conceptualised as dividing into four very distinct phases: pre-conflict (May–December 1941); the first Burma campaign (December 1941–July 1942); stalemate (August 1942–December 1944); and the second Burma campaign (January–October 1945). In each of these periods, there were constraints on SOE which affected its ability to operate effectively. Given these restraints on its freedom to operate, the book will offer suggestions to the following questions: what were the particular successes and failures of SOE in this Far Eastern colonial context? What did the organisation do well? What were the criticisms levelled at SOE both at the time and since the War? And how well do they stand up to scrutiny? What does the history of SOE in Burma tell us about command, control and the use of irregular forces in warfare in general? Since SOE worked in Burma during all phases of the War, under what conditions did it operate best? Finally, how might a study of SOE in Burma affect our understanding of the military history of the campaign as it exists?

LITERATURE REVIEW

Historians have debated SOE's military impact on the one hand and its political effects upon target countries on the other. General surveys of World War II tend to criticise SOE's military performance, if indeed it is mentioned at all.[1] This contrasts with SOE writers, such as Michael Foot, who have highlighted SOE's specialist contributions and good value relative to its cost in resources.[2]

In terms of the political debate, SOE has been accused of having helped to create the conditions for civil war or Communist insurgency. This was an accusation made both during the War, in respect of Greece and Burma, for example, and by writers since.[3] What follows is a review of how the existing literature deals with these questions for Burma, looking first at the military and then at the political debates.

The SOE in Burma: The Military Debate

In general histories of the war in Burma, SOE has tended to feature on the periphery. This is understandable as the aim has been to produce a regular military history. Where SOE has been discussed, the military contribution has usually been minimised.[4] Nevertheless, the result may be that SOE's substantive contribution to campaigns sometimes gets written out. For example, in *Defeat into Victory*, Field Marshal Slim described an important delaying action in April 1945 that he says was crucial to his drive for Rangoon, but did not attribute this action to SOE, probably because the existence of SOE was not officially in the public domain.[5] Similarly, Major General Kirby's official history of the war in the Far East, produced between 1957 and 1969, omitted SOE from the second volume, which covers the first Burma campaign of 1941–2. By 1965, when the volume dealing with the second Burma campaign of 1944–5 was published, the existence of SOE was public knowledge. Despite this, Kirby only granted SOE a mention in a footnote for the action which Slim had described as vital.

More generally, assessments of SOE's military contribution to World War II normally only relate to the war in Europe. During the War, many officers in the regular military considered that the siphoning of scarce resources in terms of men, money and materials to SOE was unjustified due to insufficient tangible returns.[6] This critical stance, which stemmed from the early years of the War as SOE established itself, seems to have persisted enough to have fed through into later military histories. In his 1989 book *The Second World War*, John Keegan concluded that SOE actions were 'a costly and misguided failure' consisting of 'irrelevant and pointless acts of bravado'.[7]

Critics of SOE's overall role in the War point, for example, to the assassination of Holocaust architect Reinhard Heydrich and the consequent Nazi retribution against the villages of Lidice and Lezaky where 5,000 civilians were murdered, to illustrate that SOE's operations were often ill-conceived.[8] Far Eastern operations (in Burma and elsewhere) make little contribution towards such overall assessments. Nigel West's *Secret War*, for instance, left the Far East out of his conclusion, despite including a chapter on both the Oriental Mission and the India Mission.[9]

Contrasting with general military histories, specialist SOE histories tend to argue that SOE operations justified the investment. Michael Foot, the first official historian of SOE, concluded that SOE was 'an admirable strategic tool', at least in Europe.[10] Examples to substantiate this interpretation include how on the Eastern Front, SOE-trained agents in Poland sabotaged or blew up around 5,000 Nazi trains during 1944–5, while on the Western Front, the D-Day landings were assisted by around 950 acts of sabotage on the French railway, which helped prevent divisions such as *Das Reich* from reaching the beach-heads in the critical days after the invasion. In early May 1945, General Eisenhower wrote that the Resistance had 'played a very considerable part in our complete and final victory'.[11] In July 1945, Eisenhower's deputies, Generals Morgan and Bedell Smith, believed that without SOE the

Resistance 'would have been of no military value'.[12] David Stafford reached a similar judgement when he concluded that '[s]trategically, SOE was a valuable bonus to the regular forces'.[13]

William Mackenzie, who wrote a European history of SOE immediately after the War (unpublished until 2000), took a cost-benefit approach which led him to surmise '[i]t is obvious that in the vulgar sense SOE showed a large military profit'.[14] More recently, Roderick Bailey has argued for a more 'rounded picture', which takes into account not only that it took time and lives to gain experience, but also that there are 'plenty of examples' of varied SOE work which aimed to shorten the War.[15] In specialist SOE overviews and literature, therefore, SOE in Europe is generally perceived as having fulfilled the Special Forces' role of accomplishing what conventional forces could not, as well as achieving significant military impact.[16]

The case for SOE's military significance and value relative to input is almost wholly informed by European case studies. Despite a notable increase in publications about SOE since the millennium, the Far East is still a relatively neglected theatre. Such neglect in favour of a more Eurocentric focus has been particularly notable in what Neville Wylie has termed the 'third phase' of SOE history writing.[17] For example, a 2006 study, *Special Operations Executive: A New Instrument of War*, contains 17 studies, only one of which is extra-European (Afghanistan).[18]

Writing in 2005, Wylie described the first phase as the history of the specific SOE country sections written during the War. Of particular relevance to this book is SOE's own history of the Oriental Mission produced in 1942, as well as a history of SOE in Burma written by the Burma Country Section (BCS) head, Richie Gardiner, in 1945.[19]

The second phase was the official histories, starting with Michael Foot's *SOE in France* in 1967, and including Charles Cruickshank's *SOE in the Far East*.[20] These official histories, according to Wylie, were largely based on the country section reports, which therefore made them to some extent '[h]istories of histories'.[21] Wylie's concern was that if there were any distortions in the original country section history, these are likely to have then been carried over into the official postwar history.[22]

Wylie's third phase was the publication of studies based upon memoirs, official histories and SOE archives, which had been made public during the 1990s. Wylie recognised that this third phase was still under way in

2005, with some areas of SOE 'awaiting serious scholarly attention'.[23] One such area is Burma, a gap which this book aims to fill.[24]

Wylie's concern about any distortions or inaccuracies from the 'first phase' of SOE histories becoming imbedded in 'second phase' histories can also be applied to Cruickshank's 'second phase' official history influencing 'third phase' work. For example, Cruickshank used, amongst others, the contemporary observers Sir George Moss (SOE London's advisor for the Far East) and Air Chief Marshal Robert Brooke-Popham (C-in-C Far East) to inform the conclusion to his Oriental Mission chapter.[25] More recently, as part of Wylie's 'third phase', Alan Ogden's *Tigers Burning Bright: SOE Heroes in the Far East*, which presents the stories of individual officers, used Cruickshank to replicate the conclusion that Killery's team achieved very little in 1941–2.[26]

Given that Cruickshank is the only 'second phase' history of SOE in the Far East, wider histories of SOE have also contributed to a perpetuation of judgements about SOE in the Far East. Nigel West's 1992 *Secret War* prefaced the chapter title on the Oriental Mission 'Exorbitant Cost', and then went on to conclude that overall 'precious little was ever accomplished'.[27]

At one level, these conclusions on the Oriental Mission are unsurprising when looking at the stark facts of British defeats during 1942: Hong Kong fell after 17 days at war; Malaya and Singapore within 70; Rangoon was evacuated within 90 days. Yet more contextualised studies of SOE's role in the Far East, such as Ian Trenowden's 1978 and Cheah Boon Kheng's 1983 studies of Malaya, included a more positive interpretation of the Oriental Mission. It was recognised that the 345 Chinese trainees who graduated from Special Training School (STS) 101 in late December 1941 and early January 1942 provided the nucleus of the wartime Malayan People's Anti-Japanese Army (MPAJA).[28] The MPAJA had grown up to 7,000 strong by 1945 and had been a major target of SOE operations into Malaya from 1943, albeit kept in reserve for an Allied combat invasion that was never needed.[29]

Focusing on the Oriental Mission more widely, Richard Gough's 1985 book, *SOE Singapore* 'was compiled mainly from the memories of those who took part'.[30] Without the access to SOE files enjoyed by later authors, Gough nevertheless concluded that, given the enormous constraints it worked under, the Oriental Mission 'accomplished more than could be expected of it', notably establishing STS 101 in Singapore, and training left-behind parties who fought on 'long after the regular army had retreated or surrendered'.[31] For both Gough and Cruickshank, had the Oriental Mission been allowed to organise left-behind parties from earlier in 1941 as intended (rather than after war started), the defeat of the Allied armies could have been 'delayed and perhaps even prevented'.[32] The more positive judgements of these two works, respectively giving a more Southeast Asian view, and a perspective based upon veterans' recollections, raises the possibility that SOE's role has been underestimated or misunderstood.

Another issue with these general histories of SOE in the Far East is that they usually give Malaya the majority of the attention, with Burma second.[33] Not only is the resulting space limited, but research for this book has revealed that sections of existing works which include the Oriental Mission in Burma contain considerable mistakes as well as inconsistencies between accounts. The mistakes range from the spelling of the names of individual British officers to the ethnicity of the Burmese that these officers were in charge of.[34] The inconsistencies concern what the officers of the Oriental Mission did, and how SOE Burma's actions integrated with the overall first Burma campaign. Two examples serve to illustrate this point.

Firstly, Cruickshank and then Ogden argued that a rear-guard action by Captain Thompson on the Toungoo–Mawchi Road in April 1942 imposed a 'critical' two-day delay on the Japanese advance, but Slim claimed that this levy force was 'swept aside'.[35] The reader is left wondering if Thompson did hold up a Japanese brigade, as proposed by Gough, and if so, how the two-day delay was 'critical'.[36]

Secondly, Cruickshank stated that 'most importantly', the Oriental Mission's Kachin levies prevented the Japanese from building an airstrip at Fort Hertz in the far north of Burma after the retreat in 1942. This airstrip would have allowed Japanese fighters to interdict the aircraft flying 'the last air link between India and China' in the period 1942–4.[37] Just how this was prevented is not explained by any of these works. Perhaps more importantly, these two actions just described might contribute to a rethink in our understanding of the Burma campaign as currently perceived.

This survey of the existing literature that includes SOE Burma thus presents several disparate works that contain a variety of confusions, errors and omissions, some of which have been perpetuated because little sustained research has so far focused on Burma. No reliable basis therefore exists for integrating Burma into overall Far Eastern accounts of SOE, and beyond that into analyses of SOE as a whole.

By focusing on Burma, this book not only provides the first comprehensive overview of the Oriental Mission in Burma to make systematic use of SOE papers held at The National Archives at Kew Gardens, but also provides a more in-depth analysis than the works cited above, focused as they are upon the wider theatre or personnel involved. This focus on Burma also allows a more detailed investigation of SOE's role in the distinct phases of the Burma campaign – pre-war, retreat, reorganisation and first operations, advance – than has been completed before. The chapters of this book are structured around the following chronological phases.

Chapter One re-examines many of the pre-war problems associated with founding SOE in the Far East that previous work, surveyed above, have emphasised. In particular, the chapter revisits problems such as the obstruction of the civil and military authorities, and provides new clarity on the personnel and their actions, but does so from the perspective of the war in Burma.

Chapter Two then looks at operations in Burma once the war started and evaluates how SOE fared in Burma compared to the extant general conclusions about the Oriental Mission.

Chapters Three (Reorganisation) and Four (Early Operations) then cover reorganisation in India and first operations in the period from the end of the first Burma campaign in June 1942, to the beginning of the second Burma campaign after the battles of Imphal and Kohima in 1944. While for 1941–2, the book must address existing myths and debates, for this next period the problem has been that rather little has been written on it at all. Cruickshank's *SOE in the Far East*, West's *Secret War*, and Ogden's *Tigers Burning Bright* devote a total of 12 pages between them to this two-year period from mid-1942 to mid-1944. A core argument of this book is that it is important that military assessments of SOE in Burma, that up to now have mainly been based upon operations in 1945, should take into account the important groundwork that was laid during this two-year period. While it is easy to be seduced by the end result, a full understanding of what is needed in order for Special Operations to succeed and what constraints had to be overcome must be recognised. This includes organisational infrastructure, support services including training and air lift, and establishing new operations in Japanese-occupied Burma.[38]

In his conclusion to *SOE in the Far East*, Cruickshank wrestled with the conundrum of whether or not SOE had fulfilled its purpose. His main criticism was based on the idea that SOE had been hamstrung by its founding charter, which had been drawn up mainly with Europe in mind. The three main objectives of this charter of July 1940 were sabotage, political subversion and subversive propaganda.[39] In Cruickshank's view, the potential to make a major contribution to such objectives did not exist in the Far East. European agents could not easily become incognito in Asian societies, and colonial Asian societies might be pushed closer into the Japanese embrace by any widespread sabotage. Japan was, after all, trying to present itself as a liberator of Asians, and had granted quasi 'independence' to Burma in August 1943.[40]

Despite this obvious difference in conditions, officials in London apparently pushed Colin Mackenzie, the commander of SOE in the Far East, to conduct sabotage operations right up until June 1945, allegedly causing SOE to fall into a 'functional vacuum' between 1942 and early 1945.[41] This vacuum was to some extent filled by SOE's attention to guerrilla and intelligence operations. In Cruickshank's opinion, however, raising guerrillas was not special operations, and therefore should have been left to the military, and intelligence was something that should never have taken precedence for SOE, as it was not part of its charter. By putting intelligence first, SOE took on the role of the Secret Intelligence Service, causing a rivalry which was wholly 'counter-productive'. Cruickshank's suggested solution was that the theatre commander, Admiral Mountbatten, should have amalgamated all the British clandestine groups along the same lines as the American Office of Strategic Services (OSS), thereby averting these problems.[42]

The tension between the limits of the original charter and the practical needs of the British military in 1943 to mid-1945 may help to explain some of the negative judgements passed on SOE in Burma. In 1944, Slim's 'huge problem' was intelligence, and he complained to 11 Army Group on 23 June that he was blind.[43] Included with other organisations operating in Burma, Slim perceived SOE as failing him in this area, and so in December 1944 he suggested having SOE closed down or amalgamated with other secret services.[44] This was because, in a theatre that was bottom of the global list for resources such as airlift and landing craft, Slim needed intelligence for an advance into Burma overland from India. Yet many of the personnel best-suited to collecting the intelligence that Slim needed were in SOE. Several questions arise from this and are addressed in this work, such as how far and how successfully did SOE extend its original remit to include intelligence?

Regarding guerrilla warfare in this period from mid-1942 and until the end of the War, SOE was responsible for organising the indigenous population to fight against the Japanese, just like the *Maquis* in France or partisans in Yugoslavia and Albania. Although guerrilla warfare was added to the India Mission's charter in August 1942, Cruickshank has argued that 'offensive action by auxiliaries', in other words partisan or guerrilla warfare, is not a Special Forces role.[45] The strategic historian Colin Gray has taken a very different line, arguing that 'special forces warriors have to function as "guerrillas in uniform"', that 'the conduct of unconventional warfare carries heavier demands', with unconventional war being a 'state of mind'.[46] By this definition, SOE was conducting Special Operations with Special Forces when raising guerrillas. As Gray points out, some generals have embraced Special Forces, but in *Defeat into Victory*, Slim concluded that Special Forces 'were wasteful'. In his view, '[t]hey did not give, militarily, a worthwhile return for the resources'.[47]

This criticism extended to Orde Wingate's 'Special Force', the Chindits. The first Chindit campaign of February to May 1943 had consisted of about 3,000 men. The second Chindit operation of March to August 1944, codenamed *Thursday*, was four times larger at 12,000 men. It took 650 sorties by Dakota to fly three-quarters of these men into Burma with 1,350 animals, 250 tons of stores, plus anti-aircraft and artillery batteries, in order to establish 'strongholds' behind the Japanese lines.[48] Robert Lyman has argued that this commitment was a 'serious threat' to Slim's plans for defeating Japan on the Imphal Plain in 1944, in a theatre that had to forfeit resources for an overall 'Europe First' grand strategy.[49]

In contrast to the Chindits, by 15 August 1945, SOE in the Far East had flown into Burma 1,430 tons of supplies and 2,000 British officers and other ranks.[50] Not only was SOE less demanding in resources, but the means by which SOE sought to exert strategic influence was entirely different. The problem here, according to Gray, is that 'strategic history which explains the effect of special operations on the course and outcome of events is not available'.[51] For example, Raymond Callahan's *Burma 1942–1945* is part of the 'Politics and Strategy of the Second World War' series, but makes no mention of SOE.[52] Debates about the Chindits, on the other hand, permeate every campaign history and have a substantial selection of books dedicated to their study in which the debate about their strategic value continues unabated.[53]

A similar argument about strategic worth can also be applied to SOE in Burma. Notwithstanding his criticism of SOE based upon a supposedly conspicuous inability to fulfil a European charter, Cruickshank concluded *SOE in the Far East* by stating that '[i]t is on its performance in Burma that Force 136 [SOE] must be judged'.[54] This is because 'by common consent its [SOE's] guerrillas had played a significant part in the Allied victory in Burma'.[55] This idea of 'common consent' must be questioned, given Slim's overall conclusion, noted above, that Special Forces had little impact. But here Slim seems to contradict his more specific assessment of parts of the campaign in 1945. In particular, he argued that action on the Toungoo–Mawchi Road during the race south towards Rangoon in 1945 had been important, despite not overtly crediting this to SOE.

If Japanese forces had been able to regroup and defend Toungoo, the XIV Army's route to Rangoon would have been blocked. Slim described how, after he gave the word to the Karen to rise, the Japanese converging on Toungoo from the northern front 'ran into ambush after ambush'.[56] Although there is no mention of SOE, it is SOE's Operation *Character* that Slim was referring to. Apart from a chapter in *Sabotage and Subversion* by Ian Dear, there is a discernible lack of investigation into SOE's military role in Burma, with even Louis Allen claiming that SOE officers dropped ahead of the British advance had 'either been ambushed and killed or had failed to rouse the local inhabitants', though 'several hundreds' were eventually raised as fighters by SOE.[57]

Tied to the lack of clarity about the role of SOE on the Toungoo–Mawchi Road in 1945 is the assertion by many of the historians of the Burma campaign that it was imperative that Slim's forces reached Rangoon before the 1945 monsoon.[58] As it happened, a seaborne invasion of Rangoon, codenamed *Dracula*, went ahead because the XIV Army was held up by determined fighting at Pegu. Rangoon had, however, been given up in order to concentrate Japanese forces in Moulmein, so the landings were unopposed. If SOE had not prevented

56 Division from reinforcing Toungoo, the XIV Army pressure might not have been enough to force Rangoon's evacuation to Moulmein, and *Dracula* would have been opposed by approximately 14,300 Japanese troops who were estimated to be in the Rangoon area in the middle of April.[59]

In summary, the work of SOE during the first Burma campaign needs to be clarified. Judgements based on Cruickshank's broad study of the Far East have been repeated, and there is confusion caused by differences in detail at various levels. The period between the retreat of 1942 and the second Burma campaign has barely received any attention, and although there has been some recognition of SOE's military contribution in 1945 in SOE works, the 'common consent' claimed by Cruickshank has not been transferred into the general campaign histories.[60] Chapters Five (*Character*) and Six (*Billet*) therefore re-examine the two major SOE operations in Burma during 1945 in order to assess the military significance of SOE in 1945.

The SOE in Burma: The Political Debate

The main argument about SOE in Burma in the relevant literature is, however, not about its military effectiveness, but about its political role. Such arguments are not confined to SOE in Burma and the Far East, and have increasingly been the subject of investigation by SOE historians. According to Neville Wylie:

> SOE's reputation largely rests on its military contribution to the Allied war effort, especially in training, equipping and finally mobilizing European resistance movements against German domination during the last years of the war. While this reputation is entirely deserved, SOE's military operations have tended to overshadow other less dramatic, or glamorous, aspects of its work. SOE's political activities fall into this category.[61]

Here there is an important distinction to be made. Wylie refers specifically to political work carried out by SOE, not the military work that had political consequences. Political work in Burma consisted of operations such as *Mahout*, where Indian agents were parachuted in to foment subversion amongst Indian dock workers, as opposed to military operations which were to raise fighters from the local population. Often, the groups that SOE armed were communists, or in the case of Palestine, Jews who intended to fight against the British mandate of Palestine once the War was over. SOE backed the communists in some European countries, such as Tito in Yugoslavia and ELAS in Greece. Roderick Bailey's work on Albania demonstrates how, on the ground, SOE personnel were pragmatic enough to work with whoever they thought would be of most benefit to the pursuit of victory. In Albania, this proved to be the communist partisans, too, but Bailey explains that this support was not a given.[62]

In the literature on Burma, the political arguments are mainly confined to the 1945 period, when SOE armed Burmese Nationalist groups, notably the Anti-Fascist Organisation (AFO) and the Burma National Army (BNA). In addition to many in the leadership of the AFO being communist, many of those in the BNA and AFO had collaborated with the Japanese since 1941. Individuals such as Kra Hla Aung, or the more widely known Aung San (who was both head of the BNA and a member of the AFO council), were also accused of having committed murder during the British withdrawal from Burma in 1942.[63] There were many civil Burma officials who wanted such men arrested, including the Chief Civil Affairs Officer, Major General F.S.B. Pearce. SOE officers have been accused, contemporaneously and since, of having acted irresponsibly, a charge which has also been levelled at the theatre commander, Admiral Mountbatten. By defying the advice of the Civil Affairs Service Burma (CAS(B)) and recognising the AFO and arming the BNA, the accusation is that SOE facilitated postwar internecine violence in Burma, much as SOE is accused of doing in Greece and Malaya.[64]

Probably the first person to criticise SOE Burma on this issue was Frank Donnison in his official history, *British Military Administration in the Far East*, which was published in 1956. Donnison had extensive experience of Burma, having worked for the Indian Civil Service from 1922. During the war he worked for CAS(B) attached to IV Corps headquarters. After the war, he finished his career as Chief Secretary to the Governor of Burma. In his book, Donnison claimed that the head of SOE in the Far East, Colin Mackenzie, made assurances to 'unrepresentative' elements of the Burmese nationalist *Thakin* party. This 'assurance' given by Mackenzie was dangerous, according to

Donnison, because it 'promised [...] sympathetic consideration for political claims in the future in return for collaboration against the Japanese'.[65] This was against British Government instructions that nationalist leaders be given no indication that their help to expel the Japanese from Burma would give them political capital in postwar Burma. Lastly, Donnison wrote that Mackenzie created this alliance without the knowledge of Mountbatten and Pearce, and although the governor, Dorman-Smith, was apparently informed, it was only through 'private channels'.

Donnison's claims were picked up in *The Union of Burma*, published by Professor Hugh Tinker in 1959. Tinker argued that:

> [SOE] worked in consultation with the Supreme Allied Commander, but by no means under his direction: in the process of fostering underground activity in Burma, Force 136 seems to have been given quasi-political undertakings which were made without prior reference to either the Supreme Commander [Mountbatten] or the Governor of Burma [Sir Reginald Dorman-Smith] or the head of the CAS(B) [Civil Affairs Service (Burma), Major General F.S.B. Pearce].[66]

This interpretation raises some important questions. Firstly, was SOE 'given quasi-political undertakings', and if so, by whom? Secondly, how much autonomy did SOE really have in the Far East? Did the organisation make promises or take actions over the heads of Mountbatten, Dorman-Smith and Pearce?

Tinker went on to state that after the Chiefs of Staff ruled in May 1945 that the BNA should be disbanded, 'once again theirs was not the effective decision'.[67] Tinker's contention was that Mountbatten, as well as SOE, acted independently of the authorities in London on more than one occasion. The picture of command and control in Southeast Asia that emerges from Tinker's account is thus one of Mountbatten, and to a lesser extent SOE, making critical decisions autonomously from accepted structures of authority.

Such claims did not go unchallenged. They were taken up in 1972 by Bickham Sweet-Escott in an exchange within the correspondence section of the *International Affairs* journal.[68] Sweet-Escott had served in SOE in both Europe and the Far East.[69] In the Far East, Sweet-Escott had been

Colonel, General Staff, from 1944 until the end of the War. This meant that he had worked at the centre, close to the command decisions. Sweet-Escott rejected Tinker's work as 'seriously misrepresent[ing]' SOE's actions during the War. Tinker only needed to have read Slim's *Defeat into Victory*, Sweet-Escott charged, to see that judgements such as that SOE acted outside the proper channels of command were false.[70] Tinker nevertheless maintained his original claims made in *The Union of Burma* and, in turn, referred Sweet-Escott to Donnison's official history, *British Military Administration in the Far East*.

This debate is briefly set out over two pages in Kirby's official history in 1967. The focus is on the difference of opinion between SOE and the civil and military authorities, and the role of Mountbatten.[71] No attempt to resolve the argument is made, and so the idea that SOE acted semi-autonomously, and dangerously on some political matters, persisted almost unchallenged until 1983, when Tinker published two volumes of documents as *Burma, the Struggle for Independence*.[72] Using selected archives from what was then the Public Records Office (now The National Archives) and the British Library, Tinker reinforced his earlier indictment of SOE. Although receiving many favourable reviews, the volumes were also criticised for abridging and omitting documents.[73] It is on this latter point that SOE and Burma veterans challenged Tinker on this issue of misrepresenting the role of SOE.[74]

Despite the concerns of veterans, Cruickshank's 1986 history *SOE in the Far East* followed closely in the footsteps of Donnison and Tinker on this matter. Although criticised by Richard Aldrich for focusing too narrowly on SOE's military activities, Cruickshank continued with the political argument that Mackenzie had promised arms and money to the nationalists 'without consulting London'.[75] He also discussed the role of Mountbatten and SOE in sidelining the Civil Affairs Service, but concluded that the decision made to work with the BNA was correct: 'It is difficult to imagine the consequences if Civil Affairs had had their way'.[76]

In a 1984 history of the Burma campaign, Louis Allen was able to use the documents in Tinker's volumes to alter the interpretation from SOE acting outside of the command structure to Mackenzie hiding plans from Pearce 'until they had been approved by higher authority'.[77] Allen also added to the debate by arguing that any interpretation also had to take into account the institutional structure of SOE Burma.

Burma section was, Allen suggested, split into two divisions 'partly for political, partly for racial reasons'.[78] One section was to liaise with the Nationalist Burmese of the AFO and BNA, and the other to work with the Karen.[79] The Karen were Burma's second largest ethnic group after the Burmans, numbering approximately 1.3 million compared to 9.6 million Burmans (out of a total population of 17 million) in the 1931 census.[80]

One explanation for the opinion that SOE acted outside the command structure could be that British writers, officials and official historians sought to distance Britain from the violence of post-colonial Burma by conveniently scapegoating SOE.[81] This distancing must be understood in the context of Burma's deeply traumatic experience in the immediate postwar years. Similar to the concurrent situation in the British Mandate of Palestine, in 1947 rival factions began a civil war in Burma even before independence. The BNA leader, Aung San, was assassinated with six other Burmese leaders in July 1947. Former Prime Minister U Saw was executed for his alleged role in the killing, while Captain David Vivian, who was rumoured to have been part of SOE's Burma section, was found guilty of organising the supply of the weapons used to carry out the assassination.[82] After independence on 4 January 1948, violence erupted between Burmese Communists and the Government of the Union of Burma, and Communist propaganda from Europe accused the British of being behind Aung San's murder.[83]

Then, after the Karen had helped to save the Union Government from a Burmese Communist coup, the Karen – this time without any doubt assisted by some former SOE Burma personnel – fought for their independence from the Union of Burma from 1949.[84] This leaves important questions for this book. How many SOE officers and men were involved and to what degree? To what extent were former SOE personnel supported by other Burma veterans, and what form did the British Government's involvement take? To what extent did minority groups in Burma decide to fight because they had been encouraged to believe, if not promised by SOE officers, that they would not be incorporated into a unified state in which they would be ruled by the majority Burmans?[85] What was the extent and nature of the involvement of former SOE personnel in the Karen challenge to the Union of Burma? These questions will be explored in the epilogue, which thus ties up the loose ends of SOE operations in Burma.

These political debates among British historians have hitherto largely neglected Burmese perspectives on SOE. The Burmese work poses its own challenges because, although reflecting the Burmese perception of SOE, the main aims of Burmese authors have been to write a history of Burmese nationalism, and to address the postwar debates pertinent to the consolidation of independence. Central to this nationalist narrative is the extent to which the BNA and AFO contributed to liberation from the Japanese with the returning British Army, and the role of the Hill Peoples in the resistance.

During the War and in the years immediately afterwards, the nationalist narrative fostered by Aung San was that the Hill Peoples only joined the fight against the Japanese after the BNA and AFO had revolted in March 1945.[86] In 1951, Maung Maung Pye, a Burmese journalist, published *Burma in the Crucible*, in which he argued that 'essential' negotiations through Thein Pe had made it possible for Burmese Nationalist forces to play a 'memorable part ... in the war of liberation, in close cooperation with the Allied forces'.[87] Thein Pe was a Burmese Nationalist who had trekked to India from occupied Burma in 1942 to secure British support against Japan, and ended up being SOE's link with the AFO in Burma.

Thein Pe's interpretation of how Burma was liberated based upon a relationship with SOE was challenged by U Maung Maung, a former BNA officer who wrote *Burmese Nationalist Movements, 1940–1948*. Published in 1989, U Maung Maung sought to illustrate how the Burmese revolt against the Japanese in 1945 was not orchestrated by, or dependent upon, SOE.[88] In March 1945, they rose up themselves, 'and neither the Communist Party, the "masters" in Force 136 [SOE] nor any higher authority could do anything about it'.[89] He continued that, due to the time it took to address the differences of opinion within the British camp, the Burmese fought with very little assistance from the British, and in particular SOE, during the first months of their rebellion from March 1945.[90]

Additionally, U Maung Maung was convinced that SOE was 'deeply penetrated by Moscow-trained British Communists', a doubly significant claim since the Communists revolted against the postwar independent Government.[91] This is used to explain, at least in part, why there was such a division in policy towards the AFO between conservative Burma government officials and the allegedly more left-leaning SOE.

The British official histories, by contrast, claim that the decisions to arm Burmese Nationalists were taken primarily by Mackenzie, while Maurice Collis, a Burma civil servant, reflected in his memoirs that 'SOE was concerned only with easing the path for the army [leaving] political complications to take care of themselves'.[92]

Burmese works can also help to fill in the story in another way. British publications and The National Archives, perhaps understandably, focus mainly on British officers and British concerns. The value of Thakin Nu's 1954 work, *Burma Under the Japanese*, is that it provides an insight into what the Burman agents sent in to Burma by SOE did after infiltration.[93] U Nu fills in some of the gaps about where these Burman agents went, whom they met, what was discussed and with what results. For example, Nu described how two Nationalist Burmans, Nyo Htun and Tin Shwe were in a position to be extracted from the Arakan in 1944 because the Japanese had sent Nyo Htun from Rangoon to Arakan to encourage the Arakanese to 'break away from the Burmese government'.[94] This reveals the interesting idea of how the Japanese might have played a significant part in encouraging racial and political divisions within Burma.[95]

Similar to SOE in various European countries, SOE in Burma is charged with having encouraged the 'wrong' side. The distinction is that, whereas in Europe those countries in which SOE had operated were left to decide their own political course as per the 1941 Atlantic charter, in Burma, the consequences were a British problem – at least until independence. The tension between war winning and colonial politics was well captured by the British Foreign Secretary, Anthony Eden, when in May 1945 he said of arming the BNA: 'Surely we should not boost these people too so [sic] much. They will give us great trouble hereafter.'[96] SOE in Burma did arguably boost the BNA and the AFO, but the extent to which SOE gave credibility to the nationalist claim to be the chief liberator of Burma is another question this book will resolve.

In summary, this overview has shown that there is considerable debate about the role of SOE in general, and of SOE in Burma in particular. It has also demonstrated that there is no single authoritative overview of SOE in Burma, and that there are considerable gaps in our knowledge of the role SOE played in the Burma campaign. This book aims to both fill these gaps and reassess these debates.

PROLOGUE

BURMA, ITS GEOGRAPHY AND ITS PEOPLE

To appreciate the context in which SOE operated in Burma, it is important that the demography and topography of the country is understood. The geography of Burma is possibly best described by a Burmese:

Burma is in many ways a country defined by its geography, at once isolated yet always with the possibility of connection, northwards to China, westward to India, and overseas to the world, a country with a stubborn and sometimes unhelpful sense of difference and uniqueness. Much of the country (a little more than half) is the valley of the Irrawaddy River, which runs from north to south, from the icy eastern curve of the Himalayas down over a thousand miles to the brackish tidal waters of the Andaman Sea. The upper portion of this valley – the heartland of successive Burmese kingdoms – is dry, almost a desert, . . . Part of the year is intensely hot and cloudless, and the rains, when they do come in late summer, come in wild and sudden downpours, concentrated over less than fifteen days a year, drenching the sandy ground and turning gullies into raging torrents. The south, on the other hand, is entirely different. The lower portion of the valley, the Irrawaddy Delta, as well as the two adjacent coastal regions of Arakan and Tenasserim, are warm and humid, with overcast skies and steady rains for weeks and months, lush and tropical with long stretches of picture-perfect beaches and little offshore islands. Around this valley is a great horseshoe-shaped arc of highlands, of terrifying chasms and soaring snow-covered mountains set alongside gently sloping hills and meandering alpine streams. Taken together, the highlands prevent any easy overland access to the outside world.[1]

Put in a European context, when superimposed on a map of Europe, Burma stretches from the highlands of northern Scotland over the Pyrenees to Madrid in Spain, a distance of approximately 1,930 km (1,200 miles). At its widest, Burma is around 750 km (470 miles) from east to west. Much of the country is covered in jungle or forest.

In 1941 when war against the Japanese began, Burma was bordered not only by India and China, but French Indochina and Siam, too. The Japanese carried out a limited invasion of Burma from Siam in 1941 to capture aerodromes in Tenasserim. The main invasion came in January 1942 across a mountainous jungle frontier that the British thought would protect their colony from invasion.[2] This assumption was swiftly proved wrong; within six months of the war starting, British and Empire forces had been forced to retreat over 1,440 km (900 miles) to the relative safety of India.

The British retreat had been further complicated by Burma's geography, for Burma is not just the 'valley of the Irrawaddy', as described. Three more great rivers, if the Chindwin is included, flow from north to south, draining out of the foothills of the Himalayas. Once the Japanese had breached the line of defence of the Salween River at Moulmein, the River Sittang lay between the Japanese and Rangoon. The British expected the Sittang to be a strong defensive line because of its strong currents and tidal bore. It had one bridge, connecting the road from Rangoon with the south of the country, and few fording points. After the bridge over the Sittang was – controversially – blown up, Rangoon was left vulnerable.[3] Occupied by the Japanese on 8 March, the evacuation of Rangoon forced British forces north into the dry area of Burma. Between the retreating Army and the safety of India were the Irrawaddy and the Chindwin rivers, and then the mountains of the Chin Hills.

The mountains that surround Burma are most often referred to as hills, such as the Chin Hills. The highest peak in the Chin Hills is just over 3,000 m (10,000 feet). Named after the people who live there, in the 1931 census, the Chins accounted for 250,000 of a total population of about 17 million.[4] Other so-called 'Hill Peoples' of Burma include the

Naga, Kachin, and Karen. Together the various hill peoples accounted for around 3.1 million, or 18 per cent of the total population. The Karen were Burma's second largest ethnic group after the Burmans, numbering approximately 1.3 million compared to 9.6 million Burmans in the 1931 census.[5]

Accurate identification of ethnicity and naming of groups was often difficult in the 1940s and remains so today. The list above is by no means comprehensive; for the sake of clarity, in this book, the description 'Burmese' has been used to indicate the people living within the British colony of Burma as a collective. Similarly, 'Arakanese' has been used to describe those living in this area of Burma, whilst it is recognised that the Arakan's (present-day Rakhine) ethnic composition is more complicated than this term allows. It is also recognised that there is differentiation within groups such as the Karen and Kachin, but this certainly would be to enter the proverbial minefield. The main groups that feature in the following account of SOE in Burma are Burman, Karen and Kachin, and are referred to as such in the same way as they were by the men of SOE in their reports in an effort to keep their perspective/sentiments clear.

Table P.1   Ethnicity in Burma, 1931[6]

Ethnicity	Population (1931 census)	
Burman	9,627,196	The majority population, and the most nationalist. It was the Burman Kingdom that Britain had fought against to make Burma part of the Empire in three wars from 1824 to 1886.
Karen	1,367,673	Consisting of Sgaw, Pwo, Bwe, Red, Black, Talaing and Striped Karens.
Kachin	400,000	Consisting of Hkahhu, Gauri, Lashi, Nung, Maru and Atzi Kachins.
Mon	336,728	
Shan or Tai	1,000,000	
Chin	250,000	21 different groups.
Naga	75,000	
Eurasian	110,000	Anglo-Burmese and Anglo-Indian.

Additional information: the table adds up to 13.1 million. Not listed are Arakanese, Chinese, and Indian communities.

Put simply, the Hill Peoples were, in the main, loyal to Britain. They were governed separately in 'Scheduled Areas' where the indirect rule of British District Commissioners allowed local headmen to run day-to-day affairs. In central Burma, where most of the majority Burman population resided, there was more formal colonial rule over a population who largely wanted independence from Britain. Britain had only completed its annexation of Burma in 1886 after a third Anglo-Burmese war. Independence from British rule was thus within living memory. When nationalist sentiment manifested itself in challenges to British authority, which it frequently did in the 1930s, the British used troops drawn from the Hill Peoples to suppress the trouble. There was, therefore, an uneasy relationship between Nationalist Burmans on the one hand, and Hill Peoples and British on the other.[7]

In particular, the Karen were close allies of the British. During the war, most of the Karen remained firmly in the British camp. This is partly because violence between Karen and Burman has a long history, but also due to legend. The legend of the Golden Book told how the Karen had been forsaken by God, but that when the 'young white brother' returned from over the seas with the golden book, their suffering would end.[8] When the American Baptist missionaries and the British arrived by boat and also arrived with a book that contained the word of God, it seemed to fit the prophecies. Many Karen willingly converted to Christianity and supported the British. The Karen helped the British in their first two Burmese wars and then to annex upper Burma in a third war in 1885. In the subsequent colonial era, the Karen helped to suppress Burman Nationalist uprisings in the 1930s.

When Japanese propaganda demanded 'Asia for the Asians', some nationalists believed that the Japanese might help them fulfil their aspirations for independence. This led to the formation of the Japanese-trained Burma Independence Army (BIA) which struck at the British with the main Japanese invasion in 1942. The BIA also took the opportunity afforded by the vacuum left between departing British and arriving Japanese to massacre Karens in Papun and Myaungmya between March and May 1942.[9] It was at this time, and later in 1945, that Aung San was accused of having murdered a village headman, a crime for which he was never brought to trial.[10] Thus, generally speaking, tensions between Burman and Karen ran high during the war, and indeed continue to do so since independence, granted in 1948.

These, then, are the conditions in which the Special Operations Executive (SOE) came to Burma in 1941: a colonial possession with some of the most difficult terrain in the world with extremes of monsoon and heat, a population that was ethnically diverse, and which included some already preparing to assist the Japanese in the cause of independence.

CHAPTER 1

THE ORIENTAL MISSION, OCTOBER 1940–DECEMBER 1941

The Special Operations Executive (SOE) was established by the British Government in July 1940. Its purpose was to strike back at Nazi-occupied Europe using clandestine means after the Army had been evacuated from France. Just three months later, in October 1940, the decision was taken by SOE headquarters, in consultation with the War Office and Foreign Office, to create a Far Eastern Mission (FEM) branch of SOE, to prepare for possible war with Japan.[1] The man chosen to lead the mission was Valentine St John Killery.[2]

The official historian of SOE in the Far East, Charles Cruickshank, argued that in the period between arriving in Singapore in May and the outbreak of war in December 1941, military and political obstructionism emanating from Singapore prevented SOE from being effectively established in any of the territories under its remit.[3] He further argued that when the Oriental Mission was finally allowed to fulfil its aims, it was too late to achieve anything meaningful. Both the General Officer Commanding (GOC) Malaya, Lieutenant General Arthur Percival, and the Commander in Chief (C-in-C) Far East, Air Chief Marshal Sir Robert Brooke-Popham were criticised by Cruickshank; Percival for his 'small mindedness', and Brooke-Popham for 'ineptitude' in dealing with Oriental Mission.[4] Cruickshank also put emphasis on what he described as the European nature of the Oriental Mission's directive to explain the 'failure of OM'.[5]

Building on this perspective, in 1992 Nigel West concluded that SOE 'played practically no useful role whatever' in Asia in 1941–2.[6] More recently, Calder Walton judged that '[t]he confusion over what Force 136's charter entailed in the Far East is part of a broader picture relating to SOE's failures during the war'.[7] These evaluations of SOE performance in the Far East generally leave the question of how far it was true of each territory, including Burma.

When Germany attacked France in May 1940, the conflict seemed a very distant prospect for the British military in Burma. To men such as John Hedley of the Burma Rifles and John Beamish, a 'teak *wallah*' with the Bombay-Burmah Trading Corporation, it was all taking place far away.[8] Yet even as the French signed an armistice with Germany in June 1940, and Britain contemplated the threat of a Nazi invasion, the situation in the Far East was changing.[9] As a result of the French surrender 6,000 Japanese troops were marched into French Indochina in August 1940. This meant that the most direct route of supply for Chiang Kai-Shek's Nationalist Chinese forces, which along with the Chinese Communists were facing an estimated 29 Japanese divisions, was now closed.[10] With Siam taking a neutral stance, another way which supplies could reach the Chinese Nationalists was through the Burmese port of Rangoon. Effectively occupying French Indochina not only placed Japanese troops in a country bordering Burma, it also gave the Japanese control of airfields from which to support a future offensive against European colonial possessions in Southeast Asia.

While the Japanese positioned themselves in French Indochina, more Burma Rifles (Burifs) units were created in case war came to the colony.[11] There was no sense of urgency, however, because the British felt relatively protected by the rugged jungle-clad hills that formed the border between Burma, French Indochina and Siam.[12] Nevertheless, by October 1940, as the immediate threat of invasion receded in Britain, planning for an SOE Far Eastern Mission began, which included Burma in its remit. By November 1940 '[t]erms of reference for an SOE group in Singapore were settled by SOE headquarters'.[13]

Looking at the period from the decision to deploy SOE in the Far East until the outbreak of war against Japan in December 1941, the main focus of this chapter is upon how far military and colonial obstructionism prevented SOE from getting to work in Burma. To do this, the chapter is divided into four main sections:

(1) FEM: Aims and Intentions.
(2) Establishment of FEM in Singapore.
(3) Civil and Military Obstruction.
(4) The Oriental Mission and Burma.

FEM: Aims and Intentions

In 1946, William Mackenzie wrote a history of SOE for the Cabinet Office. He wrote that 'no directive for SOE aims and intentions in the area as a whole [the Far East] can be found among the surviving documents: probably there never was one.'[14] Later, Cruickshank argued that the failure of the Oriental Mission was due to it having been given European 'terms of reference' which it could not fulfil.[15] In fact, a charter did exist. It was written by the head of the Oriental Mission, Valentine Killery, prior to his departure for Singapore. As far as can be ascertained, no previous writer has identified this charter and integrated it into their work.

Dated 6 April 1941, Killery's charter was entitled 'Far Eastern Mission', written for the attention of Hugh Dalton, Gladwyn Jebb and Brigadier van Cutsem. Hugh Dalton was the first Government minister responsible for SOE; Gladwyn Jebb was Dalton's assistant; Van Cutsem was head of planning for SOE:

> The whole political position in the Far East at the present time is extremely delicate, and it is clear that any precipitate or wide-scale operation may provide Japan with an excuse for direct action against Great Britain, which it is the policy of HMG, at the present moment, to avoid, or at least, postpone as long as possible. Unless therefore war breaks out between Great Britain and Japan during the course of the next year, the main functions of the Far Eastern Mission will be to build up an organisation throughout the Far East, ready to take action to counter Japanese activities in every possible way, and in the meanwhile to concentrate chiefly on the collection and coordination of intelligence and to undertake covert propaganda aimed at countering German political activities and Japanese expansion in all Far Eastern territories, and at encouraging resistance to the young military elements in Japan itself.[16]

Killery then went on to detail the 'immediate' and 'ultimate' objectives of his mission, which were: to set up in Singapore; collect political and economic intelligence; conduct subversion and propaganda; plan schemes to deny resources such as oil and mines; covert assistance to Chinese guerrillas; 'interfere' with goods exported between Germany and Japan; create labour unrest in docks handling goods bound for Germany and Japan; train personnel for Para-naval activities and smuggling.[17] All this was to be carried out 'with a view to attacking all Japanese activities and interests throughout the Far East'.

On 8 April 1941, Killery's 'outline charter' was described by Lieutenant Colonel F.T. Davies at SOE's London headquarters as 'an admirable expose of our intentions in that area', and was further endorsed on 9 April 1941 as an 'excellent document'.[18] At the same time, it was recognised that two points needed to be added, namely 'post occupational organisations in British Possessions on the lines of the Aux Units, Home Forces', and to establish a '[t]raining centre for paramilitary operations'.[19]

There are two key points to note from this charter. Firstly, Killery explicitly addressed official British policy towards Japan, which was to avoid provoking Japan as long as Britain was on the defensive against Germany, and while the United States was not in the War. Between July and October 1940, Britain had even closed the 'Burma Road' which ran from Rangoon to Chungking in Yunnan, along which supplies were transported to Chinese Nationalists fighting Japan. In this context, Brian Farrell considered the policy of non-provocation of Japan to be the major cause of the military and colonial obstructionism that prevented left-behind parties from being properly organised in Malaya.[20]

For Foreign Office (FO) staff in London, as for its representatives in the Far East, being instructed to give all possible assistance to a secret organisation whose task was to prepare for war against Japan, whilst avoiding provocation, was difficult to reconcile. Upon receipt in February 1941 of a telegram outlining SOE operations in the East, Mr Sterndale Bennett, Head of the Far Eastern Department of the FO, wrote 'I am not sure that I understand this draft telegram. It talks about preparing for anti-Japanese activities'; he was 'under the impression that activities of this nature would not be taken unless war with Japan had either broken out or was considered inevitable'.[21] This prompted the comment from someone in SOE headquarters that the 'FO are being sticky', so an assistant was sent to Mr Sterndale Bennett to 'explain matters in greater detail'.[22] It is unclear whether copies of Killery's charter were sent to the Foreign Office or to military and colonial officials in theatre.

Secondly, and linked to this opposition, Killery made it plain in the charter that all Oriental Mission work was to be undertaken only in consultation with the relevant Commanders in Chief (C-in-C) and representatives of His Majesty's Government (HMG). To that end, all the officials who needed to know, such as the governors of Singapore and Hong Kong, were informed about the existence of SOE generally, and specifically that a FEM was on its way to them, before Killery left Britain. They were also to be instructed to assist him in every way.[23]

Other documents provide information about the FEM's objectives. Previous to Killery's charter, Jebb was sent an aide-mémoire on 5 February 1941 which presented the FEM's objectives as:

(1) The disruption of Axis trade.
(2) To train guerrillas in Chungking (Chinese Nationalist head-quarters).
(3) To cause 'embarrassment to the Japanese in Manchuria' in order to get troops diverted there.
(4) To begin planning operations in French Indochina and Siam in the expectation of a Japanese occupation.
(5) To destroy oil resources in Burma and Dutch East Indies if the Japanese were to invade.
(6) To conduct sabotage in Japan.
(7) Propaganda.[24]

An elaboration of Killery's charter in May 1941 advised what FEM should do in specific countries as follows:

Malaya

In any area which is liable to be overrun it is necessary to leave behind partisans who will complete the destruction of anything which is of use to the invading forces, snipe and harry them in every way, attack the dumps, transport and small craft etc., and report information either by messenger or by wireless to aeroplanes.

Burma

(1) Partisans to be organised in the Shan states as in Malaya.
(2) Render innocuous any potential quislings.[25]

Taken together, these documents show that Killery went to the Far East
with clear and rather wide-ranging objectives, which included both the
collection of intelligence and the organisation of guerrillas.

Establishment of FEM in Singapore

After Killery was selected to head the FEM but before he was sent out to
the Far East, two men preceded him. Both A.E. Jones and Francis Nixon
had worked for the Asiatic Petroleum Company in the Far East before
the War.[26] Nixon was recruited into SOE by George Taylor in 1940 and
given the rank of temporary Major. Major Nixon then worked in Cairo
before being sent, in August 1940, 'to explain SOE to Army HQ, India,
and to investigate the possibility of manufacture of SOE stores in
India'.[27] From India, Major Nixon arrived in Singapore on Valentine's
Day, 1941, 'charged with preliminary work'. According to Nixon, he
was SOE's representative in the Far East.[28] A.E. Jones was sent to the Far
East from London, also with orders to report to the C-in-C Far East, to
explore the possibilities of a Far Eastern Mission.

The C-in-C Far East, Air Chief Marshal Sir Robert Brooke-Popham,
was informed of the existence of SOE on 24 January 1941.[29] This
telegram from the War Office revealed the plans for the FEM and its
objectives, plus command and control arrangements; SOE was to come
under Brooke-Popham for everything except political and economic
work. Furthermore, it instructed Brooke-Popham to give 'all help and
advice' to A.E. Jones, who would soon arrive in Singapore, as well as to
the Head of Mission, who would arrive later.[30] A sense of urgency is
apparent, as the C-in-C was instructed to 'reduce delay subsequent to his
[Killery's] arrival' by choosing the location for a Special Training School
(STS) and arranging the military cover for it, as well as arranging office
space for the FEM's headquarters in Singapore.[31]

Just as the Commanders in Chief India and Far East were told about
the FEM in advance of Killery's arrival, so too were the relevant civil
authorities for the countries that SOE was expected to work in.

Regarding Burma, Killery met Sir Reginald Dorman-Smith, newly appointed Governor of Burma, in London before they both left to take up their positions in the Far East.[32]

When Killery arrived on 7 May 1941, no offices had been arranged. A site had, however, been selected for the STS 'at Pula Uban [sic, Pulau Ubin], an island in the Johore Straits'. The site was considered unsuitable by Oriental Mission personnel due to the stagnant pools of water that were home to 'clouds of mosquitos'.[33] A new site was chosen at Tanjong Balai on the south-west coast of the island, and STS 101 eventually opened there in July 1941. This reception set the precedent for the next seven months, which Killery found so intensely frustrating that he offered his resignation to Brooke-Popham in October 1941.

More immediately, after Killery had set up FEM's headquarters in the Union Building in Singapore, his first problem was with Nixon.[34] On 12 February 1941, two days before Nixon arrived in Singapore, Major General Dewing, Brooke-Popham's Chief of Staff, recommended that Nixon be sent back to Bombay if he proved to be an embarrassment. Despite writing on 27 February that Nixon had 'exceeded his instructions' and sent 'verbose and unconstructive telegrams' back to India, Dewing did not have Nixon recalled.[35] Later, Nixon complained that he felt sidelined by Killery, who met Nixon just three times in the seven weeks after he arrived. Nixon wrote that Killery 'did not appear interested in my suggestions', and did not make use of his preparatory work.[36] Part of that preparatory work had been to visit senior Army officers and gain access to their files. Nixon further wrote in his report that Killery had proceeded to approach the military without him, which caused friction between the Army and SOE due to duplication. In Nixon's opinion, until Killery arrived, the military had been 'keen' on SOE.

It was obvious that SOE would need an Army liaison officer, so in April 1941 Lieutenant Colonel Alan Warren of the Royal Marines had arrived in Singapore.[37] Cruickshank would later assert that Warren should have been in charge of the FEM instead of Killery, because having a military man in charge rather than a civilian might have meant better relations with the Army.[38] However, according to Gough, Warren's relationship with the military was little better than Killery's as he struggled for six weeks to get the military 'to prepare for, or even consider the possibility of, a successful Japanese invasion of Malaya'.[39] This lack of coordination and consistency in FEM's contact with the military was probably not enough on its own to sour relations as Nixon argued, but it probably did not help matters either.

Civil and Military Obstruction

Soon after arriving in Singapore, the name 'Far Eastern Mission' was unofficially replaced with 'Oriental Mission'.[40] Perhaps this also added to the confusion for the military, after having various SOE representatives knocking on their door. Whether this influenced their actions or not, during the seven months that the Oriental Mission was in theatre until war with Japan started, senior British Army officers in Singapore and Malaya were uncooperative, to the extent that on 20 October 1941 Killery offered his resignation to Brooke-Popham:

> If you feel that our general prigramme [sic] is worthwhile, and will make a satisfactory contribution to the war effort, and are prepared to give it your full confidence and support, then we will naturally do everything we can to make it a success. If, on the other hand, you have any doubts as to the ultimate value of our efforts, and are therefore not willing to give is [sic] all the necessary support, then we must reconsider the advisability of maintaining the Mission out here; or if you feel the lack of confidence in the Mission due to any doubts as to my own personal ability to head it, I certainly would not wish to stand in the way. If I cannot be of any use here, I shall not only be willing, but anxious, to return home where I might be perhaps of more use ...[41]

Killery's offer was refused. The C-in-C promised to support him, saying that it was important for SOE to have a theatre role.[42] Killery continued, but Brooke-Popham's promised support was not forthcoming. Thirteen days after his resignation offer, meeting notes dated 24 October 1941 reveal how the leadership of the Oriental Mission felt.[43] The notes, written by Killery or his deputy, Major Grey Egerton Mott, stated that '[i]t is clear that neither HE [His Excellency the Governor, Sir Shenton Thomas] or the GOC [Percival] really want any form of OM in Malaya [...] They appear to be scared stiff of Asiatic reactions' which Oriental Mission thought was simply a 'strong weapon to defeat all arguments for an OM organisation'. Oriental Mission's critics argued that there would be a negative reaction from colonial subjects if the civil and military authorities started planning covert operations which had as their basis the idea that the Japanese might successfully conquer British possessions in the East.

This had a direct impact upon the Oriental Mission. Clandestine operations required non-Caucasian personnel, but with authorisation to recruit Asians blocked, little progress could be made. Continuing, the notes alleged that '[t]he GOC is obviously suffering from pique owing to the fact that he was not consulted [about Oriental Mission plans] in the first place.' Since Percival knew about SOE, the inference here must be that the Oriental Mission decided to persevere with the left-behind scheme without Percival's authorisation. Once Percival found out about the plans for Malayan left-behind parties by accident, towards the end of September 1941, he took offence.[44] The Oriental Mission notes of 24 October 1941 concluded with:

It is now left to the GOC to furnish OM with a memorandum setting forth the type of organisation which the Military consider might ve [sic] of use to them and OM will then consider whether such an organisation is feasible or not. If in the considered opinion of the GOC an OM organisation is not really essential, then he had better say so and save alot [sic] of time and Government money being wasted. There are plenty of other fields for our activities and if they are merely going to give us some stupid scheme to play with simply to (as they think) justify our existence, then it is much better to leave Malaya entirely alone.[45]

It took 18 days for Percival to reply to this appeal for guidance. In his memorandum to Killery, Percival wrote that he doubted that intelligence gathering for the Army and guerrilla attacks on the enemy's rear could be combined, but that he would allow the Oriental Mission to operate in both intelligence and behind-the-lines roles anyway. Percival then described what sort of intelligence he would consider useful, and what the Oriental Mission would be permitted to deny to the enemy through sabotage. Major bridges and tunnels on the Malayan Peninsula would be the responsibility of the regular military.[46] Killery's deputy, Major Egerton Mott, replied on 20 November that what Percival suggested was feasible, but since the Oriental Mission had told Percival precisely this plan on 27 August, Percival had wasted time.[47] In response, the General wrote:

> I would suggest that the loss of valuable time was due primarily to the problem being tackled from the wrong angle. Had I been consulted at the very start, the loss of time in producing a faulty scheme would have been avoided. It should be clearly understood that this scheme will become part of the military defence scheme of Malaya.[48]

Egerton Mott also sought an answer on the subject of Asian recruitment. Percival replied that this was still off-limits. While bickering continued, Major Alleyn O'Dwyer, SOE London's Overseas Liaison Officer, was sent to the Far East between 15 and 28 November 1941 to assess the situation.[49] On 20 November, in a letter which implies a maverick role for SOE, O'Dwyer wrote to Killery urging him to work separately from the civil authorities, to place a military liaison officer between Brooke-Popham and himself, and to start recruiting Asians immediately.[50] The restriction on OM's recruitment of Asians by the colonial and military authorities is difficult to comprehend when it is considered that, according to a recent study of SOE in Malaya, approximately '10,000 Malayan Asians were under arms and trained as combat troops' before the war against Japan began in December 1941.[51]

Killery had been pushing for the recruitment of Asian personnel since arrival but, according to Gough, many senior officers considered just the arrival of SOE 'to carry out blatant anti-Japanese covert operations, was rocking the boat. To make things worse they were bloody civilians belonging to SOE which "everyone knew" was Churchill's pet project which consumed essential resources they badly needed.'[52] Alert to what the Oriental Mission wished to do, and facing the conundrum of Foreign Office policy towards the Japanese, both the Governor of Singapore and the British Ambassador in Siam were bitterly opposed to Killery's mission.[53] According to Nixon, however, the military were training Malays for post-occupation work so he saw no reason why SOE should have been blocked.[54]

A further civil objection was economic in nature; men taken for SOE work would be men taken from the economy, whether Asian or Caucasian. Recognising Killery's problem with civil officials, O'Dwyer told Killery that the:

authorities at home are unaware of the extent of the restrictions imposed upon you by some diplomatic and colonial office representatives in territories in which you are intended to operate. Let them know and you will be able to get on.[55]

Later, in the post-mortem reports of the Oriental Mission written in 1942, O'Dwyer wrote that although Killery was honest and hard-working, he had been the wrong person to head the Oriental Mission because 'he went by the book and would not admit defeat'. By going 'by the book', O'Dwyer meant the charter, something O'Dwyer considered 'utterly unworkable' because of the part where Killery had written that the Oriental Mission must have the agreement of both the civil and military authorities.[56] By November 1941 it was probably too late to start distancing the Oriental Mission from the civil authorities anyway.

There were also political objections to the recruitment of Asians, which had two facets. The first specifically concerned Chinese personnel. In Singapore and Malaya there was a sizeable Chinese community, some of whom Killery wanted to train at STS 101, but the major stumbling point was that many were communist. Until recently, the Communists had sought the overthrow of the British and fomented strikes and demonstrations. For this reason, many senior British officers opposed their training for covert operations.[57] What also needed consideration was the Chinese Nationalists under Chiang Kai-shek, and how they might react to their ally training their enemy. The second facet of political concern was the training of *any* colonial subjects because later they might take up arms against Britain. By the time the Japanese attacked Malaya on the night of 7–8 December 1941, O'Dwyer's message to London advising the immediate training of Asian personnel had still not arrived, and so the issue was left unresolved.[58]

The Oriental Mission and Burma

Compared to the situation in Malaya and Singapore, Burma was in a curious position when it came to military command. In the summer of 1940, the Chiefs of Staff (COS) wanted India to come under Middle East Command, and for Burma to be under a new Far East Command.[59] This prompted the Viceroy of India, Lord Linlithgow, to write to the

Secretary of State for India, Leo Amery, advising that it was 'impossible to consider the defence of Burma and India as separate problems from a strategic aspect'.[60]

Previous to the Government of India Act 1935, this would not have been an issue since Burma had been administered as part of the Indian Empire. Now, despite Linlithgow's entreaties, the 333rd meeting of the COS in September 1941 decided to retain Burma under the jurisdiction of the Commander in Chief Far East. Throughout November and into December 1941 rankling over this decision continued, with the eventual outcome that on 11 December, three days after war with Japan started, Burma was transferred to India Command. Then, in January 1942, General Wavell, as commander of the newly created the American, British, Dutch, and Australian (ABA) Command, inherited Burma from India Command.

While Burma's military command was toyed with, its political situation further complicated matters. In April 1937 Burma was formally separated from India. This raised a further issue, which the War Office sought to clarify only in November 1940.[61] The new Burmese constitution gave control of defence to the civilian governor of Burma, which had raised concerns about a 'conflict of responsibilities' because the constitution had a 'special injunction, peculiar to Burma, that he [Commander in Chief Far East] shall ensure that the constitutional relations between the governor and the GOC are not affected, with a special reference to the question of internal security.' Brooke-Popham considered the issue important enough to stop over in Rangoon specially to discuss it with the Governor, on his way out to Singapore.[62]

Burma had two significant command difficulties then, one at a colonial level, and the other at an international/strategic level whereby the country was passed back and forth between different theatre commanders. One last problem caused by the 1935 Act was the distribution of resources for the defence of Burma. Previous to the new constitution, India had supplied Burmese needs, but the War Office noted that since 1937 'Burma is a customer and pays'.[63] The new recommendation was that Burma's defence needs should come from the UK's imperial commitment. Since Burma was not very high up the list of imperial commitments, what this meant on the ground was that in October 1941 the Burifs were reported as being inadequately supplied with light machine guns and mortars.[64] In April 1942 Leo Amery cabled Governor Dorman-Smith authorising him to spend as he saw fit.[65] By then, it was too late.

It was into this complicated Burmese command structure that the Oriental Mission arrived, but from which Killery's Burma section might have benefitted. Although the impression from most of the records is that Killery encountered little cooperation from military and civil officials alike, an Oriental Mission report of 1942 listed Dorman-Smith as helpful.[66] The GOC Burma, Lieutenant General Donald McLeod, was listed as being unhelpful. The same report reveals how in May 1941, the month Dorman-Smith became governor, he sent a representative to Singapore to discuss SOE work with Killery. As a result, Dorman-Smith approved SOE 'in principle', so that in August 1941, when Killery visited Rangoon, firm agreement was reached between Killery, the Governor and the GOC, on the functions of the Oriental Mission in Burma.[67] 'The most important functions of the organisation as agreed at this time were the establishment of left-behind parties and preparation of an organisation to undertake subversive activities across the border into Thailand.'[68] There were two further agreements: firstly, the destruction of resources in Burma that might be of value to the Japanese, and secondly, to create bases from which to supply SOE missions in China.

It was a short-lived arrangement, however, for in September Brooke-Popham went to Burma and axed two of the four agreed functions. First of all, no left-behind parties were to be allowed because 'the military had other plans which would absorb the limited personnel, both European and native, that might be available for that work'.[69] The military, starved of an effective intelligence network, and of people who intimately knew the countries of Southeast Asia, desperately needed the same people as SOE. This meant that by the outbreak of war in December 1941, according to the 'History of the Oriental Mission', there was 'virtually no actively functioning SOE organisation in Burma'.[70]

Secondly, Brooke-Popham axed the scheme for SOE to be in charge of the denial of essential resources. In Burma, this included the wolfram mines at Mawchi, the Namtu mines, the oil refineries at Syriam and the oilfields of Yenangyaung. Why the military wanted to retain control of demolitions is unclear, but SOE staff in London were incensed when they found out in January 1942. Quoting the part of Killery's charter which gave the Oriental Mission the mandate '[t]o draw up plans and make preparations for the destruction of property likely to be useful to Japan in time of war', it was asked why SOE only had advisory role.[71] Killery replied that it had been a civil and military decision.

At the same time as Killery's plans for Burma went awry, the Japanese were busy training Burmese Nationalists 'in general warfare with an emphasis on guerrilla methods'.[72] The Japanese organisation responsible was called the Minami Kikan, a secret military intelligence organisation, commanded by Colonel Keiji Suzuki. Suzuki was active in Rangoon from July 1940, but had had to leave in October when the British grew wise to his Fifth Column activities. During that time, Suzuki had arranged for a Burmese Nationalist leader, Aung San, to travel to Japan, and the two met in Tokyo on 12 November 1940.[73] In Japan, training and planning for a Burmese guerrilla army proceeded. Aung San returned to Burma in February 1941 in a disguise complete with false teeth. Between March and July 1941 Aung San and Suzuki smuggled 30 Burmese Nationalist leaders— since known as the 'Thirty Comrades' — out of Burma to Hainan Island for training. By October 1941 the Thirty Comrades were in Siam, raising the Burma Independence Army (BIA) which would assist the Japanese invasion of Burma. Thus, while Oriental Mission's plans were scuppered by the arguments in Malaya between Killery, Percival and Brooke-Popham in September 1941, Japanese plans were being implemented.

As seen above, the Governor of Burma was responsible under the 1935 Constitution (effective from 1937) for the defence of Burma, yet under Killery's charter, the mission was not allowed to act unless it also had the permission of the C-in-C Far East. Fortunately for SOE in Burma, however, Dorman-Smith seems to have been willing to go to extraordinary lengths to bolster defence, even if this meant dodging Brooke-Popham. For example, and not SOE-related, in June 1941 the first aircraft of the American Volunteer Group (AVG) arrived in Burma.[74] Ostensibly unconnected to the American Government, the AVG was part of the American commitment to Nationalist Chinese forces.

Included in the AVG's role was the protection of lend-lease goods headed for China, transported from Rangoon via the Burma Road to Yunnan. Brooke-Popham accepted AVG involvement, but ruled their aircraft must not be armed whilst in Burma for fear of precipitating war with Japan. Since the RAF presence in Burma was just 16 outdated Brewster Buffaloes of 67 Squadron, Dorman-Smith had welcomed the addition of the AVG's more modern P.40 Tomahawk aircraft. Dorman-Smith spoke to the Burmese premier, U Saw, and between them they outmanoeuvred the C-in-C by basing the US planes at a civilian aerodrome which came under the Burmese Council's jurisdiction, and not the colonial government's, thus allowing them to be armed.[75]

The second example directly concerns the Oriental Mission. Dorman-Smith had allowed Burmese levies to be recruited and trained under Captain Stevenson (sometimes erroneously spelt 'Stephenson') of the Burma Frontier Force, who was later promoted to Lieutenant Colonel and made officer commanding all Burma Levies by Dorman-Smith in December 1941. Stevenson came under the governor's control by 'special appointment' and was 'not made an Oriental Mission man' because of the need for both civil and military assistance, thereby creating the façade of separating the recruitment of Asians from the Oriental Mission.[76] However, Stevenson was given Oriental Mission code number 0.8200, and thus appears to have been *de facto* part of the Oriental Mission, despite being on the government payroll.

In the Official History, Cruickshank makes a clear distinction between Stevenson's levy organisation and SOE.[77] Further scrutiny of SOE files reveals a less clearly defined separation, as indicated above by the 'special appointment'. A table of Oriental Mission casualties differentiated between personnel not only as civilians, officers and other ranks, but also whether their membership of the Oriental Mission was 'open' or 'secret'.[78] For example, Lieutenant Hatton, whom Stevenson classed as a levy officer in his report, was recorded as a secret Oriental Mission officer. On 24 March 1942, Egerton Mott's replacement as Burma liaison officer, Major Peter Lindsay, informed Killery that the exact working relationship between the levies, the Army, and Oriental Mission could not be fixed yet, but that 'we still play an important role with the Burma Levies' as a link between the levies and the civil authorities.[79] It could be concluded from these two examples that Dorman-Smith was circumventing the complicated command and control issues that Killery faced, and the obstructionism of Brooke-Popham. Such was Dorman-Smith's approach that Major Egerton Mott wrote in 1942 that '[f]rom the end of September 1941 to early

February 1942, when I left Burma, HE [Dorman-Smith] was extremely co-operative and helpful in every respect and was very accessible'.[80]

Meanwhile, 'officially', Major W.D. Reeve was in charge of SOE Burma section from October 1941, but remained based in Singapore. In Burma, Reeve had placed L.G. Wheeler in charge of operations. Wheeler's mandate was to organise supply bases into China and prepare for over-the-border operations into Siam and French Indochina. Wheeler had organised Burma into three zones: north, central and south.[81] By November 1941 these were in the first stages of establishment, with stores in transit and personnel being trained at STS 101 in Singapore.[82] On his tour of inspection in November, Major O'Dwyer met some of the men attending STS 101. One officer was the southern zone commander, Alfred Ottaway, plus a few men from his mining company in Tenasserim. These included an Anglo-Burmese officer called Patrick Maddox, a man called Higgins, 'and one or two of the "Anglos"' (presumably Anglo-Burmese, which the author did not recognise Patrick Maddox as being). Ottaway had also recruited eight Anglo-Indians, 'and some 40 natives' from his mining company, but they were not trained at STS 101 due to the C-in-C's orders.[83]

As O'Dwyer was concluding his fact-finding mission in late November, Japanese signals were intercepted advising their nationals to leave countries that would soon be invaded.[84] War was little over a week away. Simultaneous with the pre-emptive strike upon the US fleet at Pearl Harbor on the morning of 7 December, the Japanese landed on the east coast of Siam and Malaya (where it was the night of 7–8 December) and swiftly advanced over the short Kra Peninsula into Tenasserim, in southernmost Burma. Their objectives in Burma included capturing the airstrips at Tavoy and Victoria Point that provided the strategic air link between India and Singapore. A second objective was to secure the flank as Japanese troops advanced down the Malayan Peninsula towards Singapore. Churchill's War Cabinet believed that Singapore 'must be defended until the last' in order to prevent Japanese domination of Southeast Asia and the Bay of Bengal.[85]

The vital naval base at Singapore and the dollar-earning rubber plantations of Malaya were thus the focal point of the war effort in Southeast Asia, and so at this stage Burma was not considered of primary significance. This is perhaps surprising, considering the importance attached by both sides to the flow of resources along the Burma Road to

Chinese Nationalist forces; but with Singapore the centre of gravity, in December General Smyth found his 17 Indian Division less two complete brigades, which had been sent to Malaya. The defence of Burma was left largely reliant upon the Burifs, which had recently expanded to four active battalions, and just two British battalions.[86]

James Lunt, a staff officer with 2 Burma Brigade, recalled a visit by General McLeod in October 1941:

> War with Japan was very much on the cards, he told us. Were that to happen, they could deploy overwhelming force against us. He anticipated no reinforcements. We might delay their advance – no more than that.[87]

General McLeod's sibylline speech proved correct bar one detail; Burma did receive reinforcements with the arrival of 7 Armoured Brigade in March 1942, which helped Allied forces to escape Burma. Oriental Mission also had a role in delaying the Japanese advance, which was probably due in part to Dorman-Smith's approach to defending Burma. In an effort to explain the embarrassing loss of Singapore, and through the bestselling work of Freddie Spencer Chapman, the Oriental Mission's Malayan left-behind parties have received the majority of attention.[88] It is the Burma section of the Oriental Mission, however, that could be considered to have been better prepared by the time war in the East started.

Burma had been divided into three zones, each with its own commander. At least the southern zone, centred on Tavoy, contained a team that had been put through STS 101, and totalled around 50 armed men.[89] H.N.C. Stevenson, after also completing a course at STS 101 in August 1941, had recruited and trained Kachin and Karen levies. Although a total figure for the number of levies is unknown, it is significant (as will be seen) that the Oriental Mission in Burma had been able to recruit from the local population before 7 December, unlike in Malaya. Hide-outs in the jungle had been prepared and plans made to attack the Japanese in Siam once war was declared.

Conclusions

On the eve of war against Japan in December 1941, throughout most of the territories in which it was mandated to operate, Killery's Oriental

Mission had very little to show for having been in theatre for the best part of seven months. Having established that SOE's Far Eastern Mission was in fact equipped with a charter that gave Killery the mandate to prepare for war against Japan, and that the necessary political and military officials in theatre had been briefed for Killery's arrival, it would be reasonable to conclude that the opposite should have been the case. It should be remembered, however, that SOE and its Far Eastern Mission was an immature organisation, and Killery was trying to initiate a new way of fighting the enemy, in a way that seemed not only 'ungentlemanly', but unnecessary, to traditionally minded military and civil officers.

Killery had been selected to lead FEM for his expertise and contacts in the East, and he was ably supported by officers such as Major Egerton Mott, who was described as a 'natural leader' with 'immense initiative and drive'.[90] Choice of personnel aside, in 1941, there was no tangible reason for the military to accept SOE as a weapon of war, for in Europe it was still to prove itself, and in the Middle East it had gained a bad reputation for excessive secrecy, lavish spending and poor results.[91] Indeed, Egerton Mott recognised as late as June 1943 that SOE was 'NOT an ACKNOWLEDGED WEAPON OF WAR', which it must be if it is to operate successfully.[92] Combine all this with an understandable reluctance to lose control of scarce resources, and obstruction of the Oriental Mission becomes more reasonable. Killery was right when he accused Brooke-Popham of having no confidence in SOE, for there was no evident reason why he should.

The civilian response, by comparison, was variable. Subject to different pressures than the military, some civilian officials, such as Consul General Crosby in Siam and Governor Shenton Thomas in Singapore, refused to cooperate with Killery's mission at all during peace time, while in Burma, Dorman-Smith dabbled in subterfuge to enable the levy organisation to be established. For Burma in the months preceding war, the problem was mostly with the military, rather than the politicians, and this meant in practice that Oriental Mission was better able to prepare for war in Burma than in most other British Eastern territories.

An additional problem was the apparent conflict of policy caused by the British Government's desire to avoid provoking Japan on the one hand, while supporting clandestine preparation for war on the other.

Killery had addressed this issue in the charter, which he had had approved in London, but the tension remained 'in theatre' nonetheless.

There were thus multiple reasons why FEM struggled to fulfil its objectives up to the outbreak of war, making it difficult to judge which ones were more damaging. Key military and civil authorities were obstructive (not withstanding Dorman Smith's positive attitude), its objectives clashed with the desire to avoid provoking Japan, and the organisation itself was perceived by the military as having performed badly in the Middle East. To top it all, as we have seen, there were confusions over liaison and clashes of personality, especially in FEM's main base at Singapore.

In these conditions, there were very severe limits on how far Oriental Mission could start to fulfil its objectives. Even when Killery found officials such as Dorman-Smith, who were willing to work with SOE, the obstructionism of the C-in-C Far East prevented the establishment of the straightforward relationship that was necessary for more effective preparation. This is evident from the levy scheme in Burma, where Stevenson and other officers were kept visibly detached from the Oriental Mission in order to avoid explicit disobedience of Brooke-Popham's orders. It is quite astonishing that Dorman-Smith had to manipulate structures of authority to achieve what he perceived as valuable to the defence of Burma. By making sure Oriental Mission was involved with the recruitment and training of Burmese levies, he ensured Burma was one territory in which some progress towards fulfilling Killery's charter occurred before war began.[93] The next chapter will focus on how the Oriental Mission's preparations in Burma stood up to the Japanese assault.

CHAPTER 2

THE ORIENTAL MISSION AND THE FIRST BURMA CAMPAIGN, DECEMBER 1941–JUNE 1942

In the previous chapter we saw how the Oriental Mission (OM) tried to start organising itself in the Far East from May 1941, establishing its base and a training school in Singapore, and making preparations in Burma. This chapter will examine the Oriental Mission's work in Burma from the outbreak of hostilities in December 1941 until the conclusion of the first Burma campaign in May 1942. In these six months, the British Empire lost almost all of Burma to the invading Imperial Japanese Army. British and Empire troops were forced to retreat over 16,000 km (1000 miles), from Victoria Point in Tenasserim, the southernmost tip of Burma bordering modern-day Thailand, over the Chin Hills, and into India on the north-west border of Burma.[1]

The main focus of the chapter is to establish what, if anything, the Oriental Mission contributed to the first Burma campaign. To do this, it is divided into seven sections, with the first three focusing on overall plans, and the last four on specific officers in different regions of Burma. These are, respectively:

Planning:

(1) Command and control and how this affected Oriental Mission.
(2) The left-behind plans.
(3) The recruitment of Burmese.

Operations:

(1) Tenasserim – Captain Alfred Ottaway.
(2) Karenni – Major Hugh Seagrim.
(3) The southern Shan States – Captains Neill Boyt and Arthur Thompson.
(4) Kachin State – Lieutenant Colonel Stevenson.

Command and control issues will be a recurring theme. There was little consistency of Commander in Chief (C-in-C) for the theatre, or of General Officer Commanding (GOC) for the Burma Army. Resolution of these command issues had direct consequences for SOE since the personalities involved had different ideas about its role. One of these differences was contrasting perceptions of Burmese loyalty (both of Burmans and other ethnic groups). These differences influenced opinion about the recruitment of 'natives' by Oriental Mission. As will be shown, these issues and the restraints detailed in the previous chapter continued to affect the left-behind scheme for Burma after war began.

Ascertaining just how far Oriental Mission overcame these barriers in Burma is vital, as the contribution of the Oriental Mission to the first Burma campaign is still not clear from existing works. For example, in the official history, Cruickshank wrote that a rear-guard action by Captain Thompson imposed a 'critical' two-day delay upon the Japanese advance into the southern Shan States in April 1942.[2] By contrast, Field Marshal Slim wrote that Thompson and his Karens were 'swept aside'.[3] In addition, Cruickshank stated that 'most importantly', the Oriental Mission prevented the Japanese from building an airstrip in north-east Burma at Fort Hertz after the retreat to India in 1942, yet how the Japanese were denied Fort Hertz and why this action by Oriental Mission officers and levies was important is not fully explained.[4]

Planning

In order to answer these questions about the place and role of Oriental Mission in the wider campaign, however, it is first necessary to give a brief overview of the first Burma campaign.[5] The War Office recognised four phases to the campaign.[6]

The first phase included the initial Japanese attack in Tenasserim upon Victoria Point until the fall of Tavoy on 19 January. During this period, Oriental Mission had a team in Tenasserim, but otherwise scrambled to get men and arms into the field.

In the second phase, the main events were the retreat to the Sittang River and the loss of Rangoon by 8 March 1942. The disaster at the Sittang Bridge on 23 February 1942 has been the subject of much controversy, with Louis Allen arguing that that it was at this point that 'the fate of Burma was sealed'.[7] Slim also called the Sittang 'the decisive battle of the first campaign'.[8] His reasoning was that after the Sittang battle, Rangoon could not be defended. With the capture of Rangoon, the Japanese had achieved one of their prime objectives, namely cutting supply to the Chinese along the Burma Road.

The third and fourth phases of the campaign consisted of milestones in the northward advance of the Japanese. By the 30 April the British had withdrawn from Mandalay and the Japanese had taken Lashio. By 8 May, Myitkyina in the north and Akyab Island, with its airbase on the west coast of Burma close to the Indian border, were in Japanese possession.

Some of the reasons for the Japanese victory are probably to be found in the muddle of command and control in Burma, but if indeed the battle for Burma was lost on the 23 February at the Sittang Bridge, what place does the Oriental Mission have in a history of the Burma campaign of 1942?

Command and Control

It has already been noted in Chapter One that when it came to command, Burma had been in a curious position since the Government of India Act came into effect in 1937. The new constitution made the defence of the colony the responsibility of the governor of Burma, but the creation of a Far East Command also placed Burma under Brooke-Popham as C-in-C Far East from 18 November 1940. When the plans for a Far Eastern Mission of SOE were made, it was agreed that Killery, as head of the Far Eastern Mission, would operate under the orders of the C-in-C Far East. An argument about whether or not Burma should be under the C-in-C Far East or C-in-C India had subsequently rumbled on into 1941, and on 11 December 1941, three days after the war with

Japan started, Burma was placed under the control of Wavell as C-in-C India by Churchill and the Chiefs of Staff (COS).

The next command change was made on 7 January 1942 when the American, British, Dutch and Australian (ABDA) Command was established. Command of Burma was transferred from India Command to ABDA, but remained under Wavell, who had been appointed ABDA commander. Wavell had never agreed that Burma should be part of his ABDA Command with his headquarters situated so far away in Batavia (now Jakarta), Java. After Singapore fell, Burma reverted to India Command under General Alan Hartley on 21 February 1942.

This meant that in the space of three months from December 1941 to February 1942, Burma had had three different Commanders in Chief and changed theatre command four times. Burma also had three Army commanders during the same time period. Lieutenant General McLeod was replaced by Lieutenant General Thomas Hutton from 27 December 1941, then Lieutenant General Harold Alexander succeeded Hutton from 9 March 1942.[9]

This all affected SOE because it had to conform to Army command boundaries, meaning Oriental Mission also had three Commanders in Chief, and in Burma three GOCs. With different commanders come different personalities and methods of operating, and with different commands come different responsibilities. For example, Burma had been at the forefront of India Command's concerns, but not ABDA's with its HQ in Batavia. As soon as the war started, a section of STS 101 was sent to Rangoon to do what 'work as was then permissible'.[10] The 'permissible work' altered with the start of the war because the policy of doing nothing to provoke Japan could be discarded, but it still depended upon the C-in-C and the GOC.

It was not only Wavell who had reservations over command jurisdictions. On 16 or 17 December, a cable from Singapore to London argued that the centre of gravity had shifted from Singapore to Burma and China.[11] This provoked a fresh round of disagreements. The head of SOE in London, Sir Frank Nelson, recommended that the area be divided into two missions; a northern mission under John Keswick to operate out of Chungking attached to Chiang Kai-Shek, and a southern mission under Killery, which included Burma, attached to Wavell as part of ABDA. Wavell disagreed. He thought that SOE HQ should be in Burma, with just a small liaison team to be left with him in Java.[12]

Wavell's attitude towards SOE had been shaped by his experience of SOE when he was C-in-C Middle East between 1939 and June 1941. There, SOE had been accused of incompetence and 'gross extravagance and misuse of taxpayers' money', to the extent that the head of SOE in London, Sir Frank Nelson, had flown out to Cairo to resolve the crisis.[13]

At the same time, messages urging action in Burma to prevent a fiasco like that unfolding in Malaya were sent by London, which specifically asked about plans for left-behind parties.[14] Any obstructions were to be reported immediately. Just three days before Singapore fell, on 12 February, SOE command boundaries were at last settled. A China HQ under John Keswick was to be established in Chungking. Burma was to be an independent mission under Major Lindsay, attached to General Hutton as GOC. If Burma was overrun, then this mission would be absorbed into SOE's India Mission. A southern area was to be worked out based on Japanese advances. Killery was ordered to settle personnel and equipment with Keswick and Lindsay and then proceed to London.[15]

With command in Burma settled, the War Office wired General Hutton on 25 February 1942 with a message for Lindsay. This was two days after the battle at the Sittang Bridge, where Slim said the battle for Burma was lost. The instructions were:

> Subject to the GOC's approval, you have full discretion to evacuate Rangoon office to India should this be necessary. In the meantime you will a) take such action as you consider necessary with regard 'left behind parties' and b) with the assistance of the appropriate authorities you will recruit suitable European personnel selected for their special knowledge, particularly of the Karenni districts, the northern and southern Shan states and Kachin; for e.g. police and forest officers and mining engineers. These officers should be given every facility to recruit such native personnel as they desire from their respective districts with a view to future infiltration. Our intention is that these personnel will be trained either in Burma or India as the military situation permits.[16]

It was over a year since telegrams to Army commanders and colonial officials had been sent from Britain in order to prepare for doing precisely this. It was almost a month (25–28 January 1942) since

Dorman-Smith and Hutton had allowed the Oriental Mission to recruit Asians and to organise left-behind parties.[17] Yet the first entry in SOE War Diary for March 1942 states that '[t]he story of the FEM during March is largely one of reorganisation', and 'command issues still dominated the agenda'.[18]

Major Lindsay did not want to have to act on definite orders from London because he felt that he had at last 'built up the framework of an effective organisation' which he wanted control of as 'man on the spot'. London granted Lindsay his wish. There was surprise therefore, when on 14 March, the head of SOE's India Mission, Colin Mackenzie, was cabled to the effect that he could take over the Burma organisation whenever he thought it prudent to do so. Burma's Oriental Mission officers were angry. Major W.D. Reeve cabled London to say that he was 'perfectly happy to be dismissed' if London thought that the Burma staff were not doing their job. SOE London denied that they were unsatisfied, but at this stage they considered it inevitable that SOE in Burma would have to come under Mackenzie to conform to military boundaries.

On 3 April, the War Office sent a telegram to the C-in-C India advising that SOE should have a 'bigger operational role' because more territory had come under enemy control. These sentiments were reiterated by Sir Frank Nelson between 3 and 9 April when he wrote that, as a result of Japanese victories, SOE needed to reorganise from conducting 'work of a preparatory nature' to a 'more operational character'.[19] On 4 April, Mackenzie took ownership of Oriental Mission's Burma Section, and on 9 April Wavell told the Chiefs of Staff (COS) that SOE's immediate job was to help protect Burma, India and Ceylon.[20] Less than a month later, the Japanese were in control of most of Burma.[21]

The 'Left-Behind' Scheme

The left-behind scheme had first been introduced in Britain during the summer of 1940. The idea was that in the event of invasion, specially trained groups of soldiers would emerge from secret hide-outs and attack from behind the lines. In Burma, plans for a left-behind scheme were significantly influenced by the attitude of the GOC. Where General Hutton had been agreeable but non-committal in his approach to the Oriental Mission, General Alexander was described by Lindsay as 'guerrilla-minded'.[22] Nonetheless, during Hutton's time as GOC (December 1941–March 1942), the nucleus of a dual left-behind scheme was set up. One part was based on the frontier districts, and the other for central Burma. In the frontier areas, where the population was mostly non-Burman, the left-behind scheme relied upon the recruitment of 'levies' from the Shan, Karen and Kachin peoples. In the centre, there were political considerations which necessitated the direct involvement of Dorman-Smith.

The 'levy scheme' in the frontier areas was more advanced than the left-behind scheme for central Burma. In an update sent to London from Oriental Mission headquarters in Maymyo on 3 February 1942, it was reported that extending south from Prome, all Delta Districts had a left-behind scheme in place, and that the Siamese border area from Papun north were all 'covered', albeit with 'limited arms and stores'.[23] The Papun area was led by Captain Hugh Seagrim.[24] North of Seagrim in the southern Shan States was Captain William Evans, who had been trained at STS 101 in November 1941.[25] In the frontier area of the northern Shan States, H.N.C. Stevenson had organised his Kachin districts along the 'right lines'. This included having bands of men in each frontier village to defend the area by removing livestock and destroying any supplies or bridges. These bands were also trained for offensive action against the invader.[26]

For central Burma, consultation for left-behind parties was still in progress at the end of January 1942. These districts included Rangoon and the Pegu Yomas, the hills that run north from just outside Rangoon.[27] Each district was to have a left-behind scheme with the District Commissioner from the colonial administration assisting its coordination. Instructions were to disrupt the enemy after occupation and to provide intelligence.[28] Within each district, there were to be two 'natives' 'in the know' who were to recruit and organise 'toughs'. Once the British had withdrawn, these 'toughs' would distribute British-supplied weapons. The 'toughs' were to be 'stiffened' by infiltrating specially trained 'thugs'. Since it was expected that the British would be able to maintain a frontline in central Burma, the European District Commissioner or the Superintendent of Police was to remain close behind British lines in order to oversee messages and finances. This is the plan that the governor, Sir Reginald Dorman-Smith, put before the Burmese Defence Council. The outcome was that a Burman called Tun Hla Oung was appointed its Chief Organiser.[29]

Captain Tun Hla Oung of the Burma Police was described as being the most 'trusted lieutenant' of the Home Minister, U Aye.[30] The Oriental Mission officer in charge of Burma, however, was suspicious of Captain Tun. Major Reeve thought Tun was a 'would-be leader of young Burmese' (in other words a nationalist sympathiser) and therefore unsuitable for a clandestine role. Major Lindsay also had doubts, describing Tun as an 'ambitious opportunist' who was 'not very reliable'.[31]

After an appeal to Dorman-Smith to have Captain Tun removed in favour of a European officer failed, it was decided that in order to keep control, the Oriental Mission should 'cooperate' with Captain Tun and U Aye. In order to manipulate the situation to their benefit, Reeve suggested that the task was too large for just Captain Tun to coordinate, and proposed that Frederick Wemyss of the Burma Police take half the proposed area of operations.[32] In addition, Major Reeve decided to recruit the Oriental Mission's own 'thugs', and to make contact with the District Commissioners in Captain Tun's area in an effort to get the District Commissioners 'for ourselves'. After having trained both Captain Tun's men as well as Oriental Mission's own 'thugs', left-behind parties were sent into Moulmein and Kyaikto in southern Burma.

There seems to be no record of anything specific that the left-behind scheme involving Tun and Wemyss achieved. By early April 1942, Major Reeve felt that Captain Tun was 'sitting on a fence' waiting for the Japanese. Reeve then decided to withdraw Oriental Mission support for this scheme after the Governor again refused to remove Captain Tun in an effort to keep the Burmans onside.[33] One Oriental Mission report concluded that 'the whole practicality of the scheme was smothered by that mixture of inertia, personal prejudice and politics THAT ONLY THOSE WITH EXPERIENCE OF ORIENTAL ADMINISTRATION CAN REALLY APPRECIATE'.[34]

The Recruitment of Burmese

The suspicion felt towards Captain Tun by Major Reeve is illustrative of a wider argument about the first Burma campaign. The argument about the extent to which there was a Burmese Fifth Column in 1942 is given impetus by the fact that when the Japanese invaded Burma, they did so with Burmese allies. The Burma Independence Army (BIA) commanded by Major General Aung San was only about 300 strong in January 1942, yet it had more strategic effect than it warranted.[35] The prevailing view of the British military throughout their retreat was that they were operating in an inhospitable country where 'all Burmans are our enemies'.[36] The Japanese tactic of dressing as Burmese in order to infiltrate British positions, and stories of Burmese using their *dahs* (a machete or short sword) to slit the throats of isolated British servicemen lent further credibility to this perception. Bayley and Harper, by contrast, allege that the British Army fabricated the rumour that all Burmese were traitors 'to justify and explain its failures'.[37] A further accusation is that the military scapegoated the civil administration – and particularly Dorman-Smith – in order to blame them for the humiliating reversals of 1942.[38]

Against this view of the Army, both the civil authorities and the Oriental Mission supported the Burmese population. Major Lindsay estimated that 'only 20 per cent perhaps are violently against us, a similar number are perhaps pro-us, and the remainder are anybodys [sic] – dependent upon who is the stronger'.[39] Another difference between the Oriental Mission and the military was their confidence in the Burmese as soldiers. This made an already under-supplied Army reluctant to supply weapons and officers to the Oriental Mission in order to train and arm people who the Army considered to be people of dubious loyalty and fighting qualities.[40]

As it became clear that the campaign was being lost by early March 1942, more and more Burmans decided, perhaps understandably, to take their chances with the incoming Japanese and BIA, but a distinction should be made between those who actively assisted the Japanese by force of arms and those who did not desire to be seen helping the British for fear of reprisals. According to Dorman-Smith, the BIA never exceeded 5,000 during the first Burma campaign, or 0.02 per cent of the population.[41] Stanley Short, a Bible Churchman's Missionary Society (BCMS) clergyman in the Shan States believed that 'the epithet "traitor", which was hurled by all and sundry both during and after the Burma campaign' only applied to about 10 per cent of the population.[42] That 10 per cent, he wrote, were both the educated and unemployed Burmans who placed their hope in the promises of the Japanese co-prosperity sphere.

It was not only the Burmans whose loyalty was questioned. The Thompson Po Min movement had existed for about a decade. It was a Karen group that was anti-British, and turned pro-Japanese in 1942.

Loyal Karen wanted the leaders, the brothers Thompson and Johnson Po Min, arrested. The movement was popular in the Pegu Yomas and the Yado area.[43]

The military and Oriental Mission agreed that the Thompson brothers should be arrested, and they were both arrested twice. On each occasion, those responsible for freeing the Thompson brothers were the Home Minister, U Aye, and Tun Hla Oung. Dorman-Smith refused to act on the matter because he wanted to keep Burmese Nationalists onside. In Major Lindsay's view 'the Governor's attitude and willingness to accept the Home Minister's opinion against his British advisors was fantastic'.[44] What this serves to illustrate is that sometimes the military and the Oriental Mission could see eye-to-eye on matters that the civil administration disagreed with, and that on specific matters Dorman-Smith was wilful enough to pursue his own colonial political needs in defiance of the military and SOE.

The Oriental Mission and Levy Operations

While Burman left-behind operations seem to have made relatively little headway, there is a large amount of archival evidence concerning the levy operations. The levy scheme had been started by H.N.C. Stevenson before December 1941, when it gained the official support of the Governor, Dorman-Smith, prior to war. The tasks of the levies were:

(1) To restore the rapidly deteriorating prestige of the British so as to ensure that a friendly attitude would be maintained towards our troops.
(2) To counter enemy propaganda.
(3) To organise the various districts so that guides, interpreters, transport, food, etc., would be available to our troops.
(4) To organise village watching of roads and tracks and, if found possible, local resistance to small scale enemy infiltration.
(5) Further it was hoped to train bands of picked braves to carry out reconnaissance and raids into enemy territory.
(6) So to organise the districts that, should they be overrun by the enemy, food and transport would be hidden, roads and tracks blocked and the enemy advance delayed as much as possible by booby traps, demolitions, sniping, etc.

(7)   Always to obtain the maximum intelligence and transmit it to the nearest Military HQ.[45]

Ostensibly not part of SOE, in practice the officers that led the levies were all allocated an Oriental Mission code symbol, and were either recruited directly to SOE or seconded from existing Burma military units. Each of the following sections focuses on the operations of some of the individual officers in the area in which they were given command.

Tenasserim: Captain Alfred Ottaway MM

About 27 September, shortly after Oriental Mission had divided Burma into three operational zones, Captain Alfred Ottaway was appointed commander of the Southern Zone which consisted of the Salween and Tenasserim area.[46] Ottaway was General Manager of the Tavoy tin mines, which was where he established his headquarters. First commissioned in 1936, Ottaway was an Army of Burma Reserve Officer (ABRO) serving in the Burma Auxiliary Force. As part of the Burma Auxiliary Force, Ottaway had been promoted to captain in November 1939 and then put in charge of the Tavoy District.[47] After being contacted by the Oriental Mission, Ottaway recruited employees from his mine who were then trained at STS 101 in November 1941, along with ten Australians who had volunteered in Singapore.[48]

In an agreement with the local Army commander, Lieutenant Colonel Cotton, plans were made for left-behind parties in Tenasserim. Cotton provided Ottaway with a list of objectives to blow up, and authorised mine denial. Ottaway's other task was to prepare jungle hide-outs from where his teams could provide intelligence and attack the Japanese from behind the lines.[49] Ottaway was confident that he could fulfil his objectives. Major Reeve, the officer in charge of the Oriental Mission in Burma, was less sure, though; in his opinion Ottaway was 'playing us for suckers' and 'out for himself', part of the evidence for this being that Ottaway kept on asking for more money. The Australians decided that they would not serve under him, although Reeve suspected that this might have been a case of 'coldfootedness'. Killery nevertheless believed that they should persevere with Ottaway, and Major O'Dwyer, who had been sent out on a fact-finding mission to the Far East from London, reported that Ottaway's group was 'excellent material' after he saw them at STS 101.[50]

Once the Japanese invaded Tenasserim, Ottaway's group carried out a limited denial of their tin mine before they escaped to Rangoon where they arrived in early February 1942. Major Reeve continued to be critical of Ottaway's leadership. He wrote that Ottaway and his men should have stayed behind the lines, and not made up an 'excuse' that they had led cut-off soldiers to safety. It was later verified that Lieutenant Colonel Cotton had specifically asked for Ottaway 'to rescue certain of his troops that were cut off'.[51] Another reason given by Ottaway for not staying in their jungle hide-outs was that they did not believe the local population was trustworthy.

Nonetheless, a second mission in Tenasserim was organised. Ottaway and his men had reached Rangoon by commandeering some boats in the town of Ye, about half way between Moulmein and Tavoy. The mission, consisting of a team of six led by Lieutenant Maddox, was to destroy the remaining boats that they had seen in the area. The team was infiltrated by motor launch in February 1942 with the agreement of the GOC, since these boats could have been used by the Japanese to reach Rangoon. The mission was well planned and the party had 'seemed confident of success'.[52] Upon arrival, the party decided that it was too dangerous – because of the local population – to start drawing attention to themselves by causing explosions. They therefore made for their exit rendezvous and left having achieved nothing. The report concluded that '[t]he party under MADDOX were all young and not tough enough for the task'.

Karenni: Major Seagrim

Major Hugh Seagrim became one of Burma's most famous wartime officers, with a book appearing about him as early as 1945.[53] Seagrim had been commissioned into the 1st Kumaon Rifles on 31 January 1929, and was later seconded to the 3rd Battalion Burma Rifles ('Burifs') from April 1937.[54] Promoted to temporary major in May 1941, Seagrim served with a Karen battalion. On periods of leave before the War, Seagrim would hike around Burma with half a dozen or so of his Karen troops.[55] Consequently, his knowledge of the Karen people and their environs potentially made him a valuable asset to both the Army and Oriental Mission. Seagrim was only secured for service with the Oriental Mission on 28 January 1942 after having been 'pinch[ed]' by

General Smyth for scouting duties with 17 Indian Division.[56] This annoyed Major Lindsay because it delayed the organisation of levies by several weeks.[57]

Seagrim eventually made his Oriental Mission HQ in Papun where he began training the Burma Military Police from the district and recruiting additional levies. The aim was to harass the invading Japanese along the Moulmein-Pegu-Rangoon Road. By February, Seagrim had secured 200 volunteers who were then used on patrols.[58] The problem was arms. A request for weapons was sent to Captain Noel Boyt's Oriental Mission group in the Mawchi Mine area. Although some extra weapons such as shotguns and hunting rifles, it was not much of a supplement to his meagre stock of captured Italian rifles. By March, Seagrim was behind the lines, and by the end of April he went into hiding with the Karen in the village of Mawtudo, situated just north of the Toungoo–Mawchi Road. He continued operations against the Japanese on this road until October 1942, although the surviving records don't yield any details about the success, or otherwise, of his endeavours.[59]

So what did Seagrim achieve from January to May 1942? He had gone to Papun because 'the morale of the Karen had deteriorated so rapidly and British prestige sunk very low'.[60] In the short term, Seagrim assisted British troops that had been cut off when the Sittang Bridge was blown in February 1942, and carried out limited attacks on the advancing Japanese. In the longer term, Seagrim's network of levies would eventually provide the seed of what has been called 'the most substantial military achievement of SOE's war in Asia, perhaps in any theatre of World War Two'.[61] That Seagrim was not more effective in 1942 with such a willing response to his appeal for levies was, according to Lindsay, at least partially the fault of the commander of 17 Division:

> if SMYTHE had allowed 0.8201 [Seagrim] to do as he wanted when he first reported, wrecking of enemy communications would have been possible and certainly guides and information would have been provided, which would have proved invaluable to our forces.[62]

Seagrim felt that '[h]ad the volunteer organisation been formed a month earlier, things would have been quite different'.[63] Nonetheless, Seagrim remained behind the lines from March 1942 until February 1944, when he gave himself up to the Japanese.

The Southern Shan States – Captains Noel Boyt and Arthur Thompson

After Rangoon was vacated on 7 March 1942, the main British line of retreat was up the western side of the Pegu Yomas towards Prome. Major General Bruce Scott's 1 Burma Division provided flanking protection on the eastern side of the Yomas until relieved by the Chinese V Army around the 20 March, when the latter took over the defence of Toungoo.

The road east from Toungoo goes to Mawchi, and a little further on it turns north towards Taunggyi. From Taunggyi a road goes due west into the large town of Meiktila. These two important roads are the main routes east into the Karen and Shan States. Seagrim's hide-out in the forest near Mawtudo village was north of the Toungoo–Mawchi Road, and south of the Meiktila–Taunggyi Road.

The first of two significant actions fought by the Oriental Mission and the levies during the first Burma campaign took place on the Toungoo–Mawchi Road in early April 1942. The officers in charge were Captains Noel Boyt and Arthur Thompson. Thompson had gone out to Burma in 1938, and was commissioned into the Burma Rifles in December 1939.[64] Before joining the Oriental Mission, Boyt was a forest manager for Steel Brothers & Co. After being ordered to close down the business, on 22 February, he 'met a Captain STEPHENSON [sic] . . . and accepted an invitation to join the ORIENTAL MISSION under Major LINDSAY'.[65]

Captain Boyt arrived in Mawchi on the 28 February, where he reported to Brigadier Alfred Curtis, commander of 13 Indian Brigade.[66] Curtis thought the levy idea was a 'boy-scout show'.[67] Boyt had to give Curtis 'a personal letter' from 1 Burdiv's commander 'which instructed [Curtis] in no uncertain terms, to give us his cooperation'.[68] Boyt later reported:

> During this period, I enrolled some 500 loyal Karen men and organised the thorough patrolling of all roads and paths from the SIAMESE border (E. OF MAWCHI) to BAWGALAYGYI and South into SIAM, [. . .] The Karen villagers under their leaders

were keen and hard working and some 5,000 sq. miles of wild jungle country was completely covered by these Levies. Unfortunately only about 15 per cent of the men could be armed with rifles and shot guns from the stocks I had available but the remainder armed themselves with their efficient cross bows which were, on occasions, more effective than firearms. Similarly, in BAWGALAYGYI, MCCRINDLE had recruited about the same number of Levies and was doing excellent work [...] Capt. SEAGRIM was down on the PAPUN/SHWEGYIN line and extended his activities to points well south of this line. I was in touch with SEAGRIM who had about 250 well-armed Levies under him. To the North of the MAWCHI Road, CECIL SMITH had recruited 1,750 men, well organised into companies but only 8 per cent were issued with firearms owing to lack of stocks. Summing up, in the short space of 3 weeks we had 3,000 Levies on the ground, doing first class work, patrolling; gathering intelligence; decimation of Burmese spies (some 14 men were executed); hiding of supplies cached; successful attacks on villages held by the enemy; helping stragglers from the SITTANG [...] Later we were able to give valuable help to the VI CHINESE ARMY when 13th Brigade left and all MAWCHI Road demolitions were taken over by the Levies.[69]

Curtis and 13 Brigade had retreated on Meiktila by the end of March, and the rest of 1 Burdiv had handed over Toungoo to the Chinese so that British forces could concentrate in central Burma, where General Alexander hoped to fight a decisive battle.

On 19 March 1942, General William Slim became the new Burcorps commander. His eastern flank was protected by Chinese 200 Division (the size of a British brigade) in Toungoo, and Oriental Mission's Karen Levies.[70] Further east, the Chinese VI Army's three divisions was spread out up to the Chinese border. Both the Army and Oriental Mission struggled to liaise effectively with the Chinese due to a lack of interpreters. Lindsay speculated that the Oriental Mission had been one-tenth of the use to Chinese forces that they would have been to British forces, concluding that the 'value of the levies was wasted'.[71]

The 200 Division held up the Japanese – advancing north from Rangoon – at Toungoo for 11 days until the end of March.[72] In the chaos of their retreat, the Chinese failed to blow the bridge over the Sittang, which was the entrance to the Toungoo–Mawchi Road. 'The Japanese thus gained immediate use of this road, which lead into the heart of the Karen Hills and Shan States'.[73] Slim felt that '[t]he loss of Toungoo was in fact a major disaster, second only to our defeat at the Sittang Bridge'.[74]

Now it was only Boyt's hastily organised levies and Captain Arthur Thompson's under-strength Karen company that stood between the Japanese 56 Division and Chinese 55 Division of VI Army which was assembling on the road between Loikaw and Mawchi. General Iida planned to encircle Allied forces in Mandalay by hooking up through the southern Shan States and following the road north from Mawchi towards Lashio. An unopposed advance into the southern Shan States might have made this possible.[75]

Thompson and his Karen company arrived in Toungoo about 22 March, just before the Chinese lost the town. On 23 March he was ordered by General Bruce Scott to report to Captain Boyt in Mawchi, in order to stiffen the Oriental Mission levies in Karenni with trained troops, and to help protect the flank of the retreating 1 Burma Division. He set out with 132 Karens on the afternoon of 24 March.[76] Before leaving for Mawchi, Thompson wrote that his company was relieved of their 'Bren guns, cup dischargers, tools', which went north with his battalion's other two Karen companies. Left with just rifles, four Tommy guns, and 50 rounds per man, they set off towards Mawchi. On 26 March they crossed the Paletwa Bridge and next day met Captain Boyt.[77] The following two days were spent in the town of Bawgalagyi training the levies in the use of rifle and grenades before moving back to the Paletwa Bridge on the 30 March, by which time the Chinese had blown it up. The next two days were spent covering the men blowing holes in the road above the bridge, until on 2 April at about 12.30am the Japanese arrived. Thompson wrote that there were 'several lorries, armoured cars and motor-cycles'. Later, he estimated that there was between 700 to 800 Japanese troops opposing him.[78]

With their limited fire power, Thompson's Subedar Major, Kan Choke, decided to allow the enemy to get as close as possible before opening fire.[79] At 20 metres (65 feet), battle was joined and lasted for about 90 minutes, during which 25 Karens were lost, and, according to Thompson, 30 Japanese.[80] Thompson was forced to retreat when one of his platoons was over-run and captured, threatening their route of withdrawal. Later in the day, one of the captured platoon's riflemen arrived after having managed to escape. He had grim news; the Jemadar commanding the platoon had been decapitated by the Japanese.[81]

The remainder of 2 April was spent retreating east along the road towards Kyichaung, blowing holes in the road, 'laying innumerable booby traps' and destroying two wooden bridges.[82] A passage from Thompson's novel *Desperate Journey* describes how such booby traps might have been placed:

> Twice more he placed grenades – one wedged beneath a fallen branch which he dragged out from the bank; the other in the dust under an exposed length of heavy bamboo. If they inflicted casualties, well and good, but their main purpose was to slow the Japanese down; make them hesitant.[83]

The booby traps may well have proved a nuisance to the following Japanese, as the next engagement occurred on 4 April at around 2.30 am. At Kyichaung, the Japanese used mortars from which the Burifs had little protection as they had been relieved of their 'tools' at Toungoo. By the end of the fight, three hours later, Thompson had lost 43 men, taking his force down to about 60. The unit had sustained over 50 per cent casualties since leaving Toungoo. The Japanese force they now faced was estimated at being about 1,200.[84] The Japanese could have cut them off using jungle tracks which the Karen knew about. Perhaps illustrating how the Japanese were denied these paths, in Thompson's novel the entrances to these jungle tracks were camouflaged by the Subedar Major. By 5 April, Thompson and his men reached Mawchi.

In Mawchi, the Oriental Mission handed over to the Chinese VI Army under Generals Chang and Liang. The latter would now be responsible for the demolitions in the town. The delaying action along the Mawchi Road was over. In his report, Thompson concluded:

> I am certain that if we had had some LMG's, grenade dischargers and tools for digging in we could have done much better. Without slit-trenches we had no protection at all, against mortar fire particularly. Neither had we transport to get the wounded away who had to be left. There were NO desertions while moving from

TOUNGOO to MAWCHI and the majority of our losses were either killed, wounded or taken prisoner.[85]

There were now 58 left from the original 135 Burifs. Thompson took up the story of his subsequent escape from Burma in *Desperate Journey*.[86]

Although written under his pen-name of Francis Clifford, *Desperate Journey* is billed as a true story. It begins with Thompson's recommendation for a Distinguished Service Order (DSO), written by Lieutenant Colonel Stevenson, Commandant Burma Levies:

> Capt. Thompson showed the highest quality of courage, leadership, and skilful handling of his men throughout. His determined reaction to enemy pressure during this critical period was of the utmost importance to all concerned in this very significant action. In all Capt. Thompson gained some four days time [sic] for regrouping of the Chinese 6th Army in the Southern Shan States. This enabled the 6th Army to hold up the Japs just long enough to let the Chinese 5th Army, then fighting at Pyinmana, send a division (the 200th) round to Taunggyi in time to stem the enemy's thrust westwards through Thazi-Meiktala [sic]-Yenangyaung. It is a fact that Capt. Thompson's magnificent delaying action saved the Chinese and British armies in Burma from encirclement.[87]

By contrast, in *Defeat into Victory*, Field Marshal Slim wrote of Thompson and Boyt's efforts:

> The British-led Karen Levies, newly raised and partially trained, tried to delay them, but they and the Chinese were swept away and the town [Mawchi], with some of the most valuable wolfram mines in the world, fell into Japanese hands.[88]

Gough considered Slim's judgement as 'rather unfair', though they agreed Thompson faced a Japanese brigade.[89] Both Boyt and Thompson estimated around 1,200 Japanese opposed them, about the size of one or two wartime battalions.[90] Accepting that it was a vanguard battalion of the Japanese 56 Division, most sources contradict Slim's opinion of the forces being 'swept aside'. Thompson's recommendation estimated that his actions held the Japanese for at least four days. Lindsay reported that they held up the Japanese for eight days.[91] However long the Burifs and the levies held up the Japanese, it was their actions that prevented the Japanese from driving to Mawchi unopposed, where the Chinese were able to concentrate. This rear-guard action might have saved the Allied armies in Burma from a greater mauling on their retreat, even if encirclement of the Allied armies, as asserted in Thompson's recommendation, was unlikely.[92] Lastly, and with an eye to future operations, this action had also shown that levies would fight provided they had 'a suitable minimum stuffing of trained troops with good officers'.[93]

So what explains Slim's judgement? Gough put it down to Slim never having been a supporter of Special Forces. Perhaps there is more to it. The Burifs were not considered reliable troops by the British Army after the early actions during the retreat to the Sittang. The Oriental Mission and levy scheme were viewed as a waste of resources and equipment run by untrained civilians and consisting of still more untrained 'natives' of dubious loyalty. If the Army could salvage anything of its reputation from Burma in 1942 it was the almost Dunkirk-like 'victory' of a successful retreat into India. Could that successful retreat be owed – however partially – to the action of a few Oriental Mission officers, 135 Karen Burifs and an unknown quantity of hastily raised and partially armed levies?

Kachin State: Lieutenant Colonel Stevenson

With the Japanese breakthrough at Toungoo and drive north through the Shan States in April, the last phase of the first Burma campaign began for the Oriental Mission. Although Colin Mackenzie, head of SOE's India Mission, had taken the decision to bring the Oriental Mission's Burma section under his control on 4 April, this did not immediately impact upon Oriental Mission personnel retreating north towards Kachin country. Similar to their job on the Toungoo to Mawchi Road, Oriental Mission was responsible for delaying the enemy along the main roads leading into northern Burma, covering the withdrawal of 'the last elements of the army from north-west Burma'.[94]

Even when significant actions involving the Oriental Mission are mentioned in the official history, their role remains unacknowledged.

For example, both Kirby and Slim discuss the confusion at the Shweli Bridge.[95] The Shweli Bridge was important because it was on the road north from Lashio before the town of Bhamo, beyond which are Myitkyina, Sumprabum and – in the far north – Fort Hertz. The troops responsible for the Shweli Bridge were initially Burma Frontier Force (BFF), later joined by Oriental Mission officers. The reason the Oriental Mission became involved was because after travelling north over the bridge, Captain Evans 'considered the demolition arrangements made by the BFF under Colonel WALLACE inadequate'.[96] After gaining permission from both the local Army commander and Major Lindsay, Evans returned to the bridge with a small team of men to lay new charges.

On 3 May at around 7 am, the Japanese rushed the bridge dressed in Chinese uniform, travelling in captured lorries. Although new demolition charges had been laid by Oriental Mission, no control point was set. As the Japanese crossed, an attempt was made to light the fuses to blow the bridge, but they were wet and would not ignite.[97] Once over, the road to Bhamo was open and so rapid was the Japanese advance that Myitkyina was given up without a fight. Later, post-campaign reports could not agree on who was to blame.

An argument also ensued over who could claim responsibility for successfully demolishing five bridges between Myitkyina and Sumprabum. The files reveal that Stevenson and Lindsay had fallen out.[98] Stevenson argued that six levy officers under his command, rather than the Oriental Mission *per se*, had demolished these bridges on 5–12 May.[99] Colin Mackenzie claimed Oriental Mission organised the demolitions because Stevenson was 'incapable of giving orders'.[100]

Either way, the denial of Burma north of the town of Sumprabum to the Japanese was important because the territory included an airstrip at Fort Hertz. Retention of Fort Hertz was important for three reasons. Firstly, in mid-1942, it allowed both civilians and soldiers to escape to India by air. Secondly, the reverse was also true: Allied forces could be flown into Burmese territory, from where operations were launched from early 1943. But this is not the impression given by the official history, which omits to mention the continued Allied possession of northern Burma.[101]

Lastly, Kirby noted that the supply of China was crucial to Allied strategy, and that the only way to do this was over 'some of the worst flying country in the world'. Yet in his history of SOE in the Far East, Cruickshank made it clear that retaining this northern triangle of

Burma was 'most important' to keeping that air bridge open, because retaining Fort Hertz 'prevented the enemy' from using the air strip from which Japanese fighters could have 'threatened the last air link between India and China'.[102] Later, it was also the base from which the Allies mounted offensive operations to re-open supply to the Chinese along the Burma Road.[103]

With Fort Hertz in British hands, soldiers from 153 Gurkha Parachute battalion were dropped in to reinforce it in August 1942, and the landing strip was prepared for larger aircraft so that a front could be maintained against the Japanese from within Burma. It also meant that on 26 August, Captain Thompson with Karens Kan Choke and Ba Gyaw, were flown out from Fort Hertz at the end of their journey north from Mawchi.[104]

Conclusions

In December 1942, Major Lindsay wrote a post campaign report. In it, he recognised the '[d]estruction of the five bridges under 0.8200's [Stevenson] direction on the Sumprabum Road thereby preventing the Japs penetrating North' as well as '[d]emolitions on the Mawchi Road and the delaying action fought by B.B. 257's [Thompson] Company in conjunction with the Levies', and 'The making of the airfield at Fort Hertz thereby enabling:

(a) The evacuation of a considerable number of people and
(b) The reoccupation of North Burma by our Forces and the raising of Kachin Levies.'[105]

Despite noting these achievements, in concluding this report, Lindsay claimed that the Levy and SOE officers generally felt that 'results had fallen so far short of ambitions and that their contribution to the war as a whole had been so slight that there was not much object of harping on the past'.

Lindsay was probably right when he said that the impact of the Oriental Mission and the levies on the course of the war in Burma in 1942 'slight'. In the introduction to this chapter, the question posed was: if the first Burma campaign was lost at the Sittang Bridge on 23 February 1942, what significance could the Oriental Mission have for the retreat? It is a big claim to put forth that the Oriental Mission saved the Allied armies in Burma by delaying the Japanese advance in to the Karen and Shan States, and so preventing any outflanking of the British retreat from the east. Although this is a contemporary claim, it came from officers of the Oriental Mission who had the ulterior motive of saving SOE in the Far East from being closed down. It should also be assessed against the fact that the Chinese were responsible for holding Toungoo for 11 days.

On the other hand, if there had been no opposition on the road to Mawchi, the route north would have been open to the Japanese 56 Division considerably earlier. Could it have outflanked the Allied armies, cutting them off, or trapping them in the great bend of the Irrawaddy around Mandalay?[106] Perhaps not, but both Slim and Kirby were unequivocal in their opinion that the Japanese drive into the Shan States and the consequent fragmentation of the Chinese V and VI Armies necessitated a hasty withdrawal over the Irrawaddy by the end of April in order to avoid encirclement with the river to the Army's rear.[107]

Whether this hold up allowed the Army to escape to India – or at least escape in better condition than they otherwise would have done – is perhaps something that can never be known for sure, but relatively small Oriental Mission forces had certainly had a significant delaying impact. Beyond that, and given it was achieved with levies only partially armed with modern weapons and Thompson's Burifs, who had been stripped of most of their equipment, it can legitimately be asked what more could have been done with better provision and support. As it was, General Alexander's plans for a decisive battle in central Burma never happened.

In the official history of the war in the Far East, Kirby recognised that with the confusion over command arrangements 'it was almost impossible for any plan or policy to remain consistent.'[108] The Japanese held the initiative from the beginning of the 1942 campaign, and at no point did it look like Allied forces were going to regain it. It seems, however, that as the control of the Army dissipated in the chaos of retreat, the Oriental Mission was able to work relatively unfettered. Both the fighting on the Toungoo–Mawchi Road and the demolition of the bridges leading into northern Burma saw Oriental Mission taking major roles. In both cases this relatively independent form of operating assisted the retreat of British and Chinese Divisions, and helped prevent the Japanese completely overrunning Burma. This raises the question of whether or not Special Forces usually work best independently or semi-independently of army command, while accepting that both their tactical and strategic utility is only effective when acting in some sort of wider coordination with regular forces.

In denying the Japanese northernmost Burma, the Oriental Mission did not so much have an impact upon the first Burma campaign as influence the future course of the war in Burma. It has already been noted that if the Japanese had gained Fort Hertz, aircraft flying supplies to the Chinese over 'The Hump' – the mountains of northern Burma – would have been at even greater risk of interdiction. Until the Burma Road was re-opened, this was the only way to supply Chiang Kai-Shek and ensure that the Chinese remained belligerent. Furthermore, Allied forces supplied by aircraft flown into Fort Hertz protected Stilwell's left flank as his American and Chinese forces advanced down the Ledo Road towards Myitkyina from December 1943 to re-open land communications with China. Fort Hertz also became an important staging post for later SOE and OSS missions into Kachin territory. Indeed, some of the first special operations into occupied Burma were from Fort Hertz in early 1943. However, all of this was in the future when Lindsay submitted his opinions on the first Burma campaign in his report of December 1942.

CHAPTER 3

REORGANISATION AND EARLY OPERATIONS, AUGUST 1942–AUGUST 1943

The previous chapter examined the performance of the Oriental Mission from the start of Japan's offensive in December 1941 until after the close of the first Burma campaign, when, in August 1942, the last Oriental Mission officers were flown out from northern Burma. It demonstrated the roles that rapidly shifting command structures, and conflicting priorities for personnel, equipment, and political sensitivities, had in severely limiting what Special Operations could accomplish. Yet it also showed how some SOE operations nevertheless contributed to lessening the damage inflicted during the retreat of 1942. This chapter will continue chronologically from August 1942 until the Allied *Quadrant* conference held in August 1943.[1]

The period has been framed in this way so as to cover dates when the main emphasis was on specific types of activity, namely reorganisation and subsequent experimentation. Hence this year was spent creating new infrastructure for SOE, and sending exploratory operations into occupied Burma. Country sections were formed, training centres established, and procurement and logistical systems were developed which enabled India Mission to launch substantive operations into Burma within a year of the retreat.

For India Mission and the military alike, this year was one in which confidence in, and confidence of, British and Empire forces had to be restored. Reorganisation, retraining and limited exploratory offensives were the limit of British capability in the theatre. Starved of resources and strategic direction due to the policy of dealing with Europe first, the Southeast Asian theatre had to make do.[2] Direction was eventually provided by agreements made at the *Quadrant* conference of August 1943, when South East Asia Command (SEAC) was created, and Admiral Louis Mountbatten was appointed Supreme Allied Commander South East Asia (SACSEA). With a new commander and a defined theatre which, at this point, encompassed India, Ceylon, Burma, Malaya, Siam, Sumatra and French Indochina, strategic direction was thus addressed. The supply of equipment and personnel was, however, a different matter.

The situation in June 1942, after the withdrawal from all but the northernmost parts of Burma, was likened to a Far Eastern Dunkirk.[3] The British Chiefs of Staff (COS) were told by their joint planners that 'we are in real danger of losing our Indian Empire.'[4] The situation was made all the more precarious by the absence of a maritime challenge from the Royal Navy in the Bay of Bengal in mid-1942. Similar to Britain in 1940, SOE's India Mission, under Colin Mackenzie's command, began preparing for the expected Japanese invasion of the Raj. Yet after the perceived failures of the Oriental Mission in 1941–2, and the consequent continued scepticism of many Army commanders, India Mission still had to prove itself.[5]

The mission also had to contend with the Office of Strategic Services (OSS), the American equivalent of SOE, which arrived in Karachi on 4 July 1942. From Karachi, the OSS made their journey across India by rail to Calcutta, from where they quickly established themselves in theatre with the aim of assisting the American strategy to support the Chinese Nationalists. The arrival of OSS in India complicated matters, and not just for SOE.

Cruickshank has described India Mission as being 'saddl[ed] . . . with a European charter' which put it in a 'functional vacuum' in the period covered by this chapter.[6] He argued that that the India Mission was still expected to work according to the principles of SOE's founding charter of July 1940, which emphasised sabotage of industrial targets by secret agents. Yet it had to operate in a part of the world where elements of that charter could not be implemented due to substantial operational differences.

These differences, such as a relative lack of industrial targets and obvious difficulty for a Caucasian to go undercover compared to Europe, did not prevent Mackenzie from organising groups of Indian left-behind parties that would have gone into action had the Japanese attempted to occupy India, nor did it prevent him planning operations into enemy-occupied territories. It is argued here that this year was critical to the later success of SOE in Burma, and that far from dwelling in a functional vacuum, essential infrastructure and preparatory missions were established behind the lines. Furthermore, under pressure from London to complete an operation, Mackenzie approved Operation *Longshanks*, an attack on German and Italian shipping in the Portuguese enclave of Goa, in February 1943. Although successful in that all three German ships were sunk, the operation was carried out in neutral territory, and caused such a furore that Mackenzie offered his resignation (which was not accepted). There therefore seems to have been a tension between the pressure to gain a reputation of trust and value by carrying out ill-conceived operations in the short term, and building capacity for strategic utility in the long term.

The chapter tackles this tension, and the reorganisation and related arguments, in four main sections:

(1) Reorganisation. How did Mackenzie reorganise the India Mission and enable SOE to survive in the Far East? What were the new directives for this 'vastly expanded Mission'?[7]
(2) Infrastructure: personnel, training, supply. What training establishments were set up and did they adequately provide for the mission? What specific supply issues did India Mission have to overcome?
(3) The Office of Strategic Services. What issues were associated with the arrival of the American organisation?
(4) First Operations. What was learnt, and what foundations for future missions were put in place?

Reorganisation

By February 1942, when Oriental Mission had lost its base in Singapore, arguments had already raged over the division of its organisation into sub-missions. The head of the India Mission, Colin Mackenzie, had been directed from SOE HQ in London to take charge of the Burma Section of SOE at his discretion. He chose to do so on 4 April 1942, in time to start mobilising supplies and support for Oriental Mission officers retreating to India.

The establishment of an SOE mission in India had been proposed in early April 1941.[8] From 1936 to 1943, the Viceroy of India was Lord Linlithgow, a director of the textile company J & P Coats.[9] Linlithgow had readily accepted an SOE mission when asked if he wanted one, and in June 1941 asked for Colin Mackenzie to be its head.[10] Mackenzie was recruited into SOE from the Royal Observer Corps in 1940.[11] A veteran of the Great War, in which he had lost a leg, Mackenzie was 43 when approached about the India Mission. He had been at Eton with Linlithgow, and for the past 13 years had also been a director of J & P Coats. Not only was his business background considered excellent cover for being in India, but he was described as being a man of 'most exceptional character'.[12] He was the only SOE head of mission to retain his position for the entire war. This provided India Mission with the advantage of continuity of command. Mackenzie arrived in India with his second in command, Gavin Stewart, on 1 October 1941.[13] The objectives the mission was given by SOE London were threefold:

(1) Interference and countering of enemy interests in countries bordering India.
(2) Covert propaganda.
(3) Activities in India that Government would approve.

Furthermore, Mackenzie was instructed to keep in contact with Killery's Oriental Mission. As early as August 1941, the India Mission was instructed that if the Japanese were to conquer Burma, then operations would have to be run from India and not Singapore.[14] Cruickshank described these instructions as 'singularly vague'.[15] Objective three is certainly vague, but there was clarity regarding the territory that came under Mackenzie's jurisdiction. The India Mission would operate in Iran, Afghanistan, Tibet, and in India should the Raj be threatened. This did not seem such a far-fetched proposition in October 1941. The Germans had launched Operation *Typhoon* on 2 October, and by 20 October had captured nearly a million Russians and were 160 km (100 miles) from Moscow. If the Soviet Union collapsed, the expectation was that the armies of the Third Reich would continue through the Caucasus and into the Middle East.

By April 1942, the situation which Mackenzie faced had radically changed for two reasons. Firstly, upon absorbing the Oriental Mission in April 1942, the India Mission was now 'vastly expanded'.[16] Its area of operations stretched from Tehran in the west to Saigon in the east. Secondly, India was threatened from three directions. In the west, the Germans were advancing towards the Caucasus, in the east the Japanese were advancing on India's border province of Assam, and at sea the Japanese could cruise the Bay of Bengal without serious opposition from the Royal Navy.

In addition to the external threat, the British faced internal dissent from Indian Nationalists. In March 1942 the British Cabinet sent Sir Stafford Cripps to India to secure nationalist support by offering Dominion Status after the War. The Cripps Mission failed, and while Allied forces suffered reverses in every theatre, the Indian National Congress decided to launch their latest attempt at *Swaraj* (self-rule or self-reliance). In an attempt to expel the British from India, from August 1942 the Quit India campaign targeted the infrastructure of the Raj, such as railway and police stations. It required approximately 35,000 troops to contain the disturbances, and the RAF was used to strafe rioters.[17]

Between the failure of the Cripps Mission and the start of the Quit India campaign, SOE HQ in London sent the regional head for the Far East and Russia, Lieutenant Colonel G. MacDonald, to Delhi. He arrived in May 1942 with hurriedly written notes from George Taylor, the chief assistant to the head of SOE in London. These notes recognised the importance of the India Mission, at the same time as telling Mackenzie that SOE in London did not want to dictate how SOE reorganisation should be carried out. Advice was offered based on SOE experience in Europe and the Middle East, but Mackenzie was given a free rein.[18] In August, when Taylor again wrote to Mackenzie, this freedom was reiterated:

The wide fields, both figurative and physical, in which you may have to work and your remoteness from London indicate that all instructions to you should be in the nature of a Directive rather than an exact charter. Your functions may in the most general terms be stated to be the performance of those tasks of either political or operational natures which are outside the scope or capacity of any overt organisation, or any other secret organisation now functioning.[19]

It had also been recognised that SOE had not yet devised a successful technique for operating in a war zone (as opposed to operations in occupied or neutral countries). In a war zone, SOE's directors accepted that SOE must work with military commanders, but this had been 'conspicuously unsuccessful' to date, and in the Middle East a 'complete failure'.[20] It was felt that India Mission had to 'win the confidence of the services', and one way to achieve this was to ensure that all tasks initiated by SOE, whether in London or by Mackenzie, had the approval of the Viceroy in India and the relevant Commander in Chief (C-in-C).[21] This evidence would suggest that SOE's India Mission was not hamstrung by an unworkable European charter, as argued by Cruickshank. It also suggests that, even after the difficulties that the Oriental Mission faced with obstruction from colonial and military officials, the same approach as Killery's Far Eastern charter was to be employed.

Organising the India Mission on a territorial basis was first suggested to Mackenzie in March 1942, when he found out that he was soon to absorb the Oriental Mission.[22] By July, this restructuring was complete. India Mission was divided into three groups. Burma Country Section (BCS) was part of A Group, which included Siam and French Indochina, with its HQ in Calcutta. Captain R.E Forrester, a former Bombay Burmah Trading Company employee, was head of the BCS July 1942–April 1943.[23] He was replaced by Captain Richie Gardiner, a former forestry manager for Macgregor & Co. with 17 years' experience in Burma. Gardiner then remained in charge until the end of the War.[24]

Each group was subdivided into country sections for operational purposes. Each country section had its own signals, training and technical sections. Each country section was also staffed by experts who knew the country, languages and customs. These personnel were recruited from the colonial services, or from business, and were responsible for the handling of agents and the political aspect of SOE work. For operations, personnel with military experience were required not only for the efficient planning of operations but because they were better able to work with the local Army commanders with their understanding of the military system.

Table 3.1   Organisation of the India Mission

Group A	Group B	Group C
Burma	Malaya	China
French Indochina	Sumatra	
Siam	Dutch East Indies	

The effectiveness of these country sections depended upon India Mission's relations with the military. SOE had to operate in tandem with conventional operations directed by Field Marshal Archibald Wavell as C-in-C India. As C-in-C Middle East, Wavell had witnessed the 'conspicuous failure' of SOE operationally and the conspicuous affluence of SOE officers socially.[25] One such operation had been codenamed *Yak*, and included among its personnel Captain Peter Fleming, the brother of James Bond author Ian Fleming. Sent from the UK in 'great haste in April 1941', the *Yak* team was supposed to raise a force of anti-Fascist Italians, but the scheme came to nothing, like so many others at this time in the Middle East.[26] The situation in the Middle East had got so bad that the military had placed a mole inside SOE with the task of obtaining documents to discredit SOE, and perhaps even get it closed down.[27]

Wavell was not the only senior military commander in India with preconceived ideas about SOE. As a Brigadier in Iran, the future commander of XIV Army, William Slim, had formed a similar opinion. The military generally tended to worry that SOE was expensive in money and people, and had a poor track record of successful operations.[28] Winning military confidence was now up to Mackenzie, who was explicitly told only to employ personnel who could cooperate well with the military.[29]

In August 1942, Mackenzie wrote a gloomy report. Despite having been in India for ten months, he admitted that he had 'very little to show for it'. Like Killery before him, Mackenzie placed some of the blame upon the 'incredible procrastination and indecision on the part of the authorities', but also a 'lack of first class personnel'. He finished his report by saying: 'Whether the rest of the organisation will justify its existence in the coming months remains to be seen. We shall certainly do better if we are not called upon for more than minor activity before the end of the year.'[30]

By August 1942 then, just as the last Oriental Mission personnel finally staggered into India from Burma, the India Mission had a new structure with clear command and control arrangements that included both the Viceroy and the C-in-C. The next priority was to establish the infrastructure to support missions, and get India Mission on the offensive.

Infrastructure: Training, Personnel, Supply

India Mission made it 'a *sine qua non* for operational and purely country section staff officers' to be knowledgeable of the country and languages with which they would have to work.[31] The obvious backbone of the new BCS would be provided by Oriental Mission men who had already fought in Burma, but in the chaos of the retreat their whereabouts were not always known. The India Mission War Diary had a monthly section detailing what was known about personnel.[32] Lieutenant Colonel Richie Gardiner reported that by September 1942, the remnants of Oriental Mission had arrived in India, of which just 12 were British Burma specialists.[33] Captains Thompson and Nimmo were amongst the last to arrive, flying out from Fort Hertz in northern Burma on 26 August 1942, along with Karen Subedar-Major Kan Choke and Subedar Ba Gyaw.[34] By 7 November, presumably recovered from his trek out of Burma, Ba Gyaw was sent to train Burmese personnel.[35]

The Burmese personnel that came out to India with their British or Anglo-Burmese officers were crucial to the BCS. Those that retreated with the Army provided BCS with an additional potential recruitment pool, but it was estimated that out of an approximate total of 20,000 Burmese troops at the opening of the war against Japan, just 6,140 reached India. Of this 6,140, an estimated 700 were infantry, 3,000 were Burma Frontier Force (BFF), and 140 were signallers.[36] Competition between SOE and the Army for recruits from this pool in 1942 was added to with the arrival of the OSS in India, and later by the formation of Orde Wingate's Chindits in late 1942.[37]

Of the 12 Burma experts reported by Gardiner, presumably Captains Thompson and Nimmo were two. Like many others, both were in need of recuperation. At the end of their retreat, Thompson described Nimmo as 'only 30, yet his face that of an old man'; Thompson weighed just 50 kg (8 stone).[38] While men who would later provide the nucleus of the new BCS regained fitness for active service, staff officers of India Mission started to organise the infrastructure.

India Mission's first independent training school was open by July 1942.[39] Called the Eastern Warfare School (India), EWS(I), it was located at Kharakvasla, near Poona (today's 'Pune', inland from Bombay).[40] At EWS(I), personnel could complete a paramilitary course which, in the Far East, had a large part devoted to how to live in the jungle.[41] In September 1943, Lieutenant Colonel Gardiner wrote that important jungle lessons had been learnt, such as how and where to build jungle hide-outs, how to waterproof the hide-out, and how long it took to build a suitable shelter. It was found that tobacco leaves kept leeches at bay, and that kerosene repelled ticks and fleas. Mustard oil was used to prevent wet clothes from chaffing, until it was found that ants loved it. Addressing the conception that the jungle is teeming with game, in Burma, Gardiner wrote that hunting was a full-time occupation.[42]

The rest of the syllabus was based on the A Group of SOE schools in the UK which taught 'silent killing, weapons handling, demolition, map reading and compass work, fieldcraft, elementary morse, and raid tactics'.[43] Until this facility opened, training had taken place at the Army's infantry training school in Saugor and at the base of the Assam Rifles in Kohima. At least six instructors from Special Training School (STS) 101 in Singapore had been posted to Saugor as instructors after escaping from the Japanese.[44] These men were transferred to EWS(I) when it opened.[45]

A second paramilitary training school, EWS(C), was opened in June 1943. 'C' stood for Ceylon, the facility being located in Koddiyar Bay near Trincomalee. Commonly referred to as ME25, the paramilitary courses run here were for India Mission personnel whose destination was southern Burma, Malaya or Sumatra.[46]

In May 1943 a training school for political warfare and agent training was established in Tagore, 19 km (12 miles) from Calcutta. Its cover name was the School of Eastern Interpreters (SEI). It was also known as Eastern Warfare School (Bengal) or EWS(B).[47] Training at SEI was modelled on the course run at Beaulieu in the south of England, and consisted of 'security, surveillance, agent management, and the planning of subversive organisations. There was instruction in the reconnaissance of docks and airfields, enemy identification, and intelligence reporting.

Students were taught ciphers and codes suitable for their own language.'[48] Until this facility opened,

> Any special training of agents in underground activities and cover stories etc., had to be done by the Section Head or any other odd officer who might be available, not from what they had been taught themselves (they had never had any SOE training) but purely what they could think up on their own.[49]

Personnel that had received such rudimentary training were used on operations. Operation *Flimwell* was launched in January 1943. It was BCS's first parachute infiltration and consisted of two Karens who were tasked with contacting their countrymen living in the Irrawaddy Delta region of southern Burma. Even if they had not landed on a house and been captured immediately, their chances of success could not have been high, judging by other operations. On 15 June 1943, Operation *Mahout* was launched. Sunil Datta Gupta, an Indian, was parachuted into southern Burma with the intention conducting political warfare amongst Rangoon dock workers. He was reported missing, and it was not until 21 July 1945 that he was found and re-joined his unit.[50]

From January 1943, India Mission personnel completed their parachute training at RAF Chaklala. The Chaklala base was situated near Rawalpindi, in modern Pakistan. RAF instructors were responsible for the training of SOE personnel. SOE staff consisted of an officer, a secretary and transport drivers. This small India Mission contingent at Chaklala was also known as 'Syndicate F'. In October 1944, the mission eventually got its own parachute training school at Jessore, designated ME 89.[51]

India Mission's signals training facility (designated ME 9) was located at Meerut, north-east of Delhi, until October 1943 when the strain upon the facilities proved too great. Following decentralisation to EWS(I) and EWS(C), only advanced operational signals training was retained at ME 9.

To summarise:

(1) Paramilitary training, EWS(I), Poona or EWS(C), Trincomalee.
(2) Parachute training, Syndicate F, Chaklala (subsequently at Jessore).
(3) Agent and propaganda training, EWS(B), Calcutta.
(4) Signals training, Meerut (subsequently also at EWS(I) and (C)). India Mission HQ was also situated here.

Officers of the India Mission often referred to the difference in distances in Southeast Asia compared to Europe. From Delhi to Calcutta, by rail, took 29–34 hours. From Chaklala to Colombo took 138½ hours by rail. Air travel cut this time down to 8½ and 48 hours respectively, but spare aircraft were often unavailable for shuttling around trainees.[52] The time it took to travel between training schools was shortened by the opening of India Mission's parachute facility at Jessore, but the jungle terrain that was used for training at Poona did not exist anywhere closer to Calcutta.[53]

The duration of training courses were as follows:

(1) Paramilitary training
    (a) Basic four-week course (for all personnel).
    (b) Advanced four-week course (for leaders of operations).
(2) Agent and propaganda training
    (a) Short four-week course week.
    (b) Organiser's six-week course (an 'organiser' was responsible for the agent(s) on a particular operation).
(3) Despatch training
    (a) Parachute course ten days.
    (b) Seaborne course three weeks.
(4) Signals training
    (a) Basic course four months.
    (b) Advanced course five months.[54]

The main training difficulty was 'scarcity' of everything – recruits, instructors (especially in jungle lore), interpreters, equipment and operational experience. Only in August 1944 were operatives trained with the kit that they would use in the field. To give some idea of the instructor shortage, until the expansion of EWS (C) in November 1944, there were just 15 non-commissioned officers (NCOs) split between the four training bases.[55] The prevailing concern during this period was, nonetheless, to infiltrate small numbers of personnel into Japanese-occupied territory as soon as possible, to ascertain how country sections' plans should evolve and what opportunities for raising guerrilla forces existed.

From a total of about 2,500 personnel trained by the end of the War, India Mission handled approximately 1,500 Asian personnel who did not speak English, for whom it proved extremely difficult to provide the necessary translators.[56] For Burma alone, there were 171 different languages. This included four types of Chinese and 20 different Indian languages, with the remainder indigenous to Burma.[57] Of the different ethnic groups in Burma, there are 20 different Chin languages (not dialects) alone.[58] The cover name of 'School of Eastern Interpreters' for EWS(B) was therefore fitting. This language difficulty had a significant impact upon the quality of training, especially in the early months. It also explains why SOE had to recruit so many civilians, since it was the colonial administrators and employees of the business firms in Burma who had the linguistic capability. This led to the charge from those with a military background that the India Mission officers who spoke the language were 'not always the best from the leadership or administrative point of view'.[59]

The particular difficulties attributed to Asian recruits compared to Europeans were threefold. Firstly, problems with language ranged from sheer number to the 'multi-interpretational nature' of Asiatic languages.[60] Secondly, filtering of recruits was made difficult because of a greater variation in 'initial ability'.[61] Where most Europeans had had a standard schooling, the diversity of experience amongst Asians ranged from urban-based college graduates, through to partially educated but trained soldiers, to remote, rural-based, illiterate recruits. Lastly, it was believed that Asian recruits did not learn from lectures in the same way as Europeans. Visual and practical classes were considered more effective, if only for linguistic reasons.[62]

The Chinese were singled out as the most difficult nationality to train:

> Undoubtedly the most difficult type of Asiatic to deal with was the Chinese element, recruited mainly from the ranks of the K.M.T. through the Chinese Central Government, with the exception of the Malay section's 'Dragons'.[63]

The main reason given for this was that everything centred on not 'losing face'. According to the author of the training report, '[b]y an astute wielding of the weapon of "face" these recruits, by and large, were more trouble to the schools than all other students put together'.[64] Tactics to save face included feigning understanding, and acting beneath the intelligence of their Chinese group leader. A second reason given for why the Chinese were perceived as difficult is due to international politics. Chiang Kai-Shek's Government put considerable effort into ensuring the agents he sent to SOE were 'thoroughly indoctrinated against "foreign" influence'. Other Asiatic races were only seen as problematic when they did not receive pay or promotion that had been promised when recruited.

The experience of the Oriental Mission helped Mackenzie to properly establish his India Mission between June 1942 and August 1943. Firstly, learning from the experience of Killery's mission in Singapore and Malaya, London provided more direction for military/SOE relations than before. Secondly, from May 1942 when it was thought that India faced an imminent Japanese invasion, India Mission impressed the military by helping to raise and train (at Kohima) various indigenous groups (Lushai, Naga, Kukis, Chins, Tripura) as guerrilla fighters for the defence of Bengal.[65] These groups were originally known as the East Bengal Guerrilla Force, and consisted of around 1,000 Burmese tribesmen, 'stiffened' by five battalions of the Assam Rifles.[66]

In July 1942, the military staff in India asked the War Office to clarify the relationship between India Mission, the East Bengal guerrillas and the military. Clarification was also sought on how India Mission's operations would relate to military plans, and whether SOE would operate in areas run by the military.[67] The reply from the War Office came three weeks later. The East Bengal guerrillas came under Army control because SOE should not operate in areas under Army command. The War Office agreed that SOE should complement 'military plans both in general layout and for particular operations', which would need close liaison. India Mission's task was to attack the enemy's war effort where regular forces could not.[68] In terms of command and control, well-defined parameters were now set and the importance of clear direction from London was shown. SOE now ceased to be involved in what later became V Force.

It was not just at the senior level that the role of SOE and its relationship with the regular military had to be worked out. The relatively new tool of Special Forces had to become integrated at all levels for it to become an effective part of the machinery of war. At staff level, a large volume of India Mission's administration was done through 'Army channels at GHQ India'.[69] India Mission's own HQ staff was small and remained so until July 1944. Apart from being a burden on the Army, this had an adverse effect upon the mission's training facilities, where there was:

> an absence of control over the intake of students. There was a complete lack of documentation and little standard routine covering the matter of sending parties for training or furnishing Schools with definite information regarding the probable operational tasks of their recruits. This resulted in the Schools having to attempt to cover more subjects than were really necessary or could be handled effectively by the staff available.[70]

In addition, training staff would receive orders from a 'variety of sources' because of a lack of a training directorate at India Mission HQ. Friction between the country sections and the training staff became so intense that both the Malayan and Burma country sections began to have 'secessionist tendencies', presumably meaning that they wanted autonomy.[71]

The resolution of these training problems began with the appointment of Captain Ronald Meredith (formerly an instructor at Poona) to the General Support (GS) staff in June 1943, but it was only after 'a full scale training conference was convened in August 1943 that the matter was finally thrashed out and Standing Instructions issued covering the relations between Country Sections and Training Schools'.[72] Control of training was centralised to India Mission HQ, and the training establishments had their responsibilities set out. EWS (I) became responsible for paramilitary training for French Indochina, Burma and Siam country sections, as well as filtering recruits. EWS(C) was made responsible for paramilitary training for Malaya, Netherlands East Indies and for seaborne operations. EWS(B) – the SEI – was put in charge of agent and political warfare training only. Eventually, in September 1943, Lieutenant Colonel J. Bush was sent out from the UK to be the staff officer in charge of training.[73] With the appointment of Lieutenant Colonel Bush, the procedure agreed at the August conference was implemented, successful training methods from Europe (adapted for the jungle), and a standard training syllabus introduced for each school. Thus, it was only towards the end of 1943 that the training infrastructure for operations in the Far East was rationalised.

The training schools needed supplies to train with, and operational parties needed equipment for missions. In the military, Q is the letter designated to stores and equipment. In 1941, the advice 'Get Q cracking first' was written on the wall of the British army's training college in Camberley.[74] Getting 'Q cracking' means ensuring 'an economic-logistical dimension' to warfare, which the British effort against the Japanese almost wholly lacked from 1941 until late 1944.[75] A Europe first strategy, concurrent with the German U-boat campaign, both starved British industry of resources, and made export of finished products perilous. Mobilising India as an industrial base to contribute to the war effort was essential to British fighting capability. The situation for the India Mission in June 1943 was that the allocation of SOE resources was 68 per cent for the UK and North Africa, 22 per cent for the Middle East, and 10 per cent for the Far East.[76]

In an effort to overcome supply issues, Mackenzie was instructed by London to get what he could from the Indian Army.[77] A second solution was to begin local manufacture. In 1940, munitions factories in India 'were few in number and, although most of the basic metallic ores for armament existed in India or adjacent territories, there was no means of converting them to use and all vital raw material had to be imported.' A 'shortage of supply in every direction' had been recognised in 1938, but nothing was done to address the problem.[78] With the outbreak of war in 1939, the enlargement of the Indian Army began, and like SOE, it desperately needed equipping with everything from uniforms to arms.

Competing with the needs of the expanding Indian Army was compounded by personnel taken from India to fulfil needs in North Africa and the Mediterranean. Personnel 'milked' from the Indian Army included officers that were the India Mission's procurement contacts. Such an *ad hoc* procurement system needed to be replaced by an SOE Q branch, which was only established, with trained stores officers, in September 1943.[79]

Table 3.2   The Enlargement of the Indian Army, 1939–45[80]

Date	Size of Indian Army	British Officers/Indian Officers
July 1939	183,000	2,978 / 528
July 1945	2,250,000	37,138 / 13,355

Relations between India Mission's and the military's Q branches were confused by the cover-name that SOE used in the Far East. This was GSI (K), which stood for General Service Intelligence, so, logically, the mission was attached to the Director of Military Intelligence (DMI). When faced with a request for offensive equipment, such as weapons, Army Q Branch questioned why an intelligence organisation was indenting for equipment which the Indian Army was short of. For example, 50,000 Sten guns were shipped to India Command in November 1942. India Mission was told by London to ask the C-in-C India for the 10,000 that they wanted. Expecting to be turned down, India Mission suggested that the War Office order the C-in-C to release the guns to SOE. The War Office refused, but offered to send another shipment for the mission's use if the C-in-C kept all 50,000.[81]

Getting the weapons was one thing, having ammunition another. Sten gun ammunition was in short supply. Reserve dumps in the Falkland Islands and Trinidad were sent to India, but not before they had been relieved of 145,000 rounds for STS 103 in Canada and a 'South American Security Scheme'.[82] Whether or not these stores arrived is not recorded, but in April 1943 there were just 30 rounds per Sten gun available for training purposes.[83] Achieving operational proficiency of skill at arms with just 30 rounds for live firing practice is nigh impossible. Revolvers were also in short supply; seven months after ordering revolvers, in July 1943 they had still not arrived because London was waiting for stocks to become available from the United States.[84] The shortage of equipment was not limited to arms and ammunition, with important items such as compasses and binoculars also falling short.

After the fall of Singapore in February 1942, India Mission's stores were relocated to Jubblepore (modern Jabalpur in central India), from the Indian Army depot at Ferozepore (modern Ferozepur near the border with Pakistan). It could take five months for a shipment from the UK to reach Jubblepore.[85] Port facilities in Bombay could not always cope with wartime demands, so shipments were often redirected to Karachi. From Karachi, stores were moved by rail across India. When a boat made Bombay and the port was overstretched, supplies were cleared by sending them on to any available storage depot. Without an effective Q and an accounting system to manage them, it was not always known if stores had arrived, and if they had, where they had gone. One such example is a shipment of 70 cases of incendiaries that went missing in December 1942–April 1943.[86]

Manufacturing in India was meant to have provided a solution to India Mission's Q predicament. Between 27 August and 17 October 1940, Captain Francis Nixon had been sent to India to investigate the possibility of manufacturing SOE stores locally.[87] By the time India Mission was ready to act on Nixon's proposals, the Army's Master General of Ordnance had claimed the only modern workshops in India which housed the precision tools required, and was unwilling to share with SOE.[88] India Mission considered using small shops and garages, but this was dismissed as impractical because of an inability to meet demand, uncertainty over quality and security, and a need to import key materials. More generally, equipment such as containers, flashlights, batteries, bulbs and rubber gloves could be produced in India. The services of local firms such as Alan Berry & Co. and Messrs J. Neaves & Co. were contracted, but their services needed to be overseen by trained procurement and stores officers from India Mission.[89]

The need for trained stores officers and effective administration of Q was demonstrated on 25 May 1943, when a pocket time fuse incendiary spontaneously ignited and burnt down the Jubblepore depot with the loss of all stores.[90] Such an accident had been predicted by SOE's scientific advisor in a report on India Mission's stores. He had pointed out that India Mission urgently needed trained Q officers who knew how incendiaries should be stored.[91] In August 1943, the deputy director of SOE, Major General Colin Gubbins, intervened and told Mackenzie that he should review Q and have an officer with 'thorough knowledge' put in charge of it.[92] In September 1943, Major Trevor-Jones was despatched from the UK to take up this position. This was a 'great step' towards getting Q working to 'operational requirements' for India Mission.[93]

The Office of Strategic Services

The Office of Strategic Services (OSS) was America's equivalent of SOE. Like SOE, OSS had a global role during the War. The first OSS section, activated in April 1942, was known as Detachment 101 (Det. 101) and led by Major Carl Eifler. Born in 1906, Eifler was a former policeman from Los Angeles; for his exploits with Det. 101 he later earned the epithet 'The Deadliest Colonel'.[94] Det. 101 was sent to what the

Americans called the CBI theatre (China, Burma, India) to operate under the command of Lieutenant General Joseph Stilwell, who was based with the Nationalist Chinese in Chungking, China. Stilwell was assigned to the new American CBI theatre as the US commander, and as Chiang Kai-Shek's Chief of Staff. In terms of command, he was independent of the British, and reported directly to Washington. This meant that Stilwell could pursue the American strategy of supporting China to win the war against Japan.[95]

The original intention was that Det. 101 would be based in China, from where its men would fulfil their mission of providing assistance to Chinese Nationalist forces led by Chiang Kai-Shek. American strategy included clearing northern Burma of Japanese in order to re-open the land route to China. Once supply to Chiang Kai-Shek's forces along the Burma Road was re-established, the idea was to advance upon Japan through China, while General MacArthur and Admiral Nimitz converged on Japan in the Pacific. From bases in China and the Pacific, Allied air forces would begin their offensive against the Japanese islands. This strategy meant by-passing the British colonies of Burma, Malaya and Singapore. To this end, Det. 101 was required to assist Stilwell in a limited offensive aimed only at pushing the Japanese out of northern Burma.

The original plan to base Det. 101 in China was scuppered upon arrival in India by Stilwell, who would, or could, not allow it.[96] This decision was probably due to the pressure exerted upon Stilwell by Chiang Kai-Shek's chief of intelligence, General Tai Li, who did not want an American intelligence service encroaching on his territory.[97] With China closed to Eifler, India was his only alternative. The British, however, also did not want an American intelligence organisation on their territory.[98]

In December 1941, President Roosevelt had attempted to discuss India with Churchill, who 'reacted so strongly and at such length that he [Roosevelt] never raised it verbally again'.[99] The issue was Indian independence. Roosevelt believed that the Atlantic charter of August 1941 – which promised self-determination to liberated countries after the Axis defeat – should apply to Empire as well as to Europe.[100] In the summer of 1942, the London Agreement had demarcated the global operational responsibilities of OSS and SOE, and it had been agreed that OSS would only have a liaison presence in India.[101] According to the

SOE War Diary, London was, therefore, 'surprised that EIFLER had been instructed to work into Burma from India', because this contradicted the London Agreement. If this was to be the case, it needed to be 'clearly understood that OSS were the junior partners and that their policy and major activities would be under MACKENZIE'S control'.[102]

The establishment of Det. 101 in India was facilitated by a surprising source, given the obvious American anti-colonial sentiment. The Governor of Burma, Sir Reginald Dorman-Smith, attached his friend Wally Richmond, a former Steel Brothers manager in Burma, to Eifler's unit, and arranged for Det. 101 to be based at Nazira on an Assamese tea plantation.[103] This meant that Det. 101 was well away from most SOE bases, located as it was close to the eastern border between India and Burma. Mackenzie nevertheless told London in October 1942 that he thought the Governor's actions regarding Det. 101 were 'peculiar', and asked whether Dorman-Smith would be Governor long.[104] If Det. 101 was to remain in India, Mackenzie wanted Eifler to be subordinate to him, and not the Burma Government. This desire was secured: by 30 October 1942 it was agreed that in India, SOE was the senior partner and that Det. 101 would come under Mackenzie. Eifler's unit was not permitted to operate in Burma without the approval of either the C-in-C India (Wavell) or Mackenzie, and Stilwell could not be used to overrule Wavell.

Stilwell was 'anxious' for Det. 101 to become operational. He wanted intelligence from the Myitkyina area to assist his Sino-American offensive to liberate the part of northern Burma required to re-open the Burma Road.[105] Eifler set himself the target of getting teams into the Myitkyina area by the end of 1942, so even while the wrangling over command was going on during October 1942, there were two Det. 101 teams in training. 'A Group' consisted almost entirely of Anglo-Burmese officers, some of whom were on loan from SOE.[106] The men in A Group were all Burma specialists, led by Jack Barnard.[107] 'B Group', which became known as 'O Group' because it was the initial of the leader's surname, was led by Alfred Ottaway, the tin-mine manager from Tavoy whom the Oriental Mission had made commander of the Southern Zone of Burma in 1941.[108] The reason why the British were willing to provide OSS with such valuable personnel seems clear: their temporary loan, combined with 'the arrangements which MACKENZIE had proposed, [would] virtually convert the Americans into a sub-mission'.[109] The British clearly hoped that they might be able to gain significant control over the new and inexperienced Det. 101 in Burma.

In keeping with Eifler's ambition to get an operation into the field by the end of the year, A Group left for Fort Hertz in Burma in late December 1942. Their plan was to penetrate the Japanese lines south of Fort Hertz and continue on foot to their area of operations. Once they had arrived in the vicinity of Myitkyina, they were to blow up the rail communications that supplied Japanese forces in northern Burma, including the airfield at Myitkyina that was being used to challenge aircraft supplying China over 'The Hump' from India. Fort Hertz itself was screened from a Japanese offensive by Colonel Gamble, the military commander of the Kachin Levies.[110] Cooperating with these regular forces as cover, A Group probed the Japanese lines but in the end decided to return to Fort Hertz because 'operation[s] such as ours into an enemy-occupied country must be a *vertical* penetration – that is, that we must reach our target area by parachute. The discovery was an important one.'[111]

This conclusion was reached because Colonel Peers, the Commander of Det. 101 from December 1943, believed that it had been a mistake to work with Colonel Gamble's troops as this had 'frustrated [A group's] identity' and denied them covert entry into enemy territory.[112] Colonel Gamble had wanted A Group to come directly under his command as they were in his area of operations. For Eifler, this was unacceptable, and he resolved that OSS units would not be put in this position again, and might be part of the reason why future Det. 101 operations were carried out with little reference to their British allies.

It was not just the Americans who were frustrated. In February 1943, the British Chiefs of Staff complained that OSS was conducting operations into Burma from India without being coordinated by Wavell or Mackenzie.[113] There were also political worries. In May 1943, Wavell received a communication from the India Office which accused the Americans of assisting the Japanese by undermining the British position in India:

At present American effort tends to set up organisations parallel to those existing resulting in duplication waste of effort and material and uncoordinated or even divergent action. In particular present system results in British and American staffs receiving divergent Intelligence and views. Another aspect of this is that American propaganda and publicity, unwittingly or not, though [sic] being primarily pro-American rather than pro-United Nations, tend to play into hands of Congress by implied reflection on British effort. Thus United States actions help to produce unsettled conditions in India and thereby aid Congress and Jap sponsored propaganda aimed at undermining the loyalty of Indian population in general and Indian Army in particular.[114]

The OSS, the British argued, were breaking the command and control agreement reached in September 1942 by sending missions into Burma from both China and India 'with no coordination or mutual knowledge whatever'. On 21 May, the COS decided that a resolution should wait until after bigger decisions on strategy against Nazi Germany and the Japanese had been discussed at the forthcoming *Quadrant* conference, due in August 1943.[115]

Within a year of arrival then, Eifler's Det. 101 was challenging British hegemony within the Empire by acting independently. This forced new negotiations between OSS and SOE, leading to provisional agreement on 12 August 1943. There is one essential difference between this agreement and the *modus vivendi* reached in September 1942: OSS was granted the 'free hand' to deploy into Burma from India that both the Viceroy and Mackenzie had been so wary of. In return, SOE ostensibly received the same allowance in China. This agreement has been described by Aldrich as 'a most liberal Charter', but he adds that the 'potential for trouble' should have been spotted.[116] The 'potential for trouble' was the likely possibility that OSS and SOE would compete with and compromise each other's teams in the field. In fact, this danger was pointed out on 14 August, and was considered 'quite unacceptable' by India Mission and the C-in-C India, who wanted 'unified control of authority for [a single target] ... area, irrespective of the base in which they originate'.[117]

The provisional agreement was an attempt to paper over tensions between the clandestine bodies until the *Quadrant* conference. It was only at this level of talks that the matter stood a chance of resolution, for by mid-1943 the Americans were the senior partner in the War.[118]

One way in which this new status of America was evident to India Mission was in the equipment that Det. 101 brandished. By the time of

Quadrant the OSS had put four intelligence and operational groups behind the lines in northern Burma from the Fort Hertz area (*Forward*, *Knothead*, L Group, and *Pat*) which had started recruiting Kachins, and paying them 'considerable sums'.[119] It was thought that the Kachins were 'in danger of becoming a race of cadgers' but, more damagingly, Major Wilkinson of *Forward* 'was telling the Kachins that the British had let them down, but that the Americans would not disappoint them'. Eifler considered all areas forward of Sumprabum to be 'his' despite an SOE team, *Dilwyn*, that had been in place with the Kachins since March 1943. Captain Howe, an India Mission officer based at Fort Hertz, through where these OSS missions were supplied, wrote '[w]hatever one may think of the B/B400 {Eifler} unit, the fact remains that they have the men, the equipment and the means of supplying what is wanted, when it is wanted and where it is wanted'.[120]

By the time of *Quadrant* tensions between OSS and SOE over Burma were running high, for not only had OSS resisted attempts at local British control in northern Burma, but they were undermining British/Kachin relations using the considerable means at their disposal.

First Operations

While the reorganisation and development of the India Mission's support structures got under way in late 1942, the planning and launching of operations went ahead. Keen to prove their value, Burma Country Section (BCS) was anxious to get men on the ground. On 26 August 1942, BCS commander, Captain Richard Forrester, authored an 'Appreciation for SOE Operations in Burma'.[121] In his opinion, Burma offered 'ideal hide-outs for saboteurs and partisan bands', but since most targets for sabotage were far from potential jungle bases, he recommended their use for intelligence purposes. Forrester advised against operating in just one area because Japanese reprisals would be swift and brutal, so any sabotage should be simultaneous and widespread, and ideally should coincide with a military offensive.

Eight specific target areas were identified in his appreciation, although none got beyond the planning stage. One reason for this, according to Gardiner – Forrester's replacement as BCS commander from April 1943 – was that they could not find 'native' personnel who they thought had the qualities to do the job.[122] Burmese personnel were essential in Gardiner's view because British officers had 'little or no chance' of survival except in specific areas.[123] His other reason was the arrival of OSS, and the consequent competition for personnel. Perhaps a better explanation is provided by the situation regarding India Mission's infrastructure. Personnel, training facilities, stores and the means to infiltrate were all a work in progress. It was not until January 1943 that approximately 100 recruits were trained and ready for operations.[124]

In December 1942, Captain Forrester received a 'Directive for Burma Operations' from India Mission HQ.[125] This was substantially different to Forrester's appreciation of four months previously because it specified a principal area of operations in 'that portion of Karenni within the line PYINMANA – LOIKAW – KEMAPYU – line of R.SALWEEN' to the Siamese border and south towards Moulmein. It demanded much more than just opportunistic sabotage. BCS was ordered to assist the military in the destruction of Japanese forces by attacking the 'social and economic order' in Burma. Specific tasks were: the raising of partisans; the immediate sabotage of communications, shipping and rolling stock on the Japanese lines of communication to synchronise with a planned offensive in the Arakan in 1943; to provoke the Karen into an uprising; and the assassination of Japanese supporters and staff officers. The immediate task was to get an officer and wireless transmitter (W/T) set into Karenni and find out if Captain Hugh Seagrim, who had remained with the Karen after the 1942 retreat, was still alive.[126] If the situation was favourable, Karen were to be trained in sabotage and guerrilla warfare.

Despite this directive, there was still uncertainty. The main source of this was a lack of strategic direction from London and Washington because of their differences in opinion over how to defeat Japan, and their preoccupation with the European and Pacific theatres. Strategic direction for Southeast Asia was only provided in August 1943 at the *Quadrant* conference, when South East Asia Command (SEAC) was created and Mountbatten chosen to be the commander. Until Mountbatten arrived and established himself in October 1943, SOE and OSS had to work on the assumption that the main military effort against Japan would be through China, and possibly Sumatra if landing craft for *Culverin* (the codename for a planned amphibious attack on Sumatra to strike towards Singapore and Malaya) were made available. In other words, both Burma and Siam (the countries that possessed the greatest possibilities for infiltration with the limited transport available) would be by-passed by the main military offensive which they were supposed to support. SOE operations were therefore categorised under three headings.

Short-term operations were developed to assist the military offensive in the 1943–4 season.[127] These centred upon the limited offensive in the Arakan region of Burma, which had as its aim the reclamation of Ramree Island to provide a forward airbase to support operations further south.[128] Long-term operations were to be planned and developed in order to support major offensives anticipated in the 1944–5 season. The object of these was raising guerrilla armies in the northern Shan and Karen states, in central and eastern Burma. In addition, SOE was still under the Directorate of Military *Intelligence*, and the European experience had shown that unless SOE came under the Directorate of Military *Operations*, SOE plans would not have a place in higher operational strategy.[129] Mackenzie therefore worked hard to show that India Mission was engaged in offensive operations to encourage the military authorities to make the switch.

Contacting Captain Seagrim and the Karen was one of the long-term operations planned, but getting communications established with the Karen Hills proved to be difficult. The original plan – Operation *Harlington* – consisted of parachuting in Karen personnel to whom W/T equipment would be dropped. They would then establish communications with Calcutta and indicate whether or not British officers could join them. On 19 February 1943, four Karen were landed, including Ba Gyaw. There were then three unsuccessful attempts to drop W/T equipment during the February moon period (this being the period of full moon when it was considered best to attempt parachute infiltration).

In March and April, six further attempts to drop the signals equipment failed due to weather, navigational error or aircraft trouble. Suspicion of sabotage arose when acid was found to have leaked on parachutes, but this was never confirmed.[130] In what BCS commander, Richie Gardiner, called 'quite the most depressing series of failures that we ever experienced', over 50 sorties were flown until a successful drop was eventually made in October.[131]

Operations *Flimwell* (an attempt to contact the Karen in the Irrawaddy Delta region) and *Harlington* both illustrated the need for training and development of procedure for airborne infiltration. The other major operation launched in early 1943 had similar problems.

Operation *Dilwyn* was aimed at contacting Kachins south of Fort Hertz in the Bhamo–Myitkyina region of northern Burma. The first two attempts at infiltration in February 1943 failed due to navigational error and a problem with the bomb racks, which were used to deploy men and stores.[132] A third attempt was successful, and *Dilwyn I* (Captain Kumje Tawng plus two Kachins) was successfully dropped between Myitkyina and Bhamo on 23 March 1943. Learning from *Harlington's* mistake, W/T equipment was parachuted in on the initial drop, but due to battery failure the set was useless. HQ knew nothing of the fate of this party until 4 July 1943 when a messenger arrived at Fort Hertz.

Presumably due to the unfortunate precedent set by airborne insertion, in June a party had been sent to the *Dilwyn* area overland from Fort Hertz. The party, led by Major Shan Lone, also a Kachin, took nearly six months to reach *Dilwyn*, arriving in November. In his 1945 report, Gardiner explained: 'This officer had an extremely difficult and arduous journey which can hardly be appreciated without knowing the conditions in that part of the country at the time of year'.[133] As the crow flies, the distance was only 290 km (180 miles), but unable to use the few roads available due to Japanese patrols, Major Lone was forced to travel cross country over rugged, jungle-clad hills. By November 1943, the case for faster airborne infiltration was eventually accepted by India Mission.

Conclusions

An effective network takes time to establish, but that establishment is made measurably easier and swifter when there are precise directives that set out objectives supported by central strategic control. This is essentially what the India Mission worked towards establishing during the period covered in this chapter. Mackenzie set about organising country sections, and making other plans for his area of responsibility based on advice and directives from London. There was no charter that had to be dogmatically adhered to. In this sense, the time between the retreat from Burma in the middle of 1942 until August 1943 should be seen as evolutionary. Not only were structures put in place, but important relationships had to be tried and tested to see what worked. These relationships included not just external matters such as building trust with the military and civil authorities, but internal functionality like managing the country sections' interaction with training establishments.

Both Killery's Oriental Mission in 1941–2 and Mackenzie's India Mission in 1942–3 did not enjoy the infrastructure or support for anything more than limited operations. One simple reason for this was Britain's inability to provide for a global war, even with the resources of empire. In the area of Special Operations as in regular military operations, British servicemen had to look on as Americans joined the War and mobilised, by mid-1942, an industrial behemoth to support them.[134] The speed with which American industrial might swung into action, coupled with clear instructions from the President, meant that Det. 101 was firmly rooted in India and the Southeast Asian theatre within 12 months. By June 1943, Det. 101 had 17 training camps at Nazira, and these had 150 students in training by September.[135] There were also four Det. 101 short-range operations behind the lines by that date, equipped with W/T sets, though Det. 101 was still short of aircraft and boats for long-range operations.

It quickly became apparent to the British that the OSS was not going to be easily controlled, or subordinated to SOE, as they had originally hoped. The Americans had a clear strategy for their CBI theatre, and that did not include losing American lives to help the British reclaim parts of their empire. Their goal was to re-establish an overland link with the Chinese, led by Stilwell and Eifler, both men with uncompromising tenacity and drive. The friction between OSS and SOE that began in 1942 meant that where Allies should have been coordinating their efforts and sharing their operational lessons, little happened. This relationship, however, should also be perceived as an evolutionary stage. Both SOE and OSS were new 'top secret' organisations, and there was no precedent either for their own evolution or creating a close working relationship with an ally. On top of that, divergent national strategies made cooperation more difficult.

The colonial context of this theatre, furthermore, had a significant impact upon SOE and OSS relations. Both organisations were expected to start operations when the Raj faced the external threat of the Japanese and the internal threat of Indian Nationalism. The main leaders of the latter were arguably at the pinnacle of their 30-odd years as career nationalists, and sensed their opportunity during Britain's years of crisis in 1939–43, especially after the Fall of Singapore in February 1942.

India, the base for operations to reclaim Southeast Asia from the Japanese, was far from secure during 1942. This put British commanders in an unenviable position whereby their already stretched resources had to be divided between internal security duties and fighting the Japanese, who had crossed the Chindwin River and were probing the Chin Hills on the Indo-Burmese border. It was into this melee that the fiercely anti-colonial OSS arrived with their long-term strategic and economic intentions adding to the pressure upon an already overburdened Raj.

It was in this context that Mackenzie had to prove his mission's worth and ensure its survival by defining its role. It was by demonstrating the expertise of his men in the planning of demolitions in Bengal, and the training of the East Bengal guerrilla forces in 1942 against the possibility of a Japanese invasion, that India Mission began to gain credibility with the Army. These forces were given over to military control when the role of India Mission was clearly, if open-endedly, defined as doing anything that the other services could not do to help win the War. The experience gained through their contribution to the defence of India proved tangible enough for India Mission to start building its reputation, and to persuade the Army that SOE could be useful.

All this means that Cruickshank's idea of a 'functional vacuum' is not a satisfactory description, at least for the Burma Country Section of SOE. Although getting structures right for command, coordination, training and stores is not quite so alluring for writers as the periods when SOE was in the thick of the action or involved in cloak-and-dagger operations, this period of evolution in order to support a more mature organisation is valuable for extending our understanding of how SOE was able to support XIV Army's advance to Rangoon in 1945. The experience of putting operations into Burma during that year allowed many lessons to be learnt that enabled successful later operations to develop. These lessons included such details as how best to build jungle shelters, procedure for airborne infiltration of personnel and W/T sets, and how to navigate over difficult terrain to find drop zones. Above all, perhaps, it taught confidence in the mission's ability to provide strategic value to the war effort. As an India Mission note of 14 July 1943 stated: '[t]his year was not wasted'.[136]

CHAPTER 4

GETTING BEHIND THE LINES: THE INDIA MISSION IN BURMA, SEPTEMBER 1943–DECEMBER 1944

Between September 1943 and December 1944, Burma Country Section (BCS) launched most of its operations into Burma. Some of these became well established, and developed into the operations that supported the Army in the reconquest of Burma in 1945. The work of BCS was facilitated by the extension of India Mission's supporting infrastructure and the formation of South East Asia Command (SEAC).[1] With the arrival of Admiral Louis Mountbatten, the new Supreme Allied Commander, in October 1943, steps were taken to rationalise the plethora of competing interests represented in SEAC. For the clandestine organisations, Mountbatten reinvigorated Priorities Division (P-Division) in December 1943, which had already been established to coordinate secret activities. It was intended that P-Division would prevent both the duplication of effort and the possibility of compromise by uncoordinated operations, and thus contribute to a reduction in the friction between SOE and the American Office of Strategic Services (OSS), and the Secret Intelligence Service (SIS).[2]

It was also during the timeframe of this chapter that the tide of war finally turned in the Burma campaign. During the 'campaigning season' of 1942–3, British and Empire troops attacked the Japanese in the Arakan. The coastal strip of Burma known as the Arakan is bordered by the Indian Ocean to the west, and the jungle-clad hills of the Arakan Yomas to the east. The failures of this offensive destroyed Churchill's confidence in India Command, and, in part, led to the decision to create SEAC.[3] By May 1943, after the Japanese had pushed Allied forces back to where they had started in October 1942, the myth of the 'invincible Jap' had not been dispelled, and morale amongst Allied troops plummeted. As he flew into New Delhi on 7 October 1943 to take up his appointment as SEAC commander, Mountbatten felt a 'certain thrill' at being the man chosen to be 'the visible symbol of the British Empire's intention to return to the attack in Asia and regain our lost Empire'.[4]

Before his arrival in India, Mountbatten planned how he aimed to turn the war around in the Far East. His solution was his four 'Ms'.[5] The first two stood for 'Morale' and 'Monsoon'. Concern about troop morale after the 1942–3 fighting season permeated from the Army command in theatre through to Churchill in London. The 'M' for 'Monsoon' was because Mountbatten was incredulous that there were 'fighting seasons'. He believed the monsoon should be fought through, and that it could be if his third 'M' for 'Malaria' was firmly dealt with. The final 'M' stood for 'Movement'. He wanted to devise tactics to prevent Allied troops being cut off, and if the situation did arise, he wanted the troops to have the confidence and discipline to hold their position while supplies were flown in. Mountbatten knew that getting the airlift would be the difficult part because Europe had priority on all resources, but the first Chindit campaign of 1943 had shown the efficacy of air supply in the jungles of Burma. It had also served to raise morale on the back of the Arakan campaign.

The Chindits were the brainchild of their commander, Brigadier Orde Wingate. Wingate had been requested for Burma in early 1942 by General Wavell, whom Wingate had served under in an irregular role in Abyssinia during 1941. The first Chindit campaign was codenamed Operation *Longcloth*. Launched in February 1943, its original aim was to support an offensive by the British IV Corps on the India–Burma border forward of Imphal. By operating around 320 km (200 miles) behind the lines, hitting command centres and lines of communication, it was hoped that the Chindits would divert Japanese forces from the front. The Chindit force was brigade sized, approximately 3,000 men, and went into Burma after the IV Corps offensive was called off on the insistence of Wingate, but also with his column commanders' assent. In contrast to SOE, according to Lyman, 'all the principal commanders in India recognized the value of operations of the kind Wingate espoused', so it was allowed to go ahead.[6]

In May 1943 the Chindits returned less a third of their number, but Wingate had shown that the Japanese were not the only successful practitioners of jungle warfare. For all the criticism of the Chindits and the debates about their strategic effect, they did provide a morale-boosting propaganda coup, as well as proving the viability of air supply for large forces that became a vital part of the war effort in this theatre.[7] Furthermore, when interviewed in 1945, General Renya Mutaguchi, commander of the Japanese 15 Army, said that that by penetrating Burma overland from India, the Chindit operation convinced him that an assault on Imphal in India was possible.[8] This the Japanese duly attempted from March 1944, in what was optimistically called the 'march on Delhi'. It was hoped that by using the Indian National Army (INA), Indian Nationalists would revolt within India. The result was an offensive which ended up centred upon the two Indian villages of Imphal and Kohima, and it is here that the war in Burma is said to have turned against the Japanese.[9] By 2 December 1944, Slim's XIV Army had advanced to Kalewa, a town on the Chindwin River approximately 180 km (113 miles) from Imphal. An overland re-occupation of Burma was now in the offing.

The period up until December 1944 was, for SOE's India Mission, as it was for XIV Army, one of learning the craft that would eventually enable the defeat of the Japanese Army in Burma in 1945. While the Army slowly gained confidence in its ability to fight the Japanese, India Mission's Burma Country Section (BCS) concentrated on establishing and consolidating their operations in Burma.

The five operations that feature in this chapter have been selected not only because they all continued until the end of the War, but because they emphasise the various issues that faced BCS. *Dilwyn*, *Spiers* and *Hainton* exemplify problems between what Christopher Thorne has called 'Allies of a Kind', which here applies to both the Americans and the Chinese; *Harlington* highlights difficulties of clandestine British coordination; and *Billet* demonstrates the divisions within the British camp about how to deal with Burman nationalism.[10]

The chapter is centred around these operations, and is structured as follows:

(1) Growth of Infrastructure.
(2) Operation *Dilwyn* – the Kachin Hills.

(3) Operation *Spiers* – Kokang and the northern Shan States.
(4) Operation *Hainton* – Kengtung and the southern Shan States.
(5) Operation *Harlington* – the Karen Hills.
(6) P Force patrols – the Chindwin River area.
(7) Operation *Billet* – Arakan and central and southern Burma.

P Force were SOE's Special Patrol Groups, which were sent to operate on the Imphal front in support of IV Corps. It was noted above that the Chindits enjoyed the confidence of the generals; it was these patrols that helped SOE to win some of the same support. The chapter starts, however, with a section which examines the growth of SOE's supporting infrastructure, which was critical to the operations named above, up to December 1944.

Growth of Infrastructure

In July and September 1943, it seems there were conflicting opinions about the operational readiness of SOE's India Mission. An optimistic report written in July 1943 closed with the assertion that India Mission was 'ready to get to work in earnest.'[11] In contrast, on 1 September 1943, George Taylor in London wrote that the 'whole training system [in India] is in a most unsatisfactory position.'[12] The problem was a continuing shortage of instructors, and so arguments centred on suggested ceilings for war establishments. Playing second fiddle to the European theatre of operations, India Mission did not get the extra personnel required until November 1944. Up to that date, there were just 15 Non Commissioned Officers (NCOs) available for training purposes.

While the disputes about staffing continued, the maturation – or evolution – of existing provision within SEAC proceeded. As seen in Chapter Three, in September 1943 Lieutenant Colonel Bush had been sent out from the UK to take charge of training facilities in India. In the same month, the School of Eastern Interpreters was enlarged and training was rationalised under a new commanding officer. Holding camps were also constructed for personnel waiting to go on operations.

In July 1944, paramilitary training at EWS(C) was moved from Trincomalee to Horana, 42 km (26 miles) south-east of Colombo. Subsequently, all paramilitary training was performed in Ceylon. It was at Horana that BCS teams received their jungle training from the end of

1944. These teams found themselves in the curious position of being 'old hands' of the Far East (often with operational experience in the jungle of Burma) under the tutelage of instructors fresh from Europe.

It was not just training that presented India Mission with a challenge during 1943–4. India Mission's emphasis during 1944 was upon BCS, because at this stage Burma was the only country into which airborne operations could be launched.[13] In September 1943, India Mission was awaiting delivery of a flight of six Liberators and two Catalina flying boats. Until they arrived, both SOE and SIS relied upon six Mk. III Hudsons.[14] Designated 1576 Special Duties Flight since 1 June 1943 and under the command of Squadron Leader Moore, these aircraft were based at the RAF's Air Landing School (ALS), Chaklala.[15] They had to provide for the secret services 'without prejudice to the normal functions of the ALS', which was parachute training.[16]

On 24 September 1943, the case for being equipped with Liberators was put to London: no Liberators and 'our work will come to a dead stop'.[17] On 1 February 1944, Liberators were finally allocated to India Mission and 1576 became 357 Special Duties Squadron.[18] Between June 1943 and the arrival of the Liberators in February, the Hudsons had attempted 23 sorties of which 19 had been successful in dropping supplies or men. The impact of the Liberators is obvious when seen against March 1944, when 24 sorties were attempted in that month alone, of which 20 were successful.[19] Between February and August 1944, combined Hudson and Liberator sorties totalled 109 of which 65 were successful. It is perhaps for this reason that March 1944 was described as an 'epoch making month for SD operations'.[20] Notwithstanding this steep increase in sorties, the SD squadrons still experienced more demand than they could deliver.

Once delivered into Burma, a key part of the preparatory phase was for personnel to establish communications with India. The same was true for OSS, as Saquety has written: 'Without a long-range, reliable, secure, and portable radio system, these agents could not communicate back to [India]. These groups were effectively worthless if they could not establish communications.'[21] This posed difficulties in the Far East which SOE teams in Europe did not have to contend with. In the Far East, the distances that made airborne insertion problematic also caused communications challenges. Even within India, communication between Meerut (SOE HQ) and Calcutta (Group A HQ), a distance of

Table 4.1   Target areas for the India Mission in Burma, 1943[22]

Destination (all Burma)	Distance (from Bengal)	Status of Operation
Central Burma	800–965 km (500–600 miles)	Ready to go
Bassein, Prome	965–1,125 km (600–700 miles)	Ready to go
Karenni (*Harlington*)	965–1,125 km (600–700 miles)	Party in
Northern Shan States, Kokang, Yunnan (*Dilwyn* and *Spiers*)	965–1,125 km (600–700 miles)	Party in
Tenasserim	320 km (200 miles)	Need by Nov–Dec 1943

1,400 km (900 miles), was intermittent in 1942. During the monsoon period, heavy atmospherics interfered with radio waves, and once in Burma, jungle conditions necessitated the development of 'tropic proof' equipment. From a technical point of view, powering the bulky wireless transmitter (W/T) sets also proved a challenge.[23]

The OSS swiftly overcame the same problems during 1942. Tasked with creating a receiver-transmitter and power pack of not more than 22.5 kg (50lb) in weight, their end-product weighed 24 kg (53lb) and worked over a distance of 1,900 km (1,200 miles). There were 72 sets ready to go into the field by early 1943.[24] British improvisation did not work at such speed, and nor did the OSS share.

In late 1943, five officers were dispatched to India from Britain to establish what became known as the Special Forces Development Centre (SFDC). The SFDC was tasked with three main functions: first, to be the main stores depot for SOE; secondly, to be a specialist packing centre; and lastly to develop and make specialist equipment.

The site chosen to build a research centre and workshops was near Poona in order to take advantage of its excellent port and rail communications.[25] Despite having a high 'X.X. Priority' and having the building costs covered by London, the target opening date of 1 April 1944 was not met due to a shortage of building materials.[26] The centre only became fully functional by November 1944, but from August 1944 to August 1945 it shipped out an average of 300 tonnes of stores per month.

By December 1944, the training structure for India Mission personnel was mostly complete. Only fully trained teams, that had trained together, with standardised equipment, were now sent on operations.[27] SOE had designated aircraft based at Jessore, and the lessons regarding packaging of stores and dispatch of them and personnel had largely been learnt as 1945 approached. More by accident than design, as XIV Army stood poised to advance across the Chindwin, Force 136 – as India Mission was known from March 1944 – finally had the infrastructure which made operations in support of XIV Army's offensive possible.

Operation *Dilwyn*: the Kachin Hills

At the beginning of the chapter, three issues regarding Burma operations were set out. *Dilwyn* exemplifies tension between the British and Americans, which was mostly due to divergent strategies. Originally designated *Tendon*, the operation was conceived immediately after the retreat of 1942 with the aim of contacting the Kachins in northern Burma. *Dilwyn* was launched from Fort Hertz in March 1943, and was one of the first SOE missions sent into Burma. The original tasks of the operation were sevenfold:

(1) Establish W/T communication with India.

(2) Link up with Operation *Eyemouth* (the *Eyemouth* team consisted of five Kachins who had been sent with W/T overland to the Katha area (on the Irrawaddy River approximately 250 km (155 miles) south-east of Myitkyina) from Fort Hertz in early March 1943).

(3) Provide an underground railway south to the Karen Hills based on the European model (an 'underground railway' was a series of guides and safe-houses that were supposed to ensure SOE personnel could travel to target areas overland in relative safety. The need was due to a lack of air transport).

(4) Recruit Kachins as guides and to provide intelligence for the army.

(5) Conduct 'unofficial' administration within the policy of the Burma Government.

(6) Deny the Japanese the use of river boats.

(7) Encourage ex-Burma Rifles personnel to re-enlist and serve with British forces in the north.[28]

This diverse task list was to be managed by Jemadar Kumje Tawng Wa initially, and later by Captain Shan Lone. Both were Kachins.[29] The *Dilwyn* operation was BCS's northernmost team in their plan to infiltrate missions along the length of eastern Burma, from Bhamo in the north, through to Papun in Karenni to the south.

The first *Dilwyn* Party was dropped into Burma on 23 March 1943, and consisted of four Kachins under Captain Kumje Tawng. This group was meant to provide a reception on the drop zone for Major Lone and the W/T equipment.[30] Due to navigational error on 18 March and faulty bomb racks on 21 March, Major Lone and the W/T were never dropped.[31] Lone was flown into Fort Hertz on 20 May 1943, and he set out overland for the *Dilwyn* area shortly after. He only arrived on 21 November. Explaining why he took so long, Major Lone wrote: 'Most of the time we had to follow narrow footpaths, overgrown with weeds and tall grass abounding with snakes. One can imagine untold hardships in marching during rains in the hills, with malaria, leeches, flies, mosquitos and many jungle diseases, the leeches particularly being so numerous that they dropped like hail from the trees.'[32] Before Major Lone arrived, on 20 October *Dilwyn II* had been successfully dropped by air.

While BCS struggled to get *Dilwyn* established in the Kachin Hills, the Americans made an 'intelligence push southwards' towards Bhamo and Myitkyina.[33] It was obvious that SOE and OSS were beginning to have a conflict of interest in the area, so on 3 June 1943 Kachin territory was divided using the Taiping River as a boundary. The Americans got a zone north of the river, and the British zone was south of the river. This demarcation caused disgust amongst British operational personnel, who believed that they were abandoning many of 'their' loyal Kachins to the Americans.

By early July 1943 the Americans had bypassed the agreement by inserting OSS teams into the British area south of the river under orders from their China base.[34] This precipitated a meeting later in July held at Nazira (OSS HQ in India) where a new policy was hammered out. Major Peers would be head of OSS in northern Burma, operating under the orders of OSS China. Major Noel Boyt was appointed liaison officer to coordinate all *Dilwyn* operations with Peers.[35] This agreement amounted to something of an 'armistice' between OSS and SOE for a short time.

By October 1943, when *Dilwyn II* was inserted, there were 35 OSS men already in the field.[36] They had ten functioning W/T stations in the Kachin Hills that India Mission knew about by January 1944. The three main bases from which the OSS spread into the Kachin Hills were codenamed *Knothead*, *Forward* and *Pat*. The Americans were not, as Anglo-American agreements dictated, just providing an intelligence network for Stilwell. Earlier suspicions were confirmed by early December 1943 when the *Forward* commander, Captain Curl, requested his monthly rice requirement. Investigating further, in January 1944, SOE estimated that Curl had recruited 400 Kachins for guerrilla work.[37] It thereby became obvious that the Americans were working to their own agenda, with OSS operating in a guerrilla role. This later prompted the remark that the OSS 'appeared to us like a bull in a china shop instead of a cat in the dark'.[38]

Regarding OSS intelligence, the SOE officer based at Fort Hertz, Captain Howe, complained in late November 1943 that the value of the intelligence that OSS was supplying was minimal. British reports singled out Captain Wilkinson, commander of *Forward*, for criticism as the origin of alarmist and unfounded intelligence ('flaps') about the potential of Japanese forces to advance north and take Fort Hertz.[39]

In order to defend Fort Hertz, 4 Burma Regiment was deployed to Fort Hertz at the end of 1943. Whether this was a result of the 'flaps' caused by Wilkinson is not clear, although the value of Fort Hertz to the Americans was huge. By late 1943, a large amount of American radio equipment was based there which provided weather reports, and included early warning systems to protect American air supply to the Chinese over 'The Hump'.

The pressure upon *Dilwyn* was not only American in origin. When it was learned that a second Chindit operation planned to have a diversionary force operating in the Kachin Hills from March 1944, BCS officers were concerned that the Chindits might compromise *Dilwyn*. Planning for *Dahforce*, as this decoy group commanded by Lieutenant Colonel 'Fish' Herring was known, had been kept a secret from India Mission.[40]

This lack of coordination in the first instance was compounded by the last-minute decision taken by Wingate, without informing SOE, not to land on *Dilwyn's* prepared drop zone. This unnecessarily placed the reception committee at prolonged risk. After landing in March 1944 and hiking to *Dilwyn's* area of operations, Herring's *Dahforce* enlisted Kachins to fight on the promise that the Chindits were in Burma to stay.[41] Of course, the Chindits did not stay.

When, in late April 1944, the decision to withdraw the Chindits was made, it was proposed that *Dahforce* remain. Coupled with the pressure from OSS, those in charge at BCS began to consider the position of *Dilwyn*.[42] If *Dahforce* remained and came under BCS control, then it would be their responsibility to supply the troops. Despite the arrival of six Liberators, BCS could not guarantee sufficient airlift for the supply of 340 extra men.[43] In addition, it was thought that the Japanese would be more aggressive in their anti-guerrilla operations in the Kachin Hills if the Chindits remained.

Both the OSS and the Chindits had encouraged the Kachins to fight the Japanese at a time when it was uncertain whether or not the Army would make a successful advance into the area. BCS feared Japanese reprisals against the Kachins that the Allies would be powerless to prevent.[44] Mindful of the Kachins having been let down twice already, first after the retreat in 1942, and then after the first Chindit operation in 1943, BCS was anxious to ensure the continuing loyalty of the Kachins.

The difficult decision was taken by BCS to withdraw *Dilwyn*, and 34 personnel were flown out to Calcutta in June 1944.[45] It is not clear how many *Dilwyn* men were left in the Kachin Hills, but Shan Lone's cousin, Zau June, remained with his W/T.[46] This left OSS with an open field in much of Kachin territory, which was certainly something that Stilwell desired. It was then reported that the Americans were telling the Kachins that Britain had let them down, but that they could rely on the Americans.[47] *Dahforce* commander, Lieutenant Colonel Herring, wrote to Colonel Mount Stephen Cumming, commander of SOE's A Group, in June that 'the Kachin Hills [are] being handed over to the Americans, a decision which I deeply deplore'.[48]

SOE had not given up on the mission to the Kachins though. The *Dilwyn* personnel who had been extracted in June had completed further training and were ready to go back into the field from about 18 August. It was then that relations with the Americans took a new turn. Peers was told by Colonel Taylor, the American Officer at P-Division (the body coordinating clandestine services for SEAC), that he would be 'open to a charge of meddling in British colonial policy' if he cooperated with *Dilwyn*.[49] This was because *Dilwyn* Kachins that had remained were in communications with *Spiers*, an operation which had developed into a political battle between the British and Chinese.[50] Peers wanted to work with *Dilwyn*, but considered it essential that he had Stilwell's consent.

Having had a presence in the Kachin Hills for about 18 months by August 1944, BCS staff were so reluctant to leave the Kachins to the OSS that they offered to place *Dilwyn* under American control.[51] In an effort to convince Stilwell, the idea was mooted that Peers would present *Dilwyn* plans to Stilwell as if he was in charge of them, to make it appear as if *Dilwyn* was an OSS operation, when in reality it would be a joint effort.[52] Stilwell stood firm and said that he would not accept OSS involvement with *Dilwyn*.

After this rejection by Stilwell, the matter was referred to Mountbatten by P-Division. The Americans knew that they had the upper hand, however, for it had been agreed in July that *Dilwyn* supplies would come from OSS, delivered by OSS aircraft.[53] 'A three-week battle' raged from the beginning of September in which Stilwell continued to fight for an independent American remit in northern Burma.[54] In the meantime, SOE's Station X continued to send out intelligence from the Myitkyina area, but had to watch as OSS pressed ahead with the recruitment of Kachins whom *Dilwyn* considered their personnel.

In the end Mountbatten had to order Stilwell to accept *Dilwyn* under his command, coordinated by Peers. Stilwell continued to be difficult despite this 'strong action' by Mountbatten, insisting that *Dilwyn* only undertake intelligence work, and by not using the proper channels of P-Division for coordination of OSS and *Dilwyn*. The head of BCS left Stilwell's HQ on 1 October 1944 convinced that *Dilwyn* would have to be written off due to 'the continual and deliberate obstruction of Stilwell'.[55]

Stilwell probably knew that his days in Burma were numbered at this point, enabling him to damn the consequences of defying Mountbatten. Chiang Kai-Shek had lost confidence in him and insisted that President Roosevelt recall him. Stilwell returned to the US on 27 October.[56] The damage was done by this time. Stilwell did not want SOE in 'his' area 'in the face of which we had no alternative but to cancel the operation, after having explained the situation as best we could to the Kachin chiefs and instructed them to co-operate fully with our allies'.[57]

What particularly galled BCS men was the fact that all their preparatory work was capitalised on by the Americans. Captain Zau June, who had remained when the main party was withdrawn, was particularly distressed. Captain June had worked hard to convince the Kachins in the Sinlumkaba area to start fighting; in his report, June claimed to have 5,000 Kachins ready to fight. 'Then, however, the Americans came and stepped into our shoes. Everyone on the ground was confused and puzzled.'[58] In his opinion, the Americans did not care for the Kachins they enrolled into what became known as the Kachin Rangers. For June this was the fourth time that the British had deserted the Kachins, and it was 'painfully humiliating'.[59]

With Stilwell gone, however, BCS decided to continue with *Dilwyn*. In November and December 1944, as XIV Army advanced towards the Chindwin River, *Dilwyn* teams landed in a new area of operations east of Lashio. Their task was to assist Operation *Heavy* in the northern Shan States, as well as to assist the American advance south from Myitkyina by protecting the left flank. Four *Dilwyn* stations were parachuted in by the end of the year. Named after animals, stations *Badger* (28 November 1944), *Monkey* (29 November 1944), *Gazelle* and *Squirrel* (28 December 1944) were parachuted into Monghawm and Nampakka areas. Quarrels with the Americans were replaced immediately by trouble with the Chinese: station *Monkey* landed in the middle of a battle between Kachins and Chinese guerrillas.[60]

Operation *Spiers*: Kokang and the Northern Shan States

If operation *Dilwyn* exemplifies tension between the British and their American allies, it is *Spiers* that illustrates the political intrigue between the British and Chinese. This operation was based on Kokang in the north-eastern Shan States. Kokang bordered the Chinese province of Yunnan in the north and east, and the Shan State of North Hsweni to the west across the Salween River. To the south were the Wa States, across the Nam Ting River.

The border with China had originally been agreed in 1894, but a 'Modifying Agreement' of 1897 placed Kokang in British Burma. The Chinese border was thus pushed approximately 64 km (40 miles) east, and this gave the British control of the most profitable territory in the northern Shan States.[61] The territory was controlled by a hereditary

Myosa, or ruler, who in 1942 was Yang Wen Ping.[62] He had succeeded his father in 1927. The intrigue with the Chinese was caused by Kuomintang central Government's attempt to reclaim the territory. Of the 600 villages in Kokang, 455 were Chinese.[63] The *Myosa* was in fact Chinese, the Yang family having migrated from Nanking in the seventeenth century to escape the Manchus.

The original objectives of the operation were to establish contact with operations *Eyemouth* and *Dilwyn* and assist these teams working with the Kachins to the west, as well as arming and training the Kokang Defence Force, investigating the possibility of receiving Chindits or other airborne forces, and establishing links with the Chinese Expeditionary Force. Instead, BCS found itself embroiled in a political entanglement that eventually extended to Sir Alexander Cadogan, Permanent Under Secretary at the Foreign Office in London.

During the retreat in 1942, the Government of Burma had requisitioned 320 mules from the *Myosa*. The sum owed for these was approximately Rs 100,000.[64] After the British Consul General at Kunming, Sir Alwyne Ogden – and subsequently the Burma Government – refused the *Myosa's* request that his State come under Chinese protection, the *Myosa* asked if he could be supplied with arms against the money owed. These arms would go to the *Myosa's* 'home guard', the Kokang Defence Force (KDF). This request was urgent, for in September 1942 the Japanese had launched attacks into Kokang and Chinese forces had run away without a fight. The Burma Government responded by stating that the *Myosa* could have half the money owed, but no arms because that was a matter for the commander of the Chinese Army. Privately, the policy was to give the *Myosa* 'general encouragement', and it was hoped to carry out propaganda operations through him.[65]

Herein lay the root of the problem in Kokang. The British authorities had refused to let the state come under Chinese protection because that would be tantamount to a surrender of sovereignty, yet because the northern Shan States came under the military jurisdiction of the Chinese Expeditionary Force, arming the KDF was a decision to be made by the Chinese. To resolve his dilemma, the *Myosa* went from Kunming to Chungking and obtained an audience with the Chiang Kai-Shek. A shrewd decision was made by Chiang: the *Myosa* became an honorary colonel in the Chinese Army for his leadership of independent Chinese forces (the KDF). The *Myosa*, a British subject, returned to Kokang with the title *Sze Ling Kuan*, dressed in a Chinese officer's uniform, complete with sword, presented by Chiang.[66] KDF officers were now sent to the Chinese military school at Tali in Yunnan for training, and Chinese officers were attached to the KDF.[67] The opening move to reclaim Kokang for China had been made, allowed, perhaps, by the naivety of the Burma Government and Consul General Ogden in Kunming.

The *Myosa* professed loyalty to Britain despite being forced into Chinese arms. In a meeting on 12 April 1943 at Tali with the British Assistant Military Attaché, the Myosa said that the Chinese were as bad as the Japanese. They took what they wanted from the villages and there were cases of murder. He again asked the British to supply weapons for protection against both Chinese and Japanese. The KDF had 900 men but only 300 rifles, four Bren guns and two Thompson sub-machine guns.[68] This time the head of India Mission, Colin Mackenzie, wrote to the Director of Military Operations (DMO) and said that BCS would be willing to supply the *Myosa* with arms. In return, Mackenzie said that he would want the *Myosa* to supply good men who could be used as 'bodyguards and raiding parties' for attacks on the Japanese line of communication running between Lashio and Myitkyina.[69] Importantly, he also recommended that a Political Officer should go with the BCS operation 'to avoid any unnecessary friction' because there was no government representative in either the Shan or Wa States.

The SIS was intimately involved with the *Spiers* operation from the start. It was known by the cover name of the Inter-Services Liaison Department (ISLD), and it was one of its agents who had recommended that India Mission support the *Myosa*.[70] On 7 July 1943, India Mission and ISLD representatives met and agreed to an SOE operation into Kokang.[71] Paul Hector Munro-Faure was confirmed head of the operation on 14 July 1943.

Munro-Faure was 49 in 1943 and was considered to be a China expert, having worked for the Asiatic Petroleum Company in China in 1919–41.[72] He had been commissioned into the Sherwood Foresters in 1941, and sent to Maymyo to help establish the Bush Warfare School. From 1942 until May 1943, Munro-Faure had been working for 204 Mission training Chinese guerrillas in the Third War Zone in China.[73] According to Mackenzie, Munro-Faure had been removed from his posting in China due to the machinations of OSS and ISLD.[74] When Munro-Faure was placed in charge of the Kunming Section just three months later, Mackenzie thought that ISLD were once again involved against Munro-Faure and SOE. Apparently ISLD not only tried to subordinate Munro-Faure in Kunming, but SOE's Chungking section too.

Originally, India Mission had planned the *Spiers* operation to be carried out by air as Kokang was British territory. The deficit in airlift capacity precluded this, so Munro-Faure was sent to Kunming, China, where he arrived on 6 August 1943. His directive stated that from his HQ in Kunming, SOE teams would be sent overland to Kokang.[75] This became the source of much trouble; the Chinese now had to know about the operation, and they required their British allies to have special passes to travel to Burma. While SOE was held up in Kunming without the necessary passes, ISLD got theirs and moved off into Burma. The *Spiers* mission was still stuck in Kunming on 1 October 1943, when there was an attempt on the *Myosa's* life. The *Myosa* escaped with a broken leg, but one of his sons was killed.[76]

The reason for the Chinese preventing *Spiers* from moving into Kokang became clear in the closing months of 1943. Although the Chinese denied responsibility for the attack on the *Myosa*, it was established that the Chinese had managed to subvert the *Myosa's* cousin while he was being trained at Tali, and that the Chinese 36 Division had directly supported the attack.[77] The cousin was to become a puppet *Myosa*, part of the Chinese plan to reclaim Kokang. BCS then moved fast to get personnel into Kokang by other means. If the Chinese would not allow travel overland into Burma, they could not object to a team being parachuted in. Operational instructions were sent out on 8 November 1943 for a team to be dropped on 11 November, but the sortie was aborted due to 'bad' maps.[78] In conditions of great secrecy, *Spiers I* was dropped on the night of 9 December, but it landed on the Chinese side of the border, and was arrested by Chinese troops. Complaints against SOE from the Chinese, the Americans, and British consular officials followed. To add fuel to the fire of Chinese complaint, the party had been issued with passes supplied by SEAC, which Chinese authorities did not recognise.[79]

The party was eventually allowed to proceed to Kokang, but once there the Chinese prevented the party from having any contact with the locals by threatening the latter with reprisals. Considering it pointless to stay, the *Spiers I* team withdrew to Paoshan in Yunnan at the end of

December 1943. They did so with some useful intelligence. The *Myosa's* brother, Yang Wen Tsai, was now in charge, the Chinese having detained the *Myosa's* cousin. Yang Wen Tsai was thought to be pro-British, and only working for the Chinese under duress. It later transpired that the cousin plus the Chinese officers involved in the attack had been executed in an effort to disguise Chinese intrigue.

They had also discovered that an OSS party (consisting of six Kokanese and no Americans) had entered Kokang after the attack on the *Myosa* in October. This group had found that the locals wanted the true *Myosa*, Yang Wen Pin, returned to governance so arms were flown in by OSS to this end. In response, the Chinese confiscated the arms and arrested the OSS team. General Stilwell subsequently denied all knowledge of this OSS party. This situation caused Colonel Cumming to remark: '*Spiers I* were unlucky that they found themselves put in on a wicket already stickied by OSS'.[80]

As *Spiers I* trekked out of Kokang in December 1943, Munro-Faure was walking in, having obtained passes from the Chinese at last. He met the *Spiers I* party at Paoshan. In a report on the personnel to Mackenzie, Munro-Faure wrote that Major Broadbent, the officer commanding, was 'not a leader' but should be 'a good follower'. Captain Tunney was disparagingly described as 'useful for winding the W/T generator'. The W/T operator, Corporal Sunderland, was considered a liability, and Dr Watt, a Cantonese doctor sent to treat the *Myosa*, was suspected of being under Chinese influence. Only Captain Moffat received positive comments, with the remark that he had run the operation.[81] The party was accused of having no staying power, and were withdrawn to India, with the exception of Broadbent who went back to Kokang with Munro-Faure. India Mission now placed their hopes in Munro-Faure to salvage the operation.

The Chinese provided a large escort for Munro-Faure's party as they proceeded into Kokang. Munro-Faure concluded that this was to send a signal to the locals that the Chinese were in control of the *Spiers* group. After the escort was somehow shaken off, the party was followed by some Chinese dressed in plain clothes but who had a W/T. Furthermore, Munro-Faure suspected his Hong Kong Chinese interpreters of spying for the Chinese. When he eventually arrived in Kokang, Munro-Faure reported that '[a]ny stranger visiting Kokang could only conclude he was in China.' There were pictures of Chiang

Kai-Shek everywhere, the Chinese flag was flown, and the KDF wore Chinese cap badges and sang the Chinese national anthem. In addition, the Chinese were disseminating anti-British propaganda and collecting taxes.[82]

It was suspected that the Chinese were using Kokang as a 'test case'. If they could successfully exert their authority here, then other parts of northern Burma might suffer the same fate. 'Chinese imperialism was exposed in regard to their intentions towards annexation of border states while British attention was engaged elsewhere.'[83] To regain control, three things were suggested: that *Spiers* take over the KDF; that a British political officer be installed immediately; and that the original *Myosa*, Yang Win Pen, be returned.

To help accomplish this, the British needed to establish a strong presence in Kokang. Between Munro-Faure's arrival in Kokang in February 1944 and 5 May, four more *Spiers* parties were put into the area, consisting of 11 personnel in total.[84] The *Spiers* HQ was established at Lunghtang by 26 February 1944. In the face of continued Chinese obstruction, the operation was only able to carry out a reconnaissance of the Salween River crossings and begin training and arming the KDF. Organising attacks upon the Japanese was never accomplished because the operation was so tied up with the Chinese.

In an effort to establish British political authority, after securing the release of the *Myosa* and flying him out to India, the Burma Government released a communiqué, signed by Yang Win Pen, officially recognising his brother as acting *Myosa*. BCS had stated that Kokang should have a political officer back in July 1943, but the Burma Government in exile had organised nothing. An India Mission officer, Colonel Kaulback, was therefore made Civil Affairs Officer in June 1944. The Chinese recognised this gesture for what it was, and did not afford Kaulback the usual courtesies on arrival in Kokang, despite the Chungking Government having recognised his appointment.[85]

In July 1944 the Chinese made a concerted effort to freeze out the British. At the Foreign Office in London, Sir Alexander Cadogan said that the British Government would just have to see how the situation developed.[86] Kaulback requested that two companies of Chins or Gurkhas be flown into Kokang, but the troops were not made available due to commitments on the Imphal and Kohima front. By early August 1944, Kaulback wanted to bring out most of the officers so that they could be gainfully employed elsewhere. At the end of September came 'the *coup de grace* to British prestige'. Brigadier Wilson Brand, the officer commanding the British Staff Mission created to liaise between the Chinese Expeditionary Force (CEF) and British forces in Burma, was 'berated in front of the local populace' by the CEF's Chief of Staff.[87] Within a month, *Spiers* personnel were withdrawn from Kokang. In 15 months, the operation had achieved none of its objectives, the war being between Allies rather than against the enemy.

Operation *Spiers* thus demonstrated that SOE's military objectives could be derailed by political wrangling that had a long colonial history. *Spiers* became a political operation which extended from the men on the ground up to the Generalissimo on the Chinese side, and the British Government on the other. Seeing Britain stretched by the fighting on the India–Burma border, on the China–Burma border, the Chinese were able to freeze out SOE – who in any case were not supposed to be colonial plenipotentiaries.

Operation *Hainton*: Kengtung and the Southern Shan States

Similar to *Spiers*, Operation *Hainton* (later renamed *Heavy*) was infiltrated into Burma from China, and was also the object of significant Chinese interest. Led by Major Pennell, the intended area of operations was approximately 320 km (200 miles) south of Kokang in the Wa States near the Siamese border. The objectives of the operation were to provide intelligence about Kengtung State, assess the possibility of conducting clandestine warfare in the area, and to try and link up with operation *Harlington* in the Karen Hills. The operation was approved on 19 March 1944, and *Hainton I* set out for Szemao four days later.[88] At Szemao, the Americans controlled an airstrip into which *Hainton II* were flown by 14 USAAF. The combined party then left for Burma, with a Chinese liaison officer and W/T operator attached.

It was soon found by *Hainton* personnel that, as in the *Spiers* area, the Chinese were more interested in obstructing SOE than fighting the Japanese. In July 1944 *Hainton* reported that '[o]wing to the difficulty we are experiencing with the Chinese we do not wish to become involved in any local disputes, and our plans for crossing the China border are temporarily suspended.'[89] By September, *Hainton* reported that they did not consider it safe to put Chinese SOE agents into Kengtung because they might 'come to an untimely end in the jungle'.[90]

Another way the Chinese made it difficult for *Hainton* to complete their mission was because Chinese guerrillas and the Chinese 93 Division lived off the land. Consequently, padi cultivation in Kengtung state had decreased significantly. *Hainton* needed recruits, but taking men who were needed to tend the fields when production was reduced was problematic. Supplying *Hainton* from India proved difficult, even for Liberators, during June and July, due to distance and monsoon. This failure to drop supplies was 'adversely affecting British prestige', and the food supply problem held up operational plans. In November a Liberator crashed trying to supply the operation, killing all on board. By December, the food situation was so bad that ISLD and E Group (Prisoner of War Recovery) personnel in the area came to *Hainton* for help, further diminishing their supplies. Major Pennell blamed the consequent withdrawal of his party back into China on 'insufficient support from India'.[91]

The *Hainton* operation, at least in its early stages before it became re-designated *Heavy*, reveals that Sino-British relations were difficult along the length of the China-Burma border. By September 1944, Chinese pressure had prevented SOE not only from further accessing their intended area of operations, but also from using trained Chinese personnel, and from using the local population to the desired extent. It is remarkable that despite the Chinese, as well as some reliance on the Americans, plus food shortages, the officer commanding *Hainton* still blamed failure on the lack of support from India.

Operation *Harlington*: the Karen Hills

Captain Hugh Seagrim had remained in the Karen Hills in Burma after the rest of the Army and Oriental Mission had retreated to India in 1942 (see Chapter Two). One of India Mission's first operations was to try to establish contact with Seagrim. In February 1943, therefore, four Karens were parachuted into Karenni. Attempts to drop a W/T set to them over a period of eight months were unsuccessful. At last, on 13 October 1943, Captain Jimmy Nimmo was parachuted in, and by 15 October was in communication with Calcutta. It did not take him long to locate Captain Seagrim and Lieutenant Ba Gyaw's party.

On 8 December, Seagrim and Nimmo were joined by a third British officer, Captain Eric McCrindle. All three officers had working W/T equipment which was successfully transmitting useful intelligence to BCS in Calcutta. Those in charge of BCS hoped that their section could now start proving India Mission's worth to the sceptics. The prospects looked good. It was estimated by the three British officers that around 10,000 Karens were willing to fight.[92]

What happened next had to be slowly pieced together by BCS staff over the months until the end of the War in 1945. *Harlington* had multiple sources of compromise, which ultimately led to the death of all three British officers. On 20 December 1943, a Japanese radio direction-finding van arrived in the Papun area to try and locate the W/T sets.[93] Added impetus was given to the hunt by a Burman informant and the discovery of substantial amounts of shotgun cartridges, which could only have been supplied by the British.[94] During January 1944, more Japanese arrived in the area and started asking about British officers, including a *Kempeitai* detachment on 31 January.[95] The *Kempeitai* were successful in their methods, and Seagrim's hide-out was revealed by a young Karen even before an ISLD team landed in the area on 5 February 1944.[96]

Interestingly, after McCrindle was successfully infiltrated in December, an India Mission memorandum recommended that ISLD should not be allowed to operate in the Karen Hills because the Karen scheme was considered of 'sufficient value' for it to 'go ahead undisturbed.'[97] The ISLD agents had missed their intended drop zone though, and they were compromised upon landing because one of the team landed on top of a clump of bamboo, which necessitated getting help from a nearby village.[98]

Ian Morrison, the *Times* correspondent who was given permission to write the story of Major Seagrim in 1945, made it clear, however, that in his opinion ISLD should not be held responsible for wrecking *Harlington*. He put it down to 'one of those unfortunate failures to co-ordinate', besides which, the Japanese were employing a variety of methods to hunt down Seagrim and his companions.

In February 1944, the Japanese attacked Nimmo's camp near the village of Mawtudo, north of the Mawchi Road. He was shot through the head and died instantly. At a location further south, when the Japanese attacked Seagrim's camp, McCrindle too was shot through the head.

Seagrim was able to escape. The subsequent Japanese reprisals against Karen villages pushed Seagrim into handing himself in to the *Kempeitai*, along with several other Karens, including Lieutenant Ba Gyaw, sometime in early March. The captives were taken to jail in Rangoon, where they were executed in September 1944.

In order to prevent any more reprisals against the loyal Karens, BCS decided that they would not try to re-establish *Harlington* in the short term. With the possibility of an offensive overland into Burma by the end of 1944, plans to raise the Karens were then reinitiated, with a specific plan of operations centred upon the Toungoo–Mawchi Road.[99]

P Force: the Chindwin River Area

So far, the operations described have been those that focused on raising Burmese forces from the hill tribes in the north and east of the country. At the same time as these operations far behind the lines were initiated, SOE was used in the north-west of the country on the Burma–India border. The roots of this operation go back to January 1943, when a directive was issued to Major C.B. Jones by BCS tasking him with operating in front of the Army in the Chindwin Valley. The specific tasks of this group were to create an underground route into central Burma, and to recruit agents that could be used locally to provide intelligence, and pass back potential agents for training in India.[100]

By November 1943, agents codenamed *Falstaff*, *Arrowhead* and *Wilfred* were established, though the archives yield little more about them. Presumably to build upon the success of these agents, Major Edgar Peacock received a directive in November 1943 tasking him with organising a 'string of contacts in the rear of the enemy', and founding a base camp from which to recruit and train personnel. These recruits would be used to patrol the jungle, harassing the Japanese and providing intelligence for IV Corps, on whose front they were operating. The Army was still sceptical of SOE; Peacock knew it was imperative that his group 'justify [the] confidence placed in us' which would be measured by 'cooperative efforts' with the Army.[101]

Between 24 February and 3 March 1944, Brigadier Guinness, India Mission's new second in command, went to inspect Peacock's command. Known as P Force, by February this consisted of four officers, 17 NCOs ('all native'), 104 Riflemen and 24 'other roles'.[102] He reported that

20 Division's commander, Major General Gracey, 'speaks most highly of this force'.[103] The Army's confidence in SOE had been earned by Peacock's role in supporting 20 Division's local offensives against the Japanese. This led to an agreement for Peacock to move further east at the end of March and to recruit Burmese for 'village work'. The men recruited for this role were to go about their ordinary lives in their villages, but take any opportunity to 'bump off' Japanese and Burma Traitor Army personnel. They were to be rewarded 100 Rupees for the 'production of [a] suitable bit of anatomy' from Japanese, and 50 Rupees for BTA body parts.[104]

Also operating in the Chindwin area were two other organisations, the Chin Levies, under Lieutenant Colonel Balfour Oatts, and the 'Kin Scouts', run by the exiled Burma Government. After barely a month in the field, Peacock was intensely critical of the latter. In his opinion the Kin Scouts were useless. After receiving two weeks training in a civil camp, Kin Scouts were sent back to their villages with a rifle where they were nothing but a 'liability'. Peacock saw no point in them other than to justify the existence of officials of the 'so-called government of Burma'.[105] Major General Gracey held similar views of the Kin Scouts. It seems the animosity extended to the leader of the Chin Levies too. Lieutenant Colonel Balfour Oatts' leadership of the Chin levies was criticised at the end of 1943, to the extent that one SOE officer wanted no more to do with him.[106] There were, then, at least three irregular formations working around the Army with variable success.

As Peacock won confidence in SOE, however, and prepared to move his force deeper into Burma, two things were in motion that would result in his extraction from Chindwin operations. In February 1944, the commander of IV Corps, General Scoones, was told that BCS wanted to have Peacock and Captain 'Pixie' Poles released for future operations. A shortage of officers for SOE work was cited as the pressing need to have these two officers, but it was also mentioned that the work Peacock's Special Group was doing was not considered 'a true GSI(K) role'.[107] The second factor was the Japanese offensive against India, launched in March 1944 which led to the battles of Imphal and Kohima. In May, P Force was withdrawn.[108] During the six months that he was in the field assisting IV Corps, Peacock had shown that SOE could maintain a force in the jungle, aggressively patrolling in support of regular forces.[109] This would be important to the development of operations in 1945.

Operation *Billet*: Arakan and Central and Southern Burma

While IV Corps faced the Japanese across the Chin Hills, XV Corps maintained a front facing the Japanese in the coastal Arakan region of western Burma. In this area, SOE operations could infiltrate into Japanese held territory overland or by sea, from where central and southern Burma, including Rangoon, could be reached more easily. The target population in central and southern Burma was Burmans; it was these operations which led to SOE's controversial embroilment with Burmese Nationalist forces, including the Burma National Army (BNA).

The origin of Operation *Billet* dated from immediately after the Japanese drove the British out of Burma in 1942, when a radio intercept revealed a Japanese assessment of the Burmese population.[110] The Japanese Ambassador in Bangkok reported to the Foreign Ministry in Tokyo that there was already suspicion of Japan's intentions, and a danger that the Burmese might 'swing around to hatred of Japan'. To counter this, two courses of action were recommended, either the granting of Burmese independence, or manipulation of Burmese politicians. It was considered vital to make the Burmese believe in the inevitable victory of Japan, and it was requested that the Burma Independence Army (BIA) be 'buried in oblivion'.[111]

It did not take long for Burmese Nationalists to ascertain Japanese intentions. On 1 August 1942 Dr Ba Maw was installed as head of a Burmese Government which operated 'within the wider framework' of a Japanese military administration.[112] The Burmese recognised that they had merely swapped one master for another.[113] The Japanese had read the situation correctly. From 1942 the Burmese underground, albeit divided in opinion at this early stage, and the newly named Burma Defence Army (BDA) started preparing for a possible future struggle against Japan. In July 1942, two young communists, Thein Pe and Tin Shwe, trekked out of Burma through the Arakan to India to contact the British. Their aim was to secure help from the British to defeat fascist Japan and secure Burma's postwar independence.

When they arrived in India, Thein Pe and Tin Shwe were placed under arrest. These men were considered part of the Fifth Column that had hastened the British defeat barely six weeks earlier. As Thein Pe wrote: 'We hated the English and disliked and mistrusted the Japanese. We had arranged to rise against the English with arms promised us by the Japanese, but night after night, although we waited with flashing torches, no arms arrived.'[114]

The British were naturally suspicious of the two men, thinking that the Japanese had sent them. It was over a year before permission was given by the C-in-C to send one of the men back into Burma.[115] Tin Shwe, codenamed *Lancelot*, was landed by boat on 8 December 1943, at a spot on the Arakanese coast selected during their trek out of Burma. This was the beginning of Operation *Billet*, the plan to contact the nationalist Burman population and bring the BDA (formerly the Burma Independence Army) and other anti-fascist Burmans over to the British side.

In February 1944, Tin Shwe kept to the agreed rendezvous and was picked up by boat. The exfiltration resulted in some enemy action during which a boat was sunk with the death of two Japanese and the capture of seven Burmese.[116] After debriefing, confidence in Thein Pe and Tin Shwe was strengthened. This, and the news that Aung San, head of the BDA, recognised 'the error of alliance with Japan by saying "We are finished. We are cattle now"' convinced BCS that they should exploit this opening. There had to be a radical change in attitude to make this possible. The BDA was still widely referred to in British circles as the Burma Traitor Army. Major Eric Battersby, the officer responsible for minding Thein Pe's group, was of the opinion that in France in 1940 and Burma in 1942 despite the fact that 'few soldiers' had anything good to say about the French or the Burmese, there was very little Fifth Column activity. The aim of *Billet* should be to do the same to the Japanese, and 'create [the] illusion' of a country against them.[117]

Aung San's change of allegiance was confirmed in a speech he made on 1 August 1944, when he declared the independence given by the Japanese to be a sham. Shortly afterwards, the Anti-Fascist Organisation (AFO) was formed. On both the Burmese and the British side there was confusion as to what to do. The AFO wanted to be rid of the Japanese but did not want to have the British replace them. The British did not want to arm the Burmese Nationalists only to see the guns turned against them once the Japanese were defeated. This prompted Thein Pe to write a 'thesis' in September 1944 entitled 'Toward Better Mutual Understanding and Greater Cooperation between the British and the

Peoples of Burma.'[118] In his thesis, meant for Mountbatten, Thein Pe urged the British to arm the AFO because the first task was to defeat Japan. Major Battersby agreed, as did the Governor of Burma, Sir Reginald Dorman-Smith. He believed that a relationship of trust should be built with the nationalists.

Mackenzie at HQ Force 136 (India Mission's GSI(K) cover name was replaced in March 1944 by Force 136) was unsure, and advised that BCS should work out what they wanted from *Billet*, and move forward from there. Against these views, the Civil Affairs Service, Burma (CAS(B)) was unwilling to allow the Burmese to 'work their passage home.'[119] Major Battersby described the Chief Civil Affairs Officer, General Pearce, as 'the chief nigger in the woodpile'. This was explained by the opinion that 'long residence in Burma is a well-known preservative from a dangerous spontaneity of original or enlightened thought'.[120] Thus, opinion in the British camp was divided over how to treat the Burmese Nationalists, and would remain so for the rest of the War – and beyond.

While the debate about how to deal with the Burmese Nationalists went on, BCS continued to infiltrate Burmese agents back into Arakan, and from there into upper and lower Burma. In December 1944, operation *Billet* was split into three parts. The Arakan part was called *Manual*, the upper Burma part *Grain*, and the central and lower part *Nation*. By the end of 1944, 'it seemed, at last, that we were beginning to get somewhere.' Four W/T stations, codenamed *Donkey*, *Hound*, *Camel* and *Lion*, had successfully been sent into Burma.[121] With the release of personnel from the European theatre by September 1944, these original *Billet* teams were reinforced with experienced SOE personnel, many of them Jedburgh officers and W/T operators who had recently seen action in France.

Jedburgh officers, or Jeds, were SOE officers who had served against the Nazis. It was hoped that with their experience of dealing with diverse resistance groups in places like France, the Jeds would be able to cope with the Burmese. Moreover, it was hoped that they would 'come out from England with a military reputation but with no, we hope, capitalist or Imperialistic intentions towards Burma.'[122] It was clear that the BDA was ready to turn against the Japanese, and both Force 136 and XIV Army realised that it needed to be managed. By ignoring the CAS(B) and using Jeds, there were high hopes that they would be successful as the year 1944 ended.

Conclusions

The assertion presented at the beginning of this chapter that India Mission was 'ready to get to work in earnest' made in July 1943 was premature. Over the timeframe of this chapter, from September 1943 to December 1944, not only was the training infrastructure of the India Mission deficient in personnel and procedure, but the available aircraft were limited in range to certain areas of Burma. Until these service and support requirements were in place, it is no wonder that India Mission officers were posted to the Chindwin River area on operations that were not considered 'a true GSI(K) role'. It was here, in an area that could easily be reached overland from the Indian border, that important experience was gained, and the confidence of some senior Army officers – Generals Scoones and Gracey– was secured. Both of these consequences of Chindwin patrols were hugely important to operations in 1945, as will be seen in Chapters Five and Six.

For the *Spiers* operation in Kokang in the north-east, as well as *Hainton* in Kengtung, the consequences of not having the supporting airlift ultimately resulted in both operations being withdrawn by the end of 1944. In both operational areas, British prestige was damaged; in the *Spiers* area for not having the resources to assert British colonialism over Chinese 'imperialism', and in the *Hainton* area for not being able to feed the local population. The military objectives of these two missions were never achieved, partly due to airlift, but also because India Mission was forced into a more pronounced political role where three Allies had competing political and strategic interests. Even accepting that the personnel deployed on these missions were not trained to be political officers, if there had been the supporting infrastructure behind them, the outcomes might well have been different. This support is not confined to airlift; Sir Alexander Cadogan's message from the Foreign Office to Mackenzie that the British Government could not do anything and to wait and see was hardly decisive and forward orientated. These two operations indicate that for Special Operations to best be able to fulfil their objectives, they need firm and decisive guidance from the top, a clearly defined military or political objective, and the infrastructure to support any commitment. Yet even if all of these conditions had been in place, Sino-American machinations may have been enough to derail operations.

Of the operations in this chapter, only *Dilwyn* – the operation to the Kachins in northern Burma – had any prospect of supporting an offensive by the Army in 1943–4. This it managed to a limited extent by supplying intelligence which eventually culminated in the reoccupation of Myitkyina in August 1944. Instead, *Dilwyn* was compromised by Anglo-American rivalry which was mostly caused by competing strategies, and American wariness of British colonialism. Even after spheres of influence in Kachin lands had been accepted in mid-1943, it had proved difficult for *Dilwyn* to achieve their objectives because the Americans reneged on the agreement. The picture that emerges from this study of operations to the Kachins is somewhat different to the idea that by December 1942 'an approximate geographical separation' between OSS and SOE was occurring, with OSS claiming the Kachins and SOE the Karens further south.[123] SOE remained committed to the Kachins for the duration of the War.

It should not be forgotten, however, that this was the first time that the US and Britain had conducted Special Operations alongside each other in this theatre, and lessons had to be learnt just like they still were in North Africa and Europe. The more subtle nuances of Allied cooperation had to be tried and tested, from the officers and men on the ground, up to the officers in charge at theatre level, and between the governments of the two countries. It was made all the more sensitive due to the fact that the ground was British colonial territory, and there was a sense of proprietorship over the Kachins felt by many British officers.

By the end of December 1944 the situation for BCS, while not looking quite as discouraging as a year before, was still far from achieving results. In the north around Myitkyina, most of *Dilwyn* had been withdrawn from the Kachin Hills and had only just landed in a new area of operations south-east of Bhamo. In the northeast, *Spiers* had been withdrawn from Kokang, and there were no plans to go back. South of Kokang, *Hainton* had been withdrawn for similar (and other) reasons to *Spiers*, and to the south-west of *Hainton*, *Harlington's* European and Karen officers had been killed by the Japanese. Although P Force had been withdrawn from the Chindwin area in hope of fulfilling plans to go back to the Karen Hills, at this point it was far from certain that SOE would. The operation to contact the Burmans, *Billet*, had just achieved radio contact with Rangoon by December 1944, and the first teams had gone behind the lines in the Arakan. Just two of the six operations covered by this chapter were behind the lines then, but there was now the infrastructure and resources to support operations. If the politics of the Burmese Nationalists in the BNA and AFO, as well as the Americans, were to allow, there was hope that India Mission could accomplish much more.

Yet ultimately what is the most important development, and the one most pregnant with potential for the next period, was not just how many BCS operational objectives were achieved, or men put onto the ground or Burmese recruited. As Lieutenant Colonel Gardiner wrote in 1945, this time must be thought of above all else as a 'period of very necessary experiment', when things had to be learnt the hard way because they 'were not in a book'.[124] It was a period of necessary evolution, when tactical lessons of operational procedure were learnt, and when the resources that would allow strategic effect were made available. By the end of 1944 then, it seems fair to say that the India Mission – in Burma at least – was 'ready to get to work in earnest'.

CHAPTER 5

OPERATION *CHARACTER*, NOVEMBER 1944–SEPTEMBER 1945

One of the operations that featured in Chapter Four was Operation *Harlington*, a mission based on Major Seagrim and the Karen people. Operation *Harlington* was the foundation for Operation *Character*, the focus of this chapter. Operation *Character* became SOE Burma's largest operation.

To briefly recap: in February 1943, Lieutenant Ba Gyaw was parachuted into the Karen Hills to secure a drop zone for two British officers who would follow, with the goal of contacting Major Seagrim.[1] Major Seagrim had remained in the Karen Hills since 1942, but without communications equipment. For various reasons, it was not until October 1943 that Captain Nimmo followed Lieutenant Ba Gyaw with the crucial wireless telegraph (W/T) equipment. From December 1943, after Captain McCrindle arrived, three British officers had been in communication with Calcutta, supplying intelligence from the Karen Hills.

Ultimately, however, the operation ended in disaster. In August 1944, seven months after communications from the Karen Hills stopped, the Secret Intelligence Service (SIS) informed SOE that that McCrindle and Nimmo had been killed by the Japanese, and that Major Seagrim had surrendered to prevent further Japanese reprisals against Karen villages.[2]

This chapter follows on from the troubled beginnings of Operation *Harlington* which were described in Chapters Three and Four, and details how Operation *Harlington* was resurrected as Operation *Character* in

February 1945. *Character* evolved into a complex mission during 1945, subdividing into a set of operations that were in some cases quite distinct. When Lieutenant Colonel Tulloch, commander of *Walrus* sub-area, came to write his memoir of the *Character* operation, he found that writing a 'detailed record' was 'quite impossible' because 'in practice it turned out there were virtually as many commands as there were officers in the field'.[3] For example, his own *Walrus* command broke down into headquarters, *Skunk*, *Boal*, *Red* and *White* areas. It was a similar situation for the other three commands. Despite this growth of quasi-independent commands stemming from the four groups that were originally flown in, the chapter will demonstrate how Burma Country Section (BCS) was able to dramatically turn the disaster of *Harlington* into one of SOE's 'most spectacularly successful military operations of the war.'[4]

Covering the period from November 1944 through to the end of the operation in October 1945, the chapter is divided into five sections.

(1) Personnel and Mission Objectives.
(2) Introduction of European Personnel, Training and Briefing.
(3) Operations, February–May 1945.
(4) *Character* Under Pressure, May–July 1945.
(5) The Japanese Breakout, July–September 1945.

Personnel and Mission Objectives

The personnel that formed the nucleus of *Character* were the Special Patrol Groups (SPGs) that had previously operated on the Chindwin front under the command of Major Peacock. These Special Groups, known as P Force, had been patrolling the jungle, recruiting locals to bring out to India for training, and running agents into Japanese occupied villages in the area to the front of Imphal from early 1943 through to early 1944.[5] Although these operations were not seen by BCS as proper SOE work, the experience gained would prove vital to the success of operations in the Karen Hills. Also worthy of note is the fact that P Force consisted of both Karens and Burmans, illustrating to those who needed proof that the two peoples could work together. The Burmans, Karen and British officers of P Force were extracted from Chindwin operations in May 1944. They needed to be rested and sent for parachute training before being flown into the Karen Hills for Operation *Character*.

The *Character* operation had specific objectives that originated from General Slim. Firstly, the retrained P Force, now organised into three Special Groups, had to contact the Karen and make sure that they were still loyal and willing to fight. Although *Harlington* had found the Karen willing, the reprisals of the Japanese in their search for Seagrim, and the lack of intelligence about what had happened in the intervening period, meant that there was uncertainty. It was known, for instance, that after the withdrawal of the second Chindit operation in 1944, the Kachin had become reluctant to rally to the British unless they had some guarantee that Allied forces were coming back to stay; Japanese reprisals had made their point.[6] If it was discovered that the Karen would fight, then the teams were to raise the Karen as guerrilla fighters (contemporaneously called 'levies'). It was hoped that there would be a sizeable guerrilla force ready to support XIV Army's anticipated advance.

In September 1944, BCS pondered the extent to which it was worth committing scarce specialist personnel, given the 'news' about Major Seagrim and the other *Harlington* men. The head of BCS, Lieutenant Colonel Gardiner, had planned on parachuting Honorary Lieutenant Kan Choke into the Karen Hills in October 1944 with the express purpose of ascertaining the fate of the four Operation *Harlington* officers (Lieutenant Gyaw, Captains Nimmo and McCrindle, and Major Seagrim).[7] Now that they knew, should Gardiner risk putting a rare asset – a Karen officer – into the field? BCS as a whole only had two Karen officers at this time, including Kan Choke. Two additional officers, who were serving with the Kachin Levies, had been applied for, since Gardiner considered these men essential '[i]f SEAC wish the Karens raised'.[8] Gardiner had even offered to trade the experienced Captain Jack Barnard and another officer, Captain Wilson, in return for the two desired officers, Karen Captains Saw Torry and Saw Butler.[9]

The plan to send in Lieutenant Choke was aborted in October 1944. By this point, meetings had taken place to confirm that SOE personnel from Europe would arrive in the Far East before the end of 1944, and P Force had been extracted from the Chindwin to prepare for operations in Karenni. The officer commanding 20 Division, Major General Gracey, had been impressed with the intelligence received and ambush skills of P Force. According to Gardiner, it was the work of P Force which contributed to Slim's decision to give SOE a shot at covering his flank for the advance on Rangoon.[10]

Furthermore, during its 15 months in the field, P Force had garnered the tactical experience that would facilitate the success of Operation *Character*. How the enemy reacted to ambush, Japanese patrolling habits, effective use of explosives in ambush, how to identify Japanese units, how to build an effective intelligence network, how to live in the jungle; all these tactical skills were learnt to such a level that the Japanese apparently described the men of P Force as the 'foe with fearless eyes'.[11]

Originally, there were to be three teams of P Force flown into the Karen Hills, codenamed *Otter*, *Ferret* and *Hyena*.

Otter was commanded by (newly promoted) Lieutenant Colonel Peacock. Edgar Peacock was a true child of the British Empire. He was born in Nagpur, India, in 1893, worked in Burma for 16 years in the Forestry Service until 1934, and had then gone to farm in Rhodesia.[12] By 1940, officially aged 42, he was an engineer in the Southern Rhodesian Regiment. After gaining his commission with the Officer Training Corps in Kenya, Peacock worked at Army HQ, India, in an intelligence role. He joined SOE in November 1943, and was first deployed as commander of P Force in late 1943.[13]

Group 2, *Ferret*, was commanded by Major Eustace Poles. 'Pixy' Poles was born in Yorkshire in 1902. He had also served in the Southern Rhodesian Regiment with the second battalion, as an instructor, in Salisbury. In 1941, as a platoon Sergeant with the King's African Rifles, Poles served in the Abyssinian campaign. Granted an emergency commission in October 1941, he joined SOE in April 1943, and worked with Peacock on P Force operations.[14] It was originally intended that Poles have his own command in the northern sector of the *Character* operation, but in the event he remained under Peacock's command.

The third group, *Hyena*, was commanded by Major Turrall until Lieutenant Colonel Howell took over. Rupert Turrall was born in Devon in 1893.[15] During the Great War, he served with the New Zealand Division in the Dardanelles campaign in 1915. From 1916 until 1919, he fought on the Balkan front where he was twice mentioned in dispatches. At the War's end he was a captain, holding the acting rank of major. Between the Wars, Turrall took a degree in Geology and Astronomy at Cambridge which led to his position as chief geophysicist covering first North and then South America 1922–30. During the 1930s he was in East Africa investigating mineral deposits. In World War II he had seen action in Abyssinia, where he won a Military Cross with Mission 101, an early SOE operation led by future Chindit leader, Major Orde Wingate.[16] Between the Abyssinian campaign of 1941 and arriving in Delhi to join the Chindits in January 1944, Turrall saw action in Crete and completed training courses on sabotage and parachute training. He arrived in Burma to take part in *Thursday*, the second Chindit operation, launched in March 1944. He therefore joined SOE's Force 136 in September 1944 with considerable experience in irregular warfare.[17]

Lieutenant Colonel Hugh Howell assumed command of *Hyena* from Turrall on 24 March 1945. Hugh Howell was born in India in 1904, the son of an Indian Civil Servant. When the war in Europe broke out, Howell was living with his wife and two daughters in Shanghai, employed by the Kailan Mining Company. After the War began, Howell joined the Indian Armoured Corps. He joined Force 136 on 19 September 1944. He was described in December 1944 as 'extremely painstaking' and a 'somewhat fiery character' with 'rather wild ideas'. Despite this, it was thought that he would 'do well in an operational capacity'.[18]

When it was decided to form a fourth group, the colourful character chosen to lead *Walrus* was Lieutenant Colonel John Cromarty Tulloch.[19] Apparently extracting him from a scandal concerning a cheque, Gardiner brought Tulloch back to India with him from Britain. In his late 50s, Tulloch was the oldest of the *Character* officers, so he was known as 'Pop'. Squadron Leader Terrence O'Brien, the Special Duties pilot who flew several *Character* teams into Burma, makes it clear that Pop was well known for his tall stories. One rumour is that he was a spy in 1930s Germany, selling carpets disguised as an Arab. In India, he tried to avoid parachute training by claiming that he already had his wings (and wearing them).

After deployment, Lieutenant Colonel Ronald Critchley, was placed in command of a new sub-mission codenamed *Mongoose*. Born in Edinburgh in 1905 and commissioned in 1925, Critchley was a career soldier who served abroad for most of 1929–45. In 1939 he was sent to Yugoslavia with MI(R).[20] He then served in the Abyssinian campaign with Mission 101 before going to India and organising V Force in Assam. He then served with the Chindits before returning to SOE.[21]

Introduction of European Personnel, Training and Briefing

By February 1944, shortly before P Force's extraction from the Chindwin area, Major Peacock had recruited four officers, 17 non-commissioned officers (NCOs) and 104 riflemen.[22] The majority were Burmans from the Chindwin area. In June 1944, most of this force were sent to Camp Tweed, in Eastern Bengal, which had been built specifically to accommodate P Force.[23] After parachute training, the teams went to Ceylon for jungle training, this being delayed for six weeks until November 1944 by fever contracted at Camp Tweed.[24] Their recovery coincided with the arrival of Lieutenant Colonel Musgrave, the new commandant of training at ME25 in Ceylon, and the first European personnel.

Lieutenant Colonel George Musgrave arrived back in the Far East in November 1944, and also came with a distinguished record of irregular service. After organising guerrillas in Aden and then fighting the Italians in British Somaliland in 1941, he had been sent to the Bush Warfare School at Maymyo, Burma, run by Major Mike Calvert. He had contracted black-water fever during the retreat from Burma in 1942, and as a result the doctors were set against him returning to the East for any length of time. This advice seems to have been overruled given SOE's need for people with experience of active service in the Far East, and of training Jedburgh teams in Europe.[25]

The Jedburgh concept, as developed in the European theatre, was to put specially trained teams of three men behind the lines.[26] This had been done in occupied France, Belgium and Holland. Teams usually consisted of an officer who was either a local or someone who had detailed knowledge of the area of operations, a British or American officer, and a proficient W/T operator, normally a sergeant. Their job was to train the resistance in sabotage and guerrilla tactics, and to transmit intelligence to Britain. The first Jedburgh team had left for France on the night of 5 June 1944, as the D-Day invasion forces crossed the English Channel. Their job was to provide intelligence to assist the invasion and coordinate the Resistance. With their operations in France largely complete by the summer of 1944, many Jeds then chose to go to the Far East in search of more special operations.

Musgrave had lobbied hard to be allowed to return to the Far East. At the end of August 1944 he went to India and met India Mission officers to establish the operational guidelines for those Jeds who were to

Table 5.1   Forecast of personnel needed for Burma, 1945[27]

Burma	Team to consist of:	No. of Jeds	No. of BO necessary	No. of BOs minimum	W/T operators
Billet	2 BO + 1 W/T	6	12	12	6
Character	1 BO + 1 W/T	8	16	8	8
Special			12	12	36
Groups could					
absorb					

BO = British Officers.

be transferred to the Far East. At a meeting held on 7 September 1944, general principles were agreed, and in addition three specific roles for Jeds in Burma were settled. Firstly, Jed teams would be used to develop Burmese resistance with the Anti-Fascist Organisation (AFO) in Operation *Billet*. Secondly, they would be used in the Karen Hills. Thirdly, they would be attached to P Force, which would provide protection for the Jed teams until local guerrillas had been raised.[28] By the end of September 1944, 17 British officers and 12 W/T operators had volunteered to be transferred to Force 136. It was expected that Operation *Billet* would need six Jed teams, and *Character* eight.

After this meeting on 7 September, Musgrave commented:

> Reaction of SOE India to the formation of JEDBURGHS was extremely well received and it appeared to me that owing to the speed of operations JEDS would form the main core of operational activities in India.[29]

The head of Force 136, Colin Mackenzie, wrote a directive detailing how the Jeds would be integrated with Special Groups. There should be no segregation, recognising a need for collective training.[30] Peacock was not pleased when he found out:

> that each group was to take a Jed team (recently arrived from Europe) consisting of two Officers and a Wireless Operator, with whom we had not previously associated ... Since these officers had never been in BURMA, knew nothing of the language and were

dependent entirely on the veterans of the Special Groups, the situation became confused ... The Special Groups were furious at unwanted last minute intrusions and implications against their ability to conduct jungle warfare.[31]

A certain amount of animosity towards newcomers was to be expected, but of all the post-operational reports, only Peacock's highlights any tension. Far from being 'dependent entirely' upon the old Burma hands, coupling up European experience with local agents and veterans of the Far East was seen in one 1945 report as a 'conspicuous success' both in training and in the field. The performance of the Jeds in Burma after minimal training was described as 'remarkable'.[32] Sergeant Glyn Loosmore, radio operator for *Mongoose*, argued that Peacock's negative judgement was influenced by bitterness about the possibility of losing control of his 'private army'.[33] Terence O'Brien corroborated this, writing that Peacock 'had not been happy about becoming part of a trinity having already commanded his own guerrilla force'.[34]

Training, according to Peacock, under Musgrave and the Jeds, was 'excellent' and 'good' respectively for demolitions and weapons. Not everything was so good, however, and '[o]f training in jungle warfare the less said the better, but [it] was not discreditable in instructors fresh from European theatres of war'.[35] Lieutenant Colonel Tulloch, officer commanding *Walrus*, considered training in Ceylon to have been 'a complete and absolute farce'. Even the Jed teams – operationally experienced in Western European environments – criticised the training in Ceylon in their post-operational reports. Major Alexander Campbell described his two weeks of jungle training in Ceylon as 'a complete waste of time'.[36] However, it is worth noting that Tulloch did praise the jungle training that he received at Belgaum in India, as well as parachute training.[37] If criticisms of the training in Ceylon were almost universally scathing, then criticism of the pre-operation briefing by both Jeds and the Burma veterans was damning. Major Denning, later commander of Operation *Character's Walrus Red*, said of his briefing:

> I hardly know where to begin. Several hours of verbose nothingness left us with the impression that those responsible had not the courage to admit they had no knowledge of our area or tasks, and that they were too lazy to make the effort.[38]

Major Campbell wryly wrote under 'Briefing' on his post-operational report: 'Still to come, I presume.' Peacock stated that staff in Calcutta were suffering from 'rank lunacy'. Lieutenant Colonel Tulloch's explanation was 'the absurd fetish for "security" so fanatically worshipped by nearly every staff officer in Force 136'. Others blamed it on the haste with which the teams for *Character* were dispatched on operations.[39] Such an inadequate briefing, and tension between the new arrivals and the experienced Burma personnel, was nothing new. William Mackenzie observed that in Europe, '[t]he ordinary arrangements for briefing were hardly adequate' and that 'SOE's old hands in the field complained that they would have preferred more stores rather than more inexperienced "bodies" to nurse'.[40]

If *Character* was to support XIV Army, there was a need to get the teams in quickly. A last-minute rush did, in some cases, lead to confusion. Lieutenant Colonel Peacock's first attempt at deployment had to be abandoned when fires were seen to be extinguished as they flew over the proposed drop zone. This meant that Peacock's group, along with Major Poles and his team, was parachuted into Major Turrall's drop zone at Pyagawpu. Although this proved fortuitous because the balance of men and equipment that arrived in Pyagawpu was enough to convince reluctant Karen to fight again, it did mean that Major Poles was now some 80 km (50 miles) from his intended area of operations. His *Ferret* group travelled to their allocated zone near Hoya (north of the Toungoo–Mawchi Road and south west of Loikaw), but just after they arrived about 18 March, Calcutta headquarters ordered him back to *Otter* area. Peacock reported:

> Major POLES very naturally returned into my area in a very depressed and disgusted mood, and the whole business had repercussions of the most unpleasant kind, and undoubtedly rendered my Operations North of the MAWCHI Road less effective than they might have been. I deplore most strongly the procedure adopted, which to my mind is inexcusable and might very well have led to disasters North of the Road, were it not for the level-headed conduct of Colonel TULLOCH and Major POLES.[41]

Meanwhile, Tulloch did not understand why his group were briefed as *Ferret*, and then changed to *Walrus*. With Poles gone from the *Ferret* area,

Tulloch and his team were parachuted into Burma, blind, on the 24 March 1945. After ruling out two possible drop zones, Tulloch made the decision to exit his aircraft on a third site despite the fact that there were two villages overlooking the clearing where they would land. There were also small trees, which the pilot thought would be impossible for all the parachutists to avoid.[42] A Burman soldier, Thein Maung, was found hanging from one of the trees with a broken neck. Major Lewis broke his foot.[43] Tulloch reported that all sustained minor injuries. The following two aircraft found the drop zone, but aborted as there was no reception. This was because the villages were Shan, not Karen as hoped. Runners had been sent to alert the Japanese, so Tulloch and his men had had to make a hasty exit from the drop zone. Nonetheless, with the balance of Tulloch's men successfully inserted on 28 March 1945 at Tilawsu, all four Special Groups of Operation *Character* were on the ground.

Operations, February–May 1945

The four Special Groups found themselves in terrain which was mountainous. In the *Walrus* area, which was the northern component of *Character* operations, the average 'hill' was 1,500–2,100 metres (5,000–7,000 feet).[44] These Karen Hills were covered in tropical forest or jungle, where there were few roads. This made it easy to predict the routes the Japanese would take. Of the terrain in which he was operating, Major Campbell (commanding *Walrus Skunk*) said: 'The area was absolutely God's gift and ambushes and demolitions on the Loikaw–Bawlake Road could not go wrong.' Not all teams found themselves in the right terrain; southeast of Walrus in the *Hyena White* area, Captain Barron described his area as 'unsuitable for guerrilla warfare' because it was so open and flat on the flood plains of the Sittang.[45]

The local population that the *Character* teams were to recruit from also varied across the area of operations. From *Walrus* in the north in the hinterlands of Loikaw, to *Mongoose* in the south in the vicinity of Papun, is about 185 km (115 miles). The width of *Character* territory was variable – 70–150 km (30–60 miles) – thus making a rough area of operations of about 16,800–18,000 km^2 (6,500–7,000 ml^2). Within this area, there were three main groups: the Karen, the Shan, and Burmans. The Karen were not an homogenous group, and included S'gaw, Pwo, Red, Black, Striped, and Bwe Karen. The Padaungs that

Tulloch described as the best fighters are a sub group of the Red Karens, and were particular to his *Walrus* area of operations.

The distinction is important because it accounts for the difference in traits recorded by the officers in their reports. For example, Major Lucas, *Mongoose Blue*, reported that the Karen were 100 per cent helpful, but backward, of poor physique and non-fighters.[46] This contrasts with the Lieutenant Colonel Howell of *Hyena* who observed that the Karen were good soldiers and civil administrators 'well fitted to govern themselves'.[47] Major Campbell thought that their briefing should have told them more about the people that they would be working amongst, as this 'may have prevented some of the officers from treating the Karens as "wogs"'.[48] However, evidence of this sort of treatment is not apparent in the documents, rather the opposite. It seems clear that, in the main, British officers regarded their Karen allies with great affection, and many British men continued to correspond by letter with their Karen friends after the War.

There was also inconsistency in the reports regarding the Shan. Major Denning of *Walrus Red* reported that 'all Jap. raids on us were led by Shans'.[49] Major Lucas agreed, stating that the Shan were 'on the whole, anti-British, unreliable, and often pro-Japanese', yet in the same *Mongoose* area, Lieutenant Colonel Hood noted that the Shan were very loyal, and that they had helped build an airstrip at Mewaing. Tulloch commented that the Shan and the Karen did not trust each other, but Lieutenant Colonel Hood wrote that Shan and Karen lived fine together. In the past, the Shan had not been noted by the British colonial authorities for their martial qualities, and this seemed to have been borne out by the lack of Shan recruits into the guerrilla forces raised.

In the more southern areas of the *Character* zone, such as *Hyena White*, there was a larger number of Burmans. In March 1945, the BNA changed sides and some of the *Character* teams found themselves having to fight alongside – or at least cooperate with – the Burmans of the BNA. Assessments of their new allies varied too, with some comments probably best explained by Burman nationalism. For example, Major Lucas was of the opinion that the Burmans were 'pro-Burman and nothing else', and Captain Wilson of *Hyena Orange* perceived Burmans as 'opportunists over-ready to change their policies and take advantage.'[50] Although many officers noted that in their relations with the Karen, the Burmans were 'definitely the aggressor and disturber of the peace', it is worth remembering that 80 per cent of the Special Groups that originated from P Force were Burman personnel. Lieutenant Colonel Peacock wrote in his report that prejudice against Burmans should be reconsidered because these Burmans were accepted as leaders by the Karen.[51] Yet at the same time, Captain Barron was ordered not to issue arms to Karen in areas where the AFO or BNA were present, and similarly not to arm Burmans in predominantly Karen areas.[52] Major Neville judged that relations between Karen and Burmans had 'a resemblance to the Arab-Jewish Question'.[53] In sum, the *Character* teams were expected to raise guerrilla armies from within a complicated demographic.

Some things did go right for the *Character* teams though. Raising guerrillas was made easier when many of the Karen who had been with Seagrim came to fight, and they were joined by Karen from the Burma Rifles (Burifs) who had been ordered to return to their villages in 1942.[54] Having these Burifs was 'invaluable in helping with the training'.[55] They provided the fledging guerrilla force with some welcome backbone, and former NCOs were able to reassume their leadership roles over the raw recruits that volunteered. Tulloch reported that *Walrus* had recruited 400 levies by 2 April 1945, which had grown to 2000 by 18 April; Peacock reported that within a week, *Otter* had recruited 500, which had increased to 700 by 23 March; Lieutenant Colonel Howell of *Hyena* reported that in the first month 731 arms were issued to recruits; finally, Captain Ford of *Mongoose Red* reported that by D-Day (the date for offensive operations to begin) 160 had been recruited in his area.[56] These recruits fell into two categories, 'mobiles' and 'statics'. Mobile levies were those that were willing to leave their villages and go on operations. The role of statics was to protect their villages, and deny the Japanese food and shelter.

By 9 April, around 3,000 arms had been distributed to *Character* levies. Including over 100 men parachuted in to the hills, this equates to a brigade size force sitting on the Japanese line of retreat south through central Burma, and blocking an eastward escape towards Siam.

D-Day arrived when General Slim gave the order for *Character* forces to attack the Japanese 15 Army retreating to Toungoo along the road from Loikaw via Mawchi. On 10 April, *Otter* received orders to start attacking, and on 13 April the order was received to prevent the Japanese 15 Division from reaching Toungoo.[57] *Walrus* received instructions to attack on 18 April. By this point, Peacock's *Otter* group had been in the field for six weeks, but Tulloch's *Walrus* for just 16 days. The race for Toungoo was on and according to Slim 'it looked like they [the Japanese] would beat us to it.'[58] If the Japanese were to reach Toungoo first, they would block the route to Rangoon and it was feared that if Rangoon was not captured before the monsoon, the already tenuous aerial supply of XIV Army would become impossible.

To reach Toungoo, the 15 Division of the Japanese 15 Army had to travel south on the road from Loikaw through Bawlake until meeting the River Salween just north of Kemapyu. At Kemapyu the road turned west, going through the mining town of Mawchi on its way to Toungoo. The Japanese would first have to go through Tulloch's *Walrus* area (Loikaw to Bawlake), before turning west and going through Peacock's *Otter* area. Peacock had established his headquarters on Sossisso, a ridge of 2,300 metres (7,500 feet) that overlooked the town of Mawchi 13 km (8 miles) away. Mawchi was a re-grouping point for the Japanese before continuing their journey west towards Toungoo. If the Japanese continued south along the road through Kemapyu they would travel through Turrall's *Hyena* area, towards Papun. From Papun the route continued south towards Bilin, and into Lieutenant Colonel Critchley's *Mongoose* area.

The focus in April 1945, as far as XIV Army was concerned, was on *Walrus* and *Otter* areas. Tulloch reported that between the 19 April and 10 June 'scarcely a day or night passed without an ambush, sometimes several'. By 19 April, however, advance elements of 15 Division had already passed through the *Walrus's* area and reached Mawchi. On 16 April, the Japanese left Mawchi and Peacock's *Otter* group went into action. The Japanese were forced back to Mawchi by *Otter's* guerrillas after sustaining heavy casualties. A second attempt to travel west was thwarted the next day, so on 18 April, the Japanese changed tactics sending infantry ahead of the vehicles. This began three more days of fighting, which Peacock described as an enjoyable time killing 'Japs' with no losses to his command.[59]

It was during this period of fighting that the experience of P Force operations appears to have paid dividends. Peacock wrote that with the confidence of experience, and the natural ability of the Karens in the jungle, his forces had a 'supremacy over the Jap to an almost unbelievable extent.' The preferred method of ambush devised during Chindwin operations was the Cordtex trap. To illustrate a typical

Cordtex ambush, an example is described by Lieutenant Marlam, of group *Hyena*.[60] This particular ambush consisted of 38 Mills grenades attached to 230 metres (750 feet) of Cordtex. The trap was detonated by the ambush commander who would conceal himself in an observation post so as to judge when to initiate the explosives. When Lieutenant Marlam detonated his 38 grenades simultaneously on 4 May 1945 in his *Hyena* area, he estimated around 80 Japanese were killed. In the six days of group *Otter's* engagement described above, an estimated 307 Japanese were killed and about 30 vehicles destroyed. Peacock regretted the fact that he had no medium machine guns or Hawkins grenades, and that an air strike upon the town of Mawchi never materialised: 'literally many hundreds of Japs are living today who should be dead'.[61]

While *Otter* group delayed Fifteen Division's retreat, IV Corps had been pushing south. Armoured units of 5 Division entered Toungoo on 22 April. They raced on through, leaving 19 Division responsible for securing the town and its important airfields from Japanese forces now bottled up along the road east to Mawchi. The Japanese narrowly lost the race for Toungoo, in part due to the effectiveness of Force 136 guerrillas. General Slim must have been referring to SOE when he wrote:

> [The] Japanese, driving hard through the night down jungle roads for Toungoo, ran into ambush after ambush; bridges were blown ahead of them, their foraging parties massacred, their sentries stalked, their staff cars shot up. Air-strikes, directed by British officers, watching from the ground each stick of bombs, inflicted great damage. The galled Japanese fought their way slowly forward, losing men and vehicles, until about Mawchi, fifty miles east of Toungoo, they were held up for several days by road-blocks, demolitions, and ambuscades.[62]

Despite this success, the divisions of IV Corps were held up by a stubborn Japanese defence at Pegu. This held 17 Division long enough for the seaborne forces of Operation *Dracula*, assisted by Force 136 teams, to claim Rangoon on 3 May. While the Army celebrated the liberation of Rangoon, in the Karen Hills the guerrillas of Operation *Character* fought on.

Character under Pressure: May–July 1945

After Rangoon was recaptured in early May, the campaign in Burma wound down, at least as far as the Army was concerned. Thoughts turned to the seaborne invasion of Malaya, the next major stage of the campaign against Japan. Rest, recuperation, and reorganisation were the order of the day after fighting almost uninterrupted since the start of the Japanese offensive against India back in March 1944. In this context, it is not surprising that Lieutenant Colonel Peacock was informed that 19 Division was tired.[63] As far as Force 136 was concerned, however, the war was very much still in progress. Over the coming months, considerable resentment grew within Force 136 because of the Army's perceived inactivity. On 27 June 1945, a letter was written to Brigadier John Anstey, Deputy Commander of Force 136, which summed up the SOE perspective.[64] 'For some time I have had the feeling that both you (Kandy HQ) and SACSEA have written Burma off as finished from an SOE and a military point of view.' At this point there were still 50,000 Japanese soldiers in the *Character* area of operations, with another 10,000 on the wrong side of the Sittang River, hiding in the Pegu Yomas. The author wrote that the five Allied divisions in Burma had 'developed a most depressing lack of initiative since taking Rangoon', and that as a consequence *we are killing more of the enemy than the entire 12 Army* [underlined in original].'[65] The men involved in Operation *Character* universally agreed with this in their post-operational reports, and even General Stopford, commander of XXXIII Corps, admitted in July that Force 136 had killed more Japanese than regular forces had in recent weeks.[66]

In *Walrus* area, the consequences of the Army's inertia were clear to Tulloch:

> I state categorically that had Army only maintained their presume [sic, pressure] up to the end of May or middle of June, the Jap forces in the Loikaw-Bawlake area would have disintegrated and the Karen Hills liberated three months earlier than they were. Unfortunately, after the capture of Rangoon, the Army appeared to rest on their laurels.[67]

To get to Tulloch's area, the Army could have followed the route of the retreating Japanese 15 Army south from Mandalay to approach *Walrus* from the north, or 19 Division that had been left in Toungoo could have advanced along the road into the Karen Hills. This would have taken them through *Otter* area before relieving *Walrus*. Mawchi is only 76 km (47 miles) from Toungoo. Between 7 June and 23 August, 19 Division advanced just 47 km (29 miles). According to Captain Sell, commander of *Otter Green*, contact between Force 136 and 19 Division was only achieved on 14 August 1945, at Bawgalgyi, approximately 48 km (30 miles) from Toungoo.[68] It might not have made a difference, but 19 Division had asked if there were any irregular troops to their front, and they had been told there was none.

From Peacock's perspective, not only was 19 Division advancing slowly, there was a lack of supporting airstrikes. Signals were sent, markers were put out, but only about six out of hundreds of given targets were attacked, in favour, Peacock says, of sorties against the enemy directly to the front of 19 Division.[69] The Japanese were therefore able to re-group in Mawchi and put the two northernmost *Character* teams under pressure. In the southern area, *Mongoose* soon felt the pressure too, for the Japanese were quick to realise that XIV Army was staying put. Both Major Lucas of *Mongoose Blue* and Captain Ford of *Mongoose Red* lamented the lack of advance by the Army after the fall of Rangoon. Operating furthest south of the *Mongoose* groups, Major Lucas was in the Bilin–Mokpalin area just over the Sittang River on the main road from Rangoon. His conclusion on his operation was that 'little of importance was achieved due to Army failure to advance after Rangoon'.[70]

By mid-May 1945 the Japanese started building defences and bringing troops north from Moulmein. Offensive patrols began, followed in June by a drive against *Mongoose* in 'speed and strength'.[71] *Mongoose Red* (Captains Ford and Williams, and Sergeant Dallow) reported that by the end of June, they had 1,500–2,000 Japanese hunting them.[72] Relations with the Burma National Army, or Patriotic Burmese Forces (PBF) as they were now called, deteriorated sharply as a result of British forces being on the back foot once more. They had no incentive to fight for Force 136 if the Japanese were staying and Force 136 would not arm them, so their spies led the Japanese to *Mongoose* bases.[73]

Contemporaneous with the assault on *Mongoose*, various *Walrus* bases came under attack. Captain Roy Wilson (*Walrus White*), Major Denning (*Walrus Red*) and Major Boal (*Walrus Boal*) all faced a determined simultaneous attack by the Japanese that Tulloch considered to be a 'deliberate attempt to liquidate the whole set up in the Karen Hills, possibly as a prelude to some grand counter-offensive envisaged by the Jap command'. Tulloch therefore decided to concentrate all his *Walrus* teams at Daurakhu, rather than have them picked off piecemeal. This re-grouping was complete by 27 June.[74] As the Japanese took control of territory previously held by *Walrus* teams, they razed the villages, killing, looting and burning all in their path.

The consequence of Japanese reprisals for *Otter* area to the immediate south of *Walrus* was an influx of refugees that Peacock had no capacity for sheltering or feeding. On 24 June, Captain Marchant and Sergeant Romain with 500 refugees left with two platoons of mobile levies to try and make contact with the Army further down the road towards Toungoo.[75] The next day, the Japanese attacked *Otter* headquarters. Although the attack was repulsed, it was during this attack that Major Charlesworth of Z Force was killed, and the Japanese exhibited a decapitated Karen.[76]

Only *Hyena* area seems to have been spared the attention of organised Japanese attacks. Lieutenant Colonel Howell stated in his report that 'during June and early July the main battle from HYENA point of view was not against the enemy but its own home bases'. He was complaining about how difficult it had been to obtain even basic supplies to complete his mission.[77] Due to a shortage of arms and Force 136-trained men, Howell thought that three or four times the number of Japanese from 31 and 33 Divisions of 15 Army were able to escape through his area than would otherwise have been the case. Howell's report corroborates with Lieutenant Colonel Hood's report for *Mongoose* about these Japanese regrouping south of Papun. Reflecting upon this in his post-operational report, Howell thought that this would have caused a problem had the atomic bombs not shortened the War.

The reason given for no more arms was that raising more levies meant more men to feed and equip. From Howell's point of view, food supply in *Hyena* area was plentiful – until the Japanese took it because there were not the arms to oppose them. Despite flying out to Rangoon to personally contest the order halting arms drops, the order was enforced.[78] The consequence, in his opinion, was that two air sorties of weapons would have prevented the later need for 43 air sorties of food.

The Japanese Breakout, July–September 1945

The Japanese 28 Army had been fighting in the Arakan, the western coastal strip of Burma that is separated from the central Burmese basin by the Arakan Yomas. Having crossed the Arakan Yomas, the Japanese took refuge in the Pegu Yomas in April 1945. The Pegu Yomas is a range of jungle-clad hills that run north to south between the Irrawaddy to the west and the Sittang River to the east. They rise to approximately 550 metres (1,800 feet), are 48 km (30 miles) wide and 129 km (80 miles) long.[79] The southern end of the Yomas lies to the north of Rangoon. With the advance of XXXIII and IV Corps towards Rangoon, 28 Army had been cut off from south-east Burma. In order to re-group with 15 and 33 Armies in the Tenasserim area, 28 Army had to cross the open Sittang valley, including the monsoon swelled river. They had to find a way through the XIV Army units protecting the line of communication from Mandalay to Rangoon, and the guerrillas of Operation *Character*.

By this point, *Character* teams had recruited approximately 12,000 fighters. 28 Army had been living on what the land offered them since April. The condition of some units was desperate as they now attempted to reach safety, although some were still disciplined fighting units and overall coordination of Japanese forces was still evident. As 28 Army began its breakout from the Pegu Yomas, Tulloch's *Walrus* group, now consolidated at Dawrawku, came under concerted attack. Tulloch had flown to Rangoon to secure Army support against this imminent Japanese attack, leaving Major Warren in charge. The attack developed into a five-day battle. Tulloch later wrote that 'splendid cooperation' between the Army and SOE's Rangoon office had ensured sufficient resupply of ammunition to *Walrus*. In repulsing the Japanese attack, the *Walrus* team estimated Japanese losses to be around 60 per cent. According to Tulloch '[t]his gallant action really marked the end of WALRUS operation' because after that it was just mopping up Japanese hiding in the jungle 'many of whom were so hungry that they had turned cannibal'.[80] For *Otter* too, their last serious fighting of the war was towards the end of July when the Japanese had largely passed through their area.

Further south, *Hyena* and *Mongoose* remained in the thick of it. *Hyena* commander, Lieutenant Colonel Howell, estimated that 9,000 Japanese came through his area of operations during July and August 1945. *Hyena White* (Major Saw Torry) reported that approximately 5,000 Japanese came through his zone.[81] It is during this period, the battle of the breakout, that the *Character* teams recorded their most devastating toll upon the enemy. Crossing the Sittang, and other rivers and *chaungs* (streams), the Japanese were exposed and vulnerable. In addition, Japanese plans for the breakout had been captured. The main crossing points were therefore defended, and in the words of Major Milner of *Mongoose White*, '[t]he fight was actually one-sided killing'. He wrote that their attempts to cross the Shwegyin River 'can only be described as suicidal'.[82] It was not just concentrated automatic fire upon the Japanese caught on the river; '[t]he levies went so far as to row out the boats to the rafts and shoot up the Japs on them, using their *dahs* in some cases'. Death also came from the skies with an estimated 50-plus air strikes called in, as well as artillery bombardment from the Army.

On 5 September 1945, Force 136 in Burma drew up a table detailing almost all of their operational statistics. It was called 'The Game Book of Casualties'. The section for Operation *Character* listed the following:[83]

Howell estimated *Hyena's* statistics as 5,276 Japanese killed, broken down into 1,424 on rafts crossing rivers, 1,472 from ambush, and 2,380 from 'steady sniping'.[84] This total, in Howell's opinion, was about 25 per cent below the actual total. Major Turrall was noted for his scrupulous attention to detail with statistics, due to his peacetime profession as a scientist. Although not included in the Game Book, Turrall recorded 1965 deaths caused by air and artillery attack that *Hyena* called in during the breakout in July. Even taking the total from the Game Book, *Hyena's* kill ratio was 738/1.

Table 5.2   Extract from the Game Book for Operation *Character*[85]

Operation	Enemy			Own	
Character	Killed	Wounded	POW	Killed	Wounded
Otter & Ferret	2,737	422	4	6	4
Hyena	5,166	78	113	7	2
Walrus	2,551	62	1	6	22
Mongoose	1,420	82	1	3	1
TOTAL	**11,874**	**644**	**119**	**22**	**29**

Despite these statistics, it was believed that many Japanese escaped. Along the Sittang River, some of the *Hyena* and *Mongoose* teams had worked with the BNA and AFO. The *Mongoose* teams had been warned by Saw Marshall Shwin, a Karen who used to be a recruiting officer for the Burma Rifles before the War, that the Karen this far south were different to those farther north. He said that these Karen had never produced a recruit for the Army. By 17 April, this had been confirmed as just three Karen had been recruited as mobile levies. For this reason, Captain Clark and Sergeant Shepherd were sent to recruit from the BNA.[86] A deal was made whereby the BNA would join *Character* as long as they were fed, clothed and armed. Accordingly, on 29 April, the first 60 BNA arrived and were armed.[87] Major Lucas, *Mongoose Blue*, described them as:

> A score of odd figures sprawled in their sleep: a motley group still clad in the rags of Japanese uniforms ... These were the men with whom I must work, the rabble remain of the BNA who had swum the tide of the victorious Japs and were now changing sides with the ebb. The flotsam of warfare; I was ready to use them to serve my own ends, fully aware I was playing with fire.[88]

The relationship between SOE and the BNA deteriorated when air supply failed and *Mongoose* was unable to keep their side of the deal. In addition, when the Army did not advance out of Rangoon, the Japanese consolidated and resumed offensive patrols, putting *Mongoose* under pressure in June 1945. By the time of the breakout in July, the BNA did not contest the Japanese crossing the Sittang. In Howell's opinion, most of the Burmans were 'primarily concerned with saving their own skins'.[89] At the same time, Major Lucas reported that PBF were 'warning villagers to prepare for a "second war" after the expulsion of the Japs'. Anti-British propaganda was in production which told the Burmese that the Japanese had been defeated by the Americans, but that Britain would 'reap the benefit' by using Indians to re-take Burma. In Lucas's opinion, preparation for civil war was already under way.[90]

For the *Mongoose* teams, the main action during the battle of the breakout was during August in the area of the Shwegyin Chaung. On 3 August Major Trofimov, *Mongoose Green*, received an urgent message to help Major Milner, *Mongoose White*. Milner had moved to the

River Sittang on 27 July. The aim was also to keep the Japanese caught in the open of the river plain between the towns Kyaukkyi and Shwegyin so that the RAF would have concentrated targets. For this task he had 750 men and two British officers, which was later increased to 900 plus five British officers. Force 136 was assisted by 1/6 Gurkhas, who blocked the route into Shwegyin. By 5 August, they faced 5,000 Japanese. Despite being outnumbered, Milner described the Japanese attempt to cross as suicidal, and estimated his kill ratio at 300/1 and that of the Gurkhas at 364/1. On the track to the west of the Shwegyin River the Gurkhas counted over 2,000 Japanese dead.[91]

Despite the two atomic bombs and the surrender of Japan on 15 August 1945, the battle of the breakout lasted until 9 September for the *Mongoose* teams.[92] According to Major Lucas, the reason why the Japanese continued to fight into September is not altogether due to their refusal to believe the leaflets that they were dropped by the RAF. Lucas was ordered to recall agents that he had sent to the Japanese as early as 21 August by Army HQ in Rangoon. Nearly four weeks later, after having asked the Army for specific instructions, he was told he could send an envoy, and so on 17 September Lucas eventually met the Japanese and accepted the surrender of 11,000 enemy troops.[93]

Conclusions

In all, the *Character* operation employed approximately 80 British officers and 30 non-commissioned officers, along with over 100 Burman and Karen officers and men in an area of about 16,800–18,000 sq. km (6,500–7,000 square miles). They recruited and trained some 12,000 levies. From earliest deployment in February to the latest withdrawal in November meant that the operation ran for over nine months. By 25 April 1945, a total of 179 air sorties had been flown to support the four groups.[94] Taking the surrender of 11,000 Japanese to the *Mongoose* team, as well as 11,874 killed according to the Game Book statistics, *Character* acquitted itself well militarily.

At a low cost in terms of men and equipment, Operation *Character* had helped to protect the flank of Slim's XIV Army as it advanced into southern Burma. Despite the descriptions of variable quality of training, briefings and supply, by raising the local population and operating in difficult terrain, the *Character* teams assisted regular forces by inflicting significant casualties upon the Japanese, as well as psychological damage. This was made possible by the experience gained from exploratory operations during 1943–4, which provided the necessary platform for operations of this scale. The shortfalls mentioned above can, to some extent, be put down to the griping of soldiers, and of men released from extreme pressure. In addition, when writing their post-operational reports – which inform a substantial part of this chapter – the focus was probably more on how to improve for the future than thinking about what had gone well.

Furthermore, the personnel that were deployed on *Character* had a wealth of experience and training behind them. Their experience, ability to improvise and their resourcefulness, probably went some way towards bridging the gap between operational deficiencies and what was accomplished. Operational experience might have been European, Middle Eastern or Far Eastern in terms of previous irregular or SOE operations, and although experience is a difficult factor to quantify in terms of performance in Burma, it cannot be dismissed. Men like Peacock and Poles benefitted from their experience as P Force on the Chindwin front, from learning how to live in the jungle to how the Japanese reacted to ambush. This was very different to living behind the lines in France, for example, where presumably the Germans and Italians reacted differently to being ambushed. Yet the stress and strain of being behind the lines is generic, as is being proficient with your weapon, explosives or anti-ambush drills.

As was seen from the brief biographies of men like Critchley, Poles and Turrall, many of the commanders were in their forties and fifties. Of course, higher ranks are normally held by older men, but the ranks held did not go beyond Lieutenant Colonel, and the age of the men is not one where you would expect them to be behind the lines conducting operations in one of the world's toughest environments. Finding a commonality of experience and personality that fits all the officers involved is difficult, but most had a love of the outdoors, and many had previously either soldiered or worked somewhere in the British Empire. This perhaps made them suited to the extraordinary pressures of working behind the lines.

The success of *Character* also had as a key ingredient the willingness of the Karen to fight with the British. It might have been easier for the Karen to submit to the Japanese, but that would have meant submission to the Burmans too. For most Karen, this was out of the question, not only due to the history of Karen/Burman relations but also because, according to Smith Dun, 'the character of the Karens is such that death is preferred to betrayal'.[95] In addition, there was the purported British promise of ensuring Karen independence from any autonomous Burmese state that might emerge after the War. Karen loyalty to the British in the War can therefore be explained by the colonial history of Burma, the longer history of Karen/Burman relations and hopes for postwar political protection.

If it is accepted that *Character* fulfilled its objectives where the operations examined in Chapter Four did not, what conditions were different? *Character* was not carried out in conditions of great secrecy. Whereas the Army did not really know that *Dilwyn* supplied most of the intelligence for the Americans in the north, *Character* had been asked for by General Slim. This means that the accusation that Force 136 acted autonomously of the usual command and control structures does not stand in the context of Operation *Character*. Liaison officers were put in place at the behest of General Slim, and the *Character* teams knew that they came under the tactical control of the local Army commander.[96]

Not only was this operation approved by the Army, it was given specific tasks to accomplish upon receiving the order to go into action from General Slim. Is it a coincidence that when the Army regrouped after taking Rangoon and the *Character* teams found themselves largely fighting alone, that the Japanese were able to exert sustained pressure on them? Probably not, because the enemy regained the initiative and was able to focus resources wholly upon eradicating the enemy in their midst, just as they had with previous operations such *Character's* predecessor, *Harlington*. Conditions for *Character* were, on the whole then, very different to at any other point in the history of SOE in the Far East, but probably the most important difference behind its success was the fact that *Character* had the support of an advancing army and an adequate supply infrastructure for its needs.

As a final point to this chapter, it is worth noting that because it was obvious that the Japanese were going to be defeated for good in Burma, thoughts were turned to the future. In mid-1945, there were pointers towards potential trouble between the Karen and Burman communities, which SEAC was aware of. Strict instructions were, therefore, given to BCS for the recovery of weapons distributed to Karen and Burman alike, and careful records of distribution and recovery were kept. The British were also mindful that there were those who might turn their weapons on the returning colonial power, which is something that is discussed in the next chapter.

CHAPTER 6

THE *BILLET* OPERATIONS: *NATION, MANUAL* AND *GRAIN,* NOVEMBER 1944–SEPTEMBER 1945

Operation *Character*, the subject of the previous chapter, was one of the two largest and most important operations for Force 136 in Burma. *Billet* operations, with which this chapter is concerned, was the other. Both the *Character* and *Billet* operations were specifically tasked with supporting *Extended Capital*, the Allied advance to Rangoon in 1945.

While *Character* operations defended the eastern flank of Slim's advance, the *Billet* operations were located directly in the path of the advancing Allied divisions, both in the Arakan and in central Burma. Central Burma was divided into Upper and Lower Burma. Accordingly, the *Billet* operation was subdivided into three to cover the three geographic regions that it targeted. The *Manual* operations were focused upon the Arakan, *Grain* upon Upper Burma (Mandalay), and *Nation* Lower Burma (including Toungoo and Rangoon).

Whereas Operation *Character* focused upon recruiting guerrillas from the Karen, the *Billet* operations sought cooperation predominantly from the Burman population, particularly the nationalists belonging to the Anti-Fascist Organisation (AFO), and the Burma National Army (BNA). This chapter is concerned primarily with the maturation of the *Billet* operations from November 1944 through to their conclusion in September 1945, and the difficult decisions associated with arming and fighting with the BNA and AFO.

The genesis of Operation *Billet* was introduced in Chapter Four. Briefly here, the *Billet* operations were conceived after two Burmese communists arrived in India from Burma in July 1942. Thein Pe and Tin Shwe were members of the nationalist Thakin Party. 'Thakin' was a term meaning 'master', formerly used by Burmese for Europeans, but which young Burmese Nationalists had claimed for themselves in an act of defiance. 'Sworn to protect the lives and property of the Burmese people', the Thakin Party's official name was the *Dohbama Asiayone*, which roughly translates to 'We Burmans'.[1] Through the interwar years, the *Dohbama Asiayone* 'tried to bring in a new age of radicalism and realism' to challenge British colonial rule. Their radicalism began by attempting to emulate Gandhi, but developed into a revolutionary position as student and worker strikes became favoured weapons, and as more communists joined the organisation.[2] Consisting mostly of young men of college and university age, the older Burmese politicians railed against the radicalism of the new generation of nationalists.

The Thakins should be considered a collection of Burmese Nationalists, united by their opposition to colonialism rather than by a single ideology. As Robert Taylor set out in his work, *Marxism and Resistance in Burma*, from at least 1937 through to 1942 when Thein Pe and Tin Shwe walked out to India, Thakin policy was confused.[3] One group, led by Thakin Aung San, believed that although the Japanese were Imperialists that had committed atrocities in China, the Burmese should accept the Japanese help offered by Colonel Suzuki to eject the British.[4] Aung San duly left Burma with his 'Thirty Comrades' to receive military training from the Japanese, and invaded Burma with the Imperial Japanese Army in 1942.

Another group, led by Thakins Soe, Nu, Than Tun, and Thein Pe, believed that there should be no cooperation with any Fascists. Yet within this group there was a further split, with Thakin Soe who advocated a temporary anti-Fascist alliance with the British, and Thein Pe who thought that the Burmese should fight the British when the Imperial armies of Japan and Great Britain clashed in Burma. Thein Pe's apparent change of mind to seek British support by mid-1942 is explained by Taylor as being not only 'prompted by his ideological beliefs', but 'his only practical option' once the British had been forced out of Burma.[5]

Thein Pe should not, therefore, have been too surprised when he was coolly received by the British upon his arrival in India.[6] At first suspected of being Japanese spies, Thein Pe and Tin Shwe were interrogated and placed under house arrest before being allowed to travel to China in January 1943. Ostensibly, Thein Pe went to China to assist Chiang Kai-shek and the Nationalist Chinese. While there, assisted by the Indian Communist Party, contact was made with the Chinese Communists. Thein Pe's aim was to form a broad anti-Fascist alliance, in which he gave himself four roles. The pertinent role regarding operation *Billet* is the second: 'to arrange help for the BIA when it changes into an anti-Japanese resistance movement guerrilla army, especially in regards to arms, ammunition, and equipment'.[7]

The Force 136 officer in overall charge of the *Billet* operations was Major Eric Battersby. Battersby passed his Indian Police exam in the summer of 1935 and was posted to Mandalay the same year. From 1937 until 1940, Battersby served in Maymyo and Bhamo before becoming the Governor of Burma's Aide-de-Camp in May 1940. Between November 1942 and July 1943, Battersby was in command of Number Three Forward Interrogation Centre, attached to IV Corps of what became XIV Army. It was here that Battersby first had contact with Thein Pe and Tin Shwe. In July 1943, Battersby went to the UK where he was commissioned Lieutenant on the General List, and he was then posted to SOE in January 1944. After completing political warfare training and being promoted to Major, on 1 April 1944 Major Battersby was posted to Burma to head the Political Warfare department of Burma Country Section (BCS). In this capacity, Major Battersby wrote a detailed post-operational report about *Billet*.[8]

Thein Pe and Tin Shwe returned to India from China in August 1943. Despite still harbouring doubts about the reliability of the two Thakins, in November 1943 India Mission decided that the risk of using the two men was worth it.[9] The risk was now justified by the fact that there was very little news coming out of central Burma, and India Mission was under pressure to start producing results. For Thein Pe and Tin Shwe, this decision to use them to contact the AFO in Burma was a 'gigantic victory' after all they had endured trying to get the British onside.[10]

Arrangements were swiftly made so that on 8 December 1943 Tin Shwe, codenamed *Lancelot*, landed on the Arakanese coast.[11] From there,

Tin Shwe made his way inland to contact the AFO, find out about the likelihood of a BDA revolt against the Japanese, and gather information about conditions in Burma. This was all the more pertinent since the Japanese had granted Burma 'independence' on 1 August 1943. The British wanted to know the impact of this upon the Burmese, and in particular upon the AFO and the newly named Burma National Army (BNA).[12]

On 12 February 1944, Tin Shwe kept to his rendezvous and was successfully exfiltrated, although not without incident. The extraction was compromised by a Japanese boat which the British motor launch sank, resulting in two Japanese dead and the capture of seven Burmese crew. In addition to this excitement, Tin Shwe returned with two extra Burmese. One was his new wife, Ma Mya Yi, also known as Ma Hkin Si, and soon codenamed *Guinevere*. The other Burmese, soon to be codenamed *Galahad*, was the nationalist Nyo Htun.[13]

The three Burmese were debriefed at Meerut. They provided the British with newspapers, books and other papers. They reported that life under the Japanese was intolerable. Independence was a sham, and Burmese people were disrespected, especially the women. On the strength of this information, India Mission was convinced that it was imperative that the organisation should establish an agent in Rangoon with a wireless telegraph (W/T) as soon as possible. The first *Billet* operation was therefore launched on 31 March 1944 with the intention of getting a W/T into Rangoon overland from India.[14] The party consisted of three Burmese, including Nyo Htun and an Indian W/T operator. Nyo Htun was well known in central Burma and the Arakan because of his position as regional head of the Arakan Thakins, so it was hoped that his contacts would ensure the safe passage of the party, and that the AFO would provide a safe house in Rangoon.

This first attempt at getting a W/T into Rangoon ended in failure. The *Billet 1* group ended up having to bury their stores and go on the run. This news was reported by V Force, a British intelligence organisation that operated up to 32 km (20 miles) beyond the British frontline. After three months, only Nyo Htun returned in late June 1944, the others having been captured. In a strange quirk of fate, Nyo Htun had been able to escape because he was assisted by the same men that his exfiltration motor launch had rescued from the water after sinking their boat four months previously. These men had been recruited by the Inter-Services Liaison Department (ISLD, the cover name for the Secret Intelligence Service) and were also on operations at this time.

The following month, July 1944, five Arakanese came through the lines and asked for 'GSI(K)', the cover name for India Mission.[15] SOE had sent out a message that any nationalists who wanted to turn on the Japanese should report to the British, so both V Force and the Army had been told to hand over anyone who came in asking for GSI(K). After a swift interrogation and some 'lightning' agent training, one of the men, Tun Kyaw, was sent back into Arakan. He was tasked with locating possible drop zones, sending out more agents, providing intelligence to a forward military liaison officer, and (perhaps most crucially of all), to get a W/T behind the lines. In other words, in July 1944, Force 136 was still trying to build the foundations of an underground movement by establishing long-range communications with the Burmese interior.

While Force 136 was attempting to build on its limited progress towards establishing agents within Arakan and central Burma, serious tensions arose in the British camp over the selection of Arakanese and Burman recruits that could be trained and armed by SOE. The root of the argument lay in the different perspectives and needs of Force 136 on the one hand, and the Civil Affairs Service (Burma), or CAS(B), on the other. The CAS(B) had been established in February 1943 with the purpose of providing temporary military administration of reoccupied parts of Burma until the restoration of the civil administration was possible. Many of the men in the CAS(B) were colonial officials who had served in pre-war Burma. They were given military rank in order to carry out their duties, and were attached to the forward divisions of the Army in both the Arakan and on the Chindwin front.[16] They were opposed to arming men whom they regarded as dangerous nationalists at best, and traitorous murderers at worst. This was the start of what Major Battersby called the 'prolonged war' between the colonially minded CAS(B) and the military-minded Force 136.[17] This 'prolonged war' became increasingly difficult for Force 136 through late 1944 and into 1945.

This crisis of opinion over policy towards Burman and Arakanese became manifest before the tide turned against the Japanese, having its roots in the India Mission's decision in November 1943 to use Thein Pe. However, after July 1944 when the battle for Kohima and Imphal was over and the Japanese had suffered what became their worst defeat of the War, the conflict between the various interested British parties intensified. Between July and December 1944, in the absence of resources for a seaborne landing aimed at Rangoon, General Slim took the initiative and pursued the Japanese across the Chin Hills into Burma. So began the re-conquest of Burma overland, and with it the needs of the Army commander changed. General Slim thus became embroiled in the war between SOE and CAS(B).

As XIV Army went on the offensive advancing to the Chindwin River during November 1944, General Slim was still ignorant of what forces the Japanese could deploy against him from within Burma. As far as he was concerned, both SIS and Force 136 had failed to provide the intelligence that he needed. He voiced this discontent again in November 1944, and pushed for a complete overhaul of Burma's intelligence apparatus.[18] In some accounts, Slim advocated an amalgamation of all the clandestine services along the American OSS model, and in others that Force 136 be subordinated to OSS. These suggestions were based on Slim's erroneous understanding that OSS provided all the intelligence for the American Northern Combat Area Command (NCAC) in northern Burma. A further proposal was that 'Force 136 cease to operate in Burma'.[19]

All of these 'solutions' to Slim's lack of intelligence meant that Force 136 found itself under threat of extinction as an independent organisation at the same time as coming under pressure from CAS(B) over Operation *Billet*. Yet the very intelligence from inside Burma that Colin Mackenzie's Force 136 was on the verge of achieving through *Billet* operations was exactly what the Army commander wanted. Consequently, Lieutenant Colonel Cumming, now head of Group A, Force 136, went in late December 1944 to tell General Slim what Force 136 had achieved in Burma.[20] Part of this included the explanation that much of the intelligence provided for the American area of operations was in fact from *Dilwyn*, an India Mission operation that had been in the field since 1943. It is also worth mentioning here that Force 136, concurrent with challenges from the Army and CAS(B), was locked in conflict with the Office of Strategic Services.[21]

This chapter is primarily concerned with these political problems associated with the *Billet* operations. It divides into four main sections:

(1)   Battles 'at Home'.
(2)   The Burmese Leadership.

(3) *Billet* Operations in Central and Southern Burma: *Grain* and *Nation*.

(4) Working with the AFO and BNA.

Battles 'at Home': *Manual* Force 136 and CAS(B), September 1944 to February 1945

By September 1944, Force 136 had a number of agents ready to go into the Arakan in support of XV Corps, and arrangements had been made to enable the passage of those agents through the lines. The situation in Arakan regarding the resistance was also fairly clear, at least relative to the situation in Rangoon. Links had been made with the Arakan Defence Force, and they were now ready to revolt against the Japanese in league with the British. Knowing that the British authorities needed a gentle shove, in September 1944, Thein Pe – *Merlin* – wrote a 'thesis' entitled *'Towards Better Mutual Understanding and Greater Cooperation'*. He wrote it, he said, because he wanted the British to trust the Burmans belonging to the Anti-Fascist Organisation (AFO), and arm them to help fight the Japanese. He recognised that the British were wary because as Burmese Nationalists they might turn their guns on the British once Burma was liberated.[22]

Thein Pe gave his thesis to Major Battersby, who was effectively his handler as head of the Political Warfare section for Burma. Major Battersby interpreted the work as Thein Pe had intended, a 'plea' for the British to give their 'whole-hearted cooperation with his party on a basis of trust; that we should meet all their demands for arms and ammunition', and that these resistance forces should then become the new Burma Army.[23] Moreover, Major Battersby recognised that '[a]s a result of this paper, a ruling is required on the policy to be followed for future BILLET operations'.[24] This statement was written in the covering letter which Battersby sent along with the thesis to the head of Force 136, Colin Mackenzie at the end of September 1944.

Mackenzie replied on 2 October 1944.[25] He raised two interesting points. Firstly, he said that the Chief Civil Affairs Officer (CCAO), Major General C.F.B. Pearce, had recently contacted Mackenzie about arming the Burmese, and was happy for the Hill Tribes to be armed as long as the weapons were distributed through village headmen, or preferably through British officers. Secondly, regarding Burmans and the BNA, he wrote 'we think' that General Pearce 'would oppose any general arming'. In order to 'carry the CCAO(B) with us' Mackenzie suggested that Force 136 should only arm the Burmans 'where the task to be performed can be definitely specified'.[26] In that respect, he wanted BCS to provide what they thought the precise aims of the *Billet* operations should be. It seems that Mackenzie believed that Pearce could be brought onside if Force 136 could categorically state their method and objective. Mackenzie was less sanguine about the Deputy Chief Civil Affairs Office, Brigadier Prescott. Mackenzie warned Battersby to improve the security of his Political Warfare section, as he thought Prescott was the source of a leak about plans to contact Aung San, head of the BNA; he wrote that Prescott 'must be considered hostile'.[27]

It is important to realise that for some parties on both sides, Burmese and British, an unpalatable decision had to be made. Memories of the 1942 retreat were still raw, especially the idea that a Burmese Fifth Column had hastened defeat. For many former policemen and politicians of colonial Burma, Force 136 wanted to arm traitors, Burmese who had committed a crime against the British crown. Aung San was at the top of a CAS(B) black list. For the Burmese, a decision had to be made about an alliance with the colonial master whom many had actively fought against in one form or another for half a decade or more. Memories of British colonial oppression were equally as raw, so being anti-Japanese did not automatically translate into pro-British. Yet there were some who were able to reconcile these feelings sooner in order to get on with the job of defeating the Japanese. One such man was the Governor of Burma.

Sir Reginald Dorman-Smith had also been sent a copy of Thein Pe's thesis in October 1944. In Dorman-Smith's opinion, the British should start a new relationship with the Nationalist Burmans, based on trust. He said he was 'all for trying something new'.[28] His reaction was perhaps surprising, considering the coolness of his former private secretary and the complete objection of his former head of Rangoon Police (General Pearce and Brigadier Prescott respectively). What is interesting here is how the War distorted the colonial hierarchy. In peace-time, Pearce, Prescott and Battersby would all have ultimately come under Dorman-Smith as Governor. Now, as Major General and Brigadier in charge of military administration, Pearce and Prescott exercised autonomy from the Governor.[29] Similarly, Major Battersby, as an officer in Force 136, began to behave against his erstwhile colonial superiors in a way he would probably have never entertained before the War.

In his report, Major Battersby was scathing of General Pearce for the latter's intractable attitude towards Aung San. Alerted to the possibility of Force 136 contacting Aung San, General Pearce had let his opposition be known, asserting that Aung San would never fight the Japanese because he was too anti British. In Battersby's opinion, Pearce's policy of arresting Aung San would only bring trouble, and so the policy of Force 136 should be to get the Army and the Governor onside against a less enlightened CAS(B).[30]

Major Battersby was equally critical of Brigadier Prescott. Prescott did not object to the arming of the Karen in Operation *Character*, or the Kachin in Operation *Dilwyn*. This was presumably because these people had remained steadfast Allies throughout the War. In Battersby's view, by allowing the Karen and Kachin to be armed and not the Burmese Nationalists, Prescott 'turned a blind eye to the dangers arising from this policy of racial discrimination' and he 'failed to see the bigger issues at stake'.[31] Reporting these opinions to Mackenzie, as asked, Battersby was able to undermine men who were both his peacetime colonial and, by rank at least, his wartime superior officers.[32]

On 15 November 1944, Mackenzie replied to Thein Pe's request for trust to be placed in him and his Burman anti-Fascists. The main points in his letter were that Force 136 recognised Thein Pe's organisation as the 'Anti-Axis Association of Burma' and that Force 136 would help militarily, leaving politics to the Governor. Left at that, this reply might have been enough to avoid any future trouble, but after the letter was leaked, the following became a massive point of contention for which Force 136 was accused of promising postwar recognition to anti-Fascist forces: 'it is up to the forces of the interior to show their worth, and if they fulfil the trust which we propose placing in them, then the civil government will be unable to ignore their demands.'[33]

By 15 November then, the decision to press on with *Billet* had been made, despite opposition from those in charge of CAS(B). Colin Mackenzie followed up by sending a copy of the reply to Thein Pe to SOE's Far Eastern section in London on 18 November 1944 with a letter explaining what BCS was proposing to do. It was quite open about sidelining CAS(B) and getting the Army and Governor to support *Billet* operations:

Now that the active stage has been reached MAUNG THEIN PE has inevitably raised various questions with regard to the future. His principal plea has been that the British should show confidence in them and not make the same mistake as the Japanese who promised them all sorts of things which they promptly disavowed once BURMA was conquered. We know that we cannot broach this subject to the Civil Affairs Service (BURMA), as this is mainly composed – particularly in the senior positions – of Burma civil servants who do not, and perhaps cannot, be expected to, appreciate the idea of arming people who have anti-British records, even if the quantity of arms is relatively small.

It is therefore our intention to obtain – as we believe we shall – the support of the army for our proposed actions, and from the other side we have taken up the matter on the level of principal with the Governor of Burma who has already expressed views which are definitely more enlightened than the CAS(B) and which make us fairly confident that we shall have his support. Having obtained such support from these two quarters we believe we can get the CAS(B) overruled if they attempt to interfere.[34]

By the end of November, the situation was that Force 136 knew that in the Arakan the Japanese sponsored Arakan Defence Force was ready to come over to the Allied side. Force 136 had Arakanese personnel in the field, and was ready to introduce two W/T stations, *Hound* and *Lion*, by parachute during November and December. Once these agents were established, British officers were to be introduced to direct operations in support of an offensive by XV Corps.

The situation in central Burma regarding the BNA also looked positive. Interrogation of captured BNA soldiers revealed their officers had been telling the men that the time to revolt was approaching. Other intelligence indicated that Aung San had made a 'remarkable speech' about the 'illusory' independence granted by the Japanese on the first anniversary of that 'independence' on 1 August 1944.[35] Furthermore, it was rumoured that Aung San had joined Thakin Soe and Thakin Than Tun's group, the group that believed in an alliance with the British. Force 136 was desperate to verify this intelligence by getting an agent into Rangoon to contact the AFO. Aung Myint, an Arakanese, volunteered. He went overland, without communications, but carrying a hidden microfilm message for Thakin Than Tun.

By mid-October, with no news from Aung Myint, it was decided that a Burmese called Ba Thein would be parachuted into the Rangoon area with a message similar to Aung Myint's. On the same night as Ba Thein was dropped, two Chinese with W/T were dropped near Pegu. Ba Thein was to use their W/T equipment to update Force 136 in India about the AFO. However, the two Chinese agents, codenamed Operation *Wakering*, were both killed when their parachutes failed to open. Undeterred, Force 136 decided to drop a single Burmese agent, Nagani Tun Shwe, with W/T, codenamed *Donkey*, during the November moon. This meant that at the end of November, there were possibly three agents, Aung Myint, Ba Thein and Nagani Tun Shwe in Rangoon, but still no confirmed contact with the AFO. Station *Donkey* eventually made contact on 1 December 1944. Force 136 at last had communications with Rangoon.

The Force 136 plan thus far had been to introduce Burmese agents first. Once these agents were established with W/T, European personnel would be sent in to provide leadership and expertise. In September 1944, it had been decided that Jedburgh teams from Europe – freed from service in France – would be used to increase *Billet* effectiveness.[36] It was thought that the Jedburgh teams would be able to overcome negative Burmese traits that some British officials thought characteristic, such as 'vanity' and a 'lack of discipline' because of their experience in France working with Gaullists, Communists and followers of Giraud. Furthermore, unlike Burmese-speaking British officers, it was hoped that they would 'come out from England with no … capitalist or Imperialist intentions towards Burma'. The first Jedburgh team to go on operations in the Far East was *Billet/Camel*, which was dropped to a reception hosted by *Hound* in the Arakan. The team, dropped on 27 December 1944 south of Kyauktaw, consisted of Major Carew, Captain John Cox and Sergeant John Sharp (W/T operator) with Nyo Htun (*Galahad*) and four Arakanese.

On 30 December, three days after *Camel* was deployed, Lieutenant Colonel Cumming made his way to Army HQ for an audience with General Slim, in his capacity as head of Group A, Force 136. Cumming told Slim about the three W/T sets on air behind the lines in the Arakan (*Hound*, *Lion*, and *Camel*), now reinforced with a Jedburgh team. He also told Slim that they had *Donkey* in Rangoon, who had made contact with the AFO through Thakin Than Tun in mid-December. Cumming set out Force 136's future plans, including the projected operations to the Mandalay area (*Billet/Grain*) and the Karen Hills (Operation *Character*). The consequence, according to the head of BCS, Lieutenant Colonel Richie Gardiner, was that this interview with Slim 'cleared the air'.[37] Sidelining the CAS(B) and going ahead with *Billet* had enabled Force 136 to report tangible progress to Slim.[38] There were two important consequences of this meeting. It was agreed that Force 136 operations would now come under the operational control of the Army, and that the primary task of operations was to provide General Slim with intelligence.

Five days later on 4 January 1945, an important meeting was held at advanced Allied Land Forces, South East Asia (ALFSEA) HQ at Barrackpore where General Browning and his staff met Captain Garnons-Williams, the head of Priorities Division (P-Division). P-Division had been established in late 1943 by Mountbatten to coordinate the various secret services in SEAC. General Slim was not present, and it is not known whether those that were knew of the meeting between Cumming and Slim.[39] At Barrackpore there were three objectives, one of which was to examine General Slim's earlier proposals regarding closing down or amalgamating Force 136.

Garnons-Williams said that Slim's proposals regarding OSS were 'impractical', and that amalgamation 'betrayed an ignorance of the functions of the clandestine services'.[40] Garnons-Williams's views were accepted at ALFSEA, which, combined with Cumming and Slim's December agreement, meant Force 136 was secure for now. Despite this progress with ALFSEA and the *modus vivendi* between Force 136 and General Slim, CAS(B) had not given up the fight on limiting the role of 'radical' Burmese Nationalists and 'collaborators', so conflict at home for Force 136 continued into 1945.

With Slim and ALFSEA onside, in January 1945 future operations in Arakan and central Burma depended upon *Camel*. Major Carew's experience with the AFO would set the precedent. Despite Slim having been persuaded that Force 136 had the potential to support the advance of his army, this still needed to be converted into results. At first it looked like *Camel* would not deliver for Force 136. After travelling 64 km (40 miles) into the Arakan and recruiting no guerrillas, Major Carew was ready to close down his operation in early January. What turned the mission into a success was an airstrike that was called in on a concentration of about 800 Japanese troops at Minzegyaung. At approximately 16.30 on 2 January, 30 RAF Thunderbolts killed approximately 100 Japanese. After this the volunteers came 'pouring' in.[41]

Amongst the men that Major Carew recruited were Kra Hla Aung and a monk called Pyinnyathiha (also known as Hiawatha).[42] Kra Hla Aung was head of the Arakan Defence Force (ADF) in the Kaladan area, and was described by Carew as a 'robber chieftain and a real ruffian'. As Burmese Nationalists, according to Carew, these men regarded themselves as 'the Irish of the East', so when it was revealed that Carew was Irish, their friendship was sealed. Both Kra Hla Aung and Pyinnyathiha turned out to be great assets to the *Camel* team, providing leadership, useful contacts and intelligence. Unfortunately, these men were also at the top of the CAS(B)'s black list. Kra Hla Aung was wanted for his leadership of the previously collaborationist ADF, and for allegedly bayoneting three British soldiers to death after they had surrendered to him in 1942. Pyinnyathiha was wanted for his part in leading the communal violence between Buddhists and Muslims in the Arakan in 1942.[43]

By mid-January, CAS(B) officers attached to the forward units of the Army had started arresting men that Carew had recruited. The situation became so serious that Carew had to come through the lines to try and resolve it. Upon arrival at Army HQ, Carew said 'Astonishment was expressed to see me', because it was thought that Kra Hla Aung and Pyinnyathiha were holding him 'under duress'.[44] In a series of meetings at Cox's Bazaar (on the Indian side of the border with Burma), Major Carew spoke to General Pearce, XV Corps commander, General Christison and Christison's intelligence officer, Major Paterson. Major Paterson declared himself satisfied with the intelligence received from *Camel*. General Christison was informed that the prospects for 'running a secret army' in Burma were 'better than in France', but that arresting Carew's men would probably prevent this from happening.[45] In Carew's account of this meeting, he told the general that he would refuse to go back on operations if the arrested men were kept in custody. Christison then showed Carew a map which detailed all his intelligence assets, to which Carew said 'they are all mine', and that if he did not go back the whole lot would collapse.[46] Christison therefore agreed that the men should be released, and to persuade General Pearce of the necessity to do so. The result was an amnesty for the Arakanese recruited by *Camel* signed by Pearce on 15 January 1945:

> With reference to the Arakanese now working under you, you are authorised to inform them that provided they continue to serve to your satisfaction until discharged and then surrender their arms, they will not be brought before a Court of the Military Administration on a charge of crimes against the state or of assisting the King's enemies.[47]

With General Pearce signing this amnesty, and General Slim endorsing the decision to cooperate with Burmese Nationalists, by January 1945 Force 136 might have expected their war with the CAS(B) to be over. This was not to be the case. With the formation of ALFSEA in November 1944, the command structure had changed so that XIV Army and XV Corps were separated and both reported to ALFSEA. ALFSEA in turn came under Mountbatten as Supreme Allied Commander, South East Asia (SACSEA). Brigadier Prescott, deputy chief of CAS(B), changed the angle of his attack from Generals Slim and Christison, to General Leese at ALFSEA on 13 February 1945. He wrote to Leese informing him that arming the Burmese in the Irrawaddy Delta region of southern Burma would cause 'a wave of serious crime' which would require a 'minor military operation' to suppress. Furthermore, he predicted communal trouble between Burman and Karen in this region that would require a prolonged troop deployment.[48] Of the AFO request to trade help for arms and training, he wrote that arming the AFO would create an 'awkward legacy' using the Greek civil war to substantiate his opinion.[49] In Prescott's opinion the AFO was 'pro-Burman only'. He described the Burmans as gamblers who had backed the wrong horse (the Japanese) and now wanted their money back.[50] His tactics and reasoning prevailed: on 15 February General Leese ruled 'that NO members of the Anti-Fascist Organisation in Burma will be armed by any military forces'.[51]

For Force 136 the timing of this ruling was critical. There were Burmese Nationalist reception parties standing by to receive *Billet* teams at Allanmyo, Pyinmana, Tharawaddy, Pyapon, Thaton and Tavoy. There were already Burmese teams on the ground at Kyaukse, Toungoo, and Pegu.[52] Having already anticipated that CAS(B) might continue to oppose their plans, at the end of January, Gardiner and Battersby had agreed that they would approach Mountbatten for a final decision.[53] On 18 February 1945, Colin Mackenzie wrote to Mountbatten, who reversed the ALFSEA decision on 24 February. On 27 February, Mackenzie had to write to Mountbatten again because no reversal of the order had been effected. Mountbatten sent a telegram to General Leese the same day:

> Due to an oversight by my staff you were not repeat not informed that I reserve political decisions to myself and in reaching them take into consideration views which the Governor of Burma and his Chief Secretary Sir John Wise have expressed to me from time to time. The advice which you have received does not fit into the broad policy for Burma which I have decided upon.
>
> In view of the above considerations I have ruled that political considerations such as those which have been presented to you are not repeat not to limit the activities of Force 136. I should be obliged therefore if you would issue immediate instructions to Force 136 to proceed with their planned operations so that present moon period is not lost.[54]

Mackenzie explained Mountbatten's reversal in a letter to his deputy on 28 February. As SAC, Burma was Mountbatten's responsibility until civil government was restored, and until then Mountbatten believed that the CAS(B)'s job was to carry out the military administration, not make decisions on that administration. In addition, Mountbatten did not want to be accused of having refused help from forces opposed to the Japanese. The letter ended: 'Pearce and Prescott have apparently been under fire for some time and if one can produce suitable successors believe they would receive short shrift. Have you any suggestions?'[55]

The Burmese Leadership

By the end of February, the Army had broken out of their bridgeheads over the Irrawaddy. To the south, IV Corps began their attack on Meiktila. Meiktila was the main Japanese supply centre for their divisions in the north. Meiktila was thinly defended because the

Japanese had fallen for Slim's ruse that XIV Army's main attack would come from the north, where XXXIII Corps was pushing for Mandalay. By 3 March 1945 Meiktila was in Allied hands, forcing the Japanese to respond to this threat to their lines of communication. With Meiktila and Mandalay captured by 14 March, XIV Army had 645 km (400 miles) to advance in ten weeks if it was to reach Rangoon before the rains.

Slim had nothing to lose by accepting any assistance Force 136 could offer towards achieving Rangoon in this limited timeframe. After Mountbatten overturned Leese, the *Character* Special Groups meant to protect the Army's left flank were hurriedly deployed towards the end of February. If the *Character* teams were unable to establish themselves and raise a guerrilla army from the Karen in time, then *Billet's Nation* and *Grain* teams were to cause as much damage as possible with the assistance of the AFO and BNA. By the end of February, *Nation* and *Grain* had deployed five groups along the line of the Army's advance from Mandalay to Rangoon, with a further two in the Tenasserim area (*Rabbit* and *Hare*). Contact had been made with local BNA and AFO headquarters in most of the towns near which the five teams had been dropped, and the BNA was on the verge of rebelling.

As seen above, SOE had believed that Aung San had given a speech in August 1944 which indicated a new attitude towards the Japanese.[56] This intelligence had been part of the impetus behind getting an agent into Rangoon as quickly as possible in September 1944. However, in his memoirs, Dr Ba Maw, the *Adipati* (Head of State) and Premier of 'independent' Burma wrote that Aung San spoke 'clearly' in August 1944 about continuing to work with the Japanese, quoting Aung San's speech.[57] In Ba Maw's opinion, '[t]he general feeling on that anniversary of independence and during the months that followed was definitely for resisting the return of the British to Burma', but that '[t]he British, however, were doing their best to displace the anti-colonial resistance against them with a new antifascist resistance directed against the Japanese, and they were succeeding'.

By contrast, Thakin Nu has claimed that Aung San's allegiances had clearly shifted at an earlier stage. Shortly after Tin Shwe (*Lancelot*) returned to India in early February 1944, a conference was held at Thakin Nu's house, attended by Thakin Than Tun and Aung San. According to Thakin Nu, at this meeting 'the Burma Defence Army was systematically linked up with the revolutionaries outside the army' (in other words, the AFO).[58] Thus, it is a rather muddled picture of what Aung San was up to, even from the Burmese side. Whether this was real oscillation or deliberate obfuscation by Aung San (with various people making one or other side of his equivocation Aung San's 'real' position for their own purposes) can only be guessed at. He was either genuinely unsure, or playing a carefully calibrated game, or a mix of both. Whatever the truth, his stance made the British all the more suspicious.

There was a real fear on the British side that as soon as the Japanese had been defeated in Burma, Aung San and the BNA would turn on the British. According to Ba Maw, in September 1944:

> We explained our plan to Aung San. As much as possible the Burmese and Indian forces would stay out of the actual fighting that would start with the final British offensive and would leave it mainly to the Japanese to do it, they alone being effectively trained and armed for such highly mechanised combat. Meanwhile, we could keep our two forces poised in certain strategic areas. Upon the Japanese withdrawal from Burma, which was now a certainty, we would be ready to start an anti-British resistance with the arms the Japanese would leave behind. Thus, before the British would be able to stabilise their hold on Burma again, we could keep up a joint guerrilla attack from a line stretching into Bengal, Bose's stronghold, till the postwar situation would come to our rescue in India and Burma.[59]

Aung San's response as recorded by Ba Maw was favourable, but he did not commit himself. The BNA was 'deeply split' over how best to win independence, and Aung San needed to consult his officers. In his work, *Burmese Nationalist Movements*, U Maung Maung confirmed this complicated situation. The 'deep split' went further than simply communist followers of Thakin Soe and those following Aung San. Within the BNA there was a group called 'The Young Officers', consisting of 'second-level Underground leaders' and 'student leaders'.[60] They did not care for Thakin Soe's left-wing dogmatism, and believed even Aung San was stalling in organising a revolt against the Japanese. These officers believed that since the British had made no statement about Burmese independence, the British would have to be fought too.[61]

This postwar autobiographical evidence of planning to attack the British corroborates what Force 136 claimed in 1945. During April, Force 136 infiltrated an agent into the AFO headquarters in Pegu. The documents obtained showed that Thakin Than Tun had written a directive in August 1944 for an armed struggle against the British to be started in September 1945. Another document, entitled 'From Fascism to Freedom' dated April 1945, championed a peaceful strategy against the British.[62] Something had altered AFO plans in the intervening period. Major Battersby had argued that gaining the trust of the AFO and BNA would prevent future disorder in Burma. Cooperation, rather than the mass arrests and trials advocated by the CAS(B), was Battersby's solution. On 29 May, Thakin Than Tun wrote to Mountbatten showing – on the face of it at least – exceptional willingness to cooperate with the British.[63] Some semblance of trust was therefore probably achieved through the increased intensity of *Billet* operations during March and April 1945. It is to those operations which the next section of this chapter now turns.

Billet Operations in Central and Southern Burma: *Grain* and *Nation*

The *Nation* part of *Billet* operations that were focused on the Rangoon and Irrawaddy Delta regions deployed the most teams to the field. It was intended that both *Nation* and *Grain* would be able to build on the experience of *Manual* operations in the Arakan.[64] The Arakan operations had indeed set the precedent, trialling the model of first sending in a single person or a small team of Burmese with an AFO leader to establish local contacts, which then provided a reception for a Jedburgh team. In total, in December 1944–April 1945, 16 *Nation* teams were deployed. By comparison, it seems that *Grain* operations consisted of just one mixed Burman and Chinese group of four being parachuted into upper Burma.

Grain's team *Elephant* was parachuted into Burma just to the south of Mandalay on 2 January 1945. The four-man team included Tin Shwe (*Lancelot*), originally chosen to go back to Mandalay with his wife, Ma Mya Yi (*Guinevere*), because of their contacts with the resistance. However, Tin Shwe decided to travel 400 km (250 miles) south to Toungoo in order to get instructions from Thakin Soe, which illustrates

Table 6.1 Billet Operation details, *Nation, Manual* and *Grain* [65]

Billet	**Nation** (Lower Burma)	*Donkey* Dec 1944 Burmese	*Elk (later Yak), Terrier* Jan 1945 Burmese	*Rabbit, Vole & Hare* Feb 1945 Burmese	*Weasel, Pig, Jackal, Zebra & Reindeer* Mar 1945 Jedburghs	*Chimp, Dog & Giraffe* April 1945 Jedburghs	*Panda & Cow* May 1945 Jedburghs
	Grain (Upper Burma)	*Elephant* Jan 1945 Burmese					
	Manual (Arakan)	*Hound & Lion* Nov 1944 Burmese	*Camel* Dec 1944 Jedburghs	*Leopard* Jan 1945 Jedburghs	*Mouse, Rhino & Fox* Feb 1945 Jedburghs		

how far the nationalists were acting autonomously of Force 136.[66] The outcome was that Force 136 did not want to risk sending in the Jedburgh team that was supposed to join *Elephant*, despite a signal on 5 March which said that Tin Shwe was in Mandalay, and in control of a battalion of the BNA that had already started to revolt. Nine days later, Mandalay was retaken by XIV Army. According to Gardiner, although the results of this BNA uprising were 'negligible', the Army realised the possibilities of a coordinated BNA uprising. General Slim started to urge Force 136 to get Aung San out to Allied lines so that BNA units could advance with Allied troops.[67]

The first Jedburgh team to be deployed on Operation *Nation*, on 20 March 1945, was *Weasel*. *Weasel* was a three-man Jed team, commanded by Major Carew, accompanied by two non-Europeans.[68] His Burmese reception party was *Terrier* at a DZ 65 km (40 miles) south of Toungoo. Carew's first message from inside Burma advised that, as in Mandalay over a fortnight before, the BNA and AFO were about to rise against the Japanese, with or without the British. The Young Officers of the BNA had been restive for over a year, having decided in December 1943 for a revolt in February 1944. That rising never happened because Aung San and Colonel Ne Win had not been persuaded. Disillusioned, the young officers had turned to Thakin Soe and his Communists to discuss a joint uprising in mid-1944. Ultimately, Thakin Soe had let this group down too, fearful of rising prematurely.[69] Now, in March 1945, the Young Officers could not be contained any longer, so they forced their leaders' hands. On 27 March the BNA officially mutinied against the Japanese.[70]

In a hurry to now harness the BNA and the AFO, five Jedburgh teams were set to deploy on the one night of 30 March 1945. Only four – *Pig*, *Jackal*, *Reindeer* and *Zebra* – made it into the field to join *Weasel* because the aircraft carrying *Hart* crashed on take-off, killing all those on board.[71] By late March then, there were five Jedburgh teams in central Burma.

With 15 experienced European officers and non-commissioned officers (NCOs) on the ground ready to coordinate Burmese Nationalist forces, on the face of it prospects looked positive. *Weasel* had been dropped ahead to make contact with Thakin Than Tun, but Than Tun proved to be difficult. Major Carew had concluded on 24 March that Than Tun did not trust the British, and planned on turning on them once the Japanese were defeated.[72] It was into this environment that the four Jedburgh teams landed on 30 March, and perhaps began the process of persuading Than Tun that he should not fight the British after the Japanese.

Of the four teams dropped on 30 March, *Pig* and *Reindeer* were received by *Weasel*. *Pig* did not have a great start: the team's Burman, Maung Tin, broke his leg and all their kit was lost. With Than Tun continuing to be difficult because he did not want British officers in charge of his men, *Pig* was forced to stay with *Weasel* until 12 April. The team's run of ill fortune continued when they left *Weasel*. An Indian National Army (INA) unit captured the party after their bullock cart driver betrayed them. Majors Cox and Reid and Sergeant Tack were able to escape after standing 'shoulder to shoulder' and firing upon the INA, killing four.[73]

Meanwhile, Major Dave Britton's *Reindeer* had fared better. Leaving the political wrangling behind, *Reindeer* left for their area of operations near Kywebwe which is roughly half way between Pyu and Toungoo, where they found the local Burmans most cooperative. According to Sergeant Brierley's post-operation report, training began immediately. Men were organised into squads of nine, each of which was armed with five Sten guns, two rifles and eight grenades. Three squads made a section, and each section of 27 was issued a Bren gun and a mortar. Projectile Infantry Anti-Tank, or Piats, were issued for ambushes on the roads. Training lasted five days and was completed in batches of 100. By 12 April, 300 men were organised, including a good intelligence network.[74] In an interview in 1988, Sergeant Brierley said that this intelligence network was 'quite incredible'; they even knew when a Japanese soldier went to the toilet. He attributes this to the cooperation of the Burmans who 'had had enough of the Japs'.[75] On 19 April, the Army told *Reindeer* to go all out in the Toungoo area.

Attacks on the Japanese line of communication from Rangoon to Toungoo had actually commenced ten days earlier than the Army's order. According to Brierley's report, between 9–23 April, *Reindeer* killed 216 Japanese soldiers, destroyed 20 trucks, a car, a motorbike, one motor train and two boats. Brierley claimed that no Japanese trains were able to get north of Kywebwe to reinforce and supply Toungoo. Full details of Japanese positions around Toungoo were reported and airstrikes were called in that caused 'colossal damage to MT [Motor Transport], and other stores, and destroying several Jap HQs'.[76] XIV Army arrived in Toungoo on 24 April, by which time *Reindeer* had been in action for 15 days. Brierley thought that of his three Jedburgh operations, the one in Burma was the most successful in terms of the 'damage and mayhem' his team created.[77]

Operations continued through May after Rangoon had been reoccupied on 3 May, with Brierley writing that they 'had a good party on the river [Sittang] on 27 May killing 53'. A week later, on 3 June 1945, *Reindeer*'s commanding officer, Major Dave Britton, was killed. He was shot through the neck while on patrol in long grass near the River Sittang.[78] That same day, Major Rubinstein arrived to help *Reindeer* operations, his own *Chimp* area having been absorbed by the advancing army. Major Rubinstein therefore took command of *Reindeer* in time for when the Japanese 54 and 55 Division began their break out from the Pegu Yomas.

This was the start of a very busy period for many of the *Nation* teams, but like their colleagues on Operation *Character*, some officers and non-commissioned officers (NCOs) on *Nation* felt that the Army considered the war in Burma won after Rangoon was recaptured. Conversely, Kirby's official history says that, post Rangoon, the Army 'continued to press the campaign forward in Burma', with the objective of capturing Moulmein on the Salween. It boasts that XII Army killed 20,000 Japanese in three months (June–August 1945) with a kill ratio of 64:1.[79]

Captain Craster (*Zebra*) recalled that, by June 1945, the Army had two words circulating, 'demob' and 'repat', so there was no interest in 'chasing' the Japanese.[80] Major Rubinstein agreed that the Army did not want to 'chase' the Japanese and, further, that Force 136 was told to get on with it.[81] Similarly, Teams *Giraffe* and *Cow* had been dropped into the Bilin–Thaton area of southern Burma on 27 and 30 April. Sergeant Fred Bailey, the W/T operator with *Cow*, considered the first few weeks of the operation very successful, hitting Japanese motor transport with Piats and calling in airstrikes.[82] But when the Japanese realised that the Army was not going to advance beyond the Sittang, Japanese forces focused on rounding up the Force 136 teams. *Cow* and *Giraffe* were chased north where they joined Lieutenant Colonel Critchley, commander of *Character/Mongoose*.[83]

Cooperation and support from the Army seems to have been variable. Where *Character* complained about a lack of support from 19 Division, Captain Waller from *Reindeer* thought it was 'good'. Waller described 'artillery shoots' where a whole regiment of guns would fire when a signal pistol was fired by Force 136, and how the Army used armoured cars to chase the Japanese across the open area between the hills and the Sittang River; this 'was the first time that Army had really fought side by side with our men and both sides liked it'.[84] This was not the case for *Chimp*, though, where there were incidents of 'friendly fire' after Indian troops arrived in the area. When the soldiers left on 31 July 'CHIMP and the guerrillas breathed a sigh of relief'.[85]

At the same time as *Chimp* personnel were sighing with relief, their former commanding officer, Major Rubinstein, was attacking the Japanese as they left the Pegu Yomas to escape to southern Burma. Rubinstein described the fighting as 'carnage time'; he recalled that the River Sittang had bodies floating down it for three days.[86] Some *Nation* personnel described the Japanese at this time as 'in a bad way' or in 'pathetic condition'.[87] Japanese troops were lightly armed, which meant that Force 136 guerrillas were able to take them on despite the observation by Captain Houseman (*Hyena Purple*) that it took 'three villagers and two mags of Sten ammunition to kill one Jap'.[88] Yet the Japanese 'still had a fanatical zeal to die for the emperor', so Force 136 remained committed to guerrilla tactics.[89]

The overall results of *Billet's* contacts with the enemy were compiled by Major Battersby into what was called the Game Book.[90] A full Game Book was produced by HQ A Group Force 136 in September 1945, with a disparity of 565 between the totals. The higher total gives a kill ratio of 118/1; the lower 102/1. These figures exclude the 7,500 Japanese that Major Battersby estimated were killed by the BNA.[91] The commander 98 Indian Infantry Brigade, Brigadier Charles Jerrard, wrote to commander 19 Division, General Rees, 'to place on record [his] appreciation of the achievements of Force 136'. In particular, this applied to *Reindeer*, with specific mention of Majors Britton and Rubinstein. Without the intelligence supplied by *Reindeer*, 'such successes as we have had would scarcely have been possible'.[92]

Table 6.2   Extract from the Game Book for Operation *Billet*[93]

Operation	Killed (Japanese)	Killed (Own)
MANUAL		
Camel & Mouse	133	1
GRAIN		
Elephant	19	2
NATION		
Terrier	43	
Reindeer	1,941	23
Chimp	809	
Weasel & Pig	150	
Zebra & Jackal	816	5
Panda	250	
Dog	9	
Hart	–	5
Giraffe & Cow	58	
Rabbit	20	
TOTAL	4,248	36

Working with the AFO and BNA

Once the largely communist leadership of the AFO were convinced of the need to work with the British, they seem to have disseminated this message efficiently to their district leaders across Burma. Force 136 reports were pretty much unanimous in their praise of AFO cooperation. The BNA – the military force that had emerged from the BDA and openly turned against its Japanese sponsors in March – was a different matter. Major Boiteux of *Panda* claimed that the BNA consisted 'mainly of bad hats and dacoits, they were deceitful, liars, thieves, undisciplined, and thoroughly unreliable'.[94] This seems to have been the prevailing opinion throughout the Force 136 reports. This difference between the AFO and BNA is perhaps difficult to understand if it is accepted that, according to Thein Pe, most officers in the BNA were also members of the AFO, including Aung San.

This is not to say that the Force 136 men necessarily felt safe with all AFO groups compared to the BNA units. Even Major Carew, who said he 'was made' when he told the Burmese that he was Irish, took measures to protect himself because he did not doubt that they would hesitate to kill him or his team if they thought it necessary.[95] By contrast, when team *Dog*, a Jed team dropped on 24 April in the Pyapon area of the Irrawaddy Delta area, were told that the BNA were going to murder them, the AFO guarded them against that possibility.[96] It was clear to *Dog* that the BNA were in control of the delta area, and that their intention was to attack the British once the Japanese were dealt with.

As seen above, Force 136 Intelligence confirmed that the AFO had planned to turn on the British once the Japanese were defeated, and that the order had been rescinded in April 1945. Major Battersby thought that it took some time for this news to filter through to all AFO and BNA units, and with varying levels of acceptance.[97] Aung San himself only went to meet General Slim on 16 May.

General Slim 'admired his [Aung San's] boldness' at that first meeting on 16 May 1945. Aung San claimed to represent a Provisional Government of Burma as established by the AFO.[98] Slim told Aung San that there was no way that the British could accept this, His Majesty's Government (HMG) being the legitimate authority through Mountbatten as Supreme Allied Commander (SAC), and later through Dorman-Smith. It was this assumption by Aung San that, by taking part in the liberation of Burma, the AFO would have a claim to political authority that had been feared by CAS(B). The contest for control of postwar Burma thus began in mid-May 1945, with at least 50,000 Japanese troops still in the country.

The British determined that they should make their strength visible, and one way of doing that was through the spectacle of a victory parade.[99] The parade was held in Rangoon on 15 June 1945. This 'opportunity' for the Burmese to appreciate British power was necessary because the British feared the possibility of 10,000 BNA creating havoc with plans to use Rangoon as a base for the invasion of Malaya.[100] Force 136 'very rightly suggested' that a lot depended upon getting the *Thakins* involved in government as soon as possible.[101] This was not possible while the country was under military administration, awaiting the return of civil government from Simla. There was, meanwhile, little chance of civil government being restored in June or July because of the 50,000 Japanese troops in central Burma who were preparing to breakout of their hide-outs in the Pegu Yomas.

While the Force 136 *Nation* and *Character* teams fought the battles of June to September 1945, discussions concerning Burma's political future were held in Rangoon. At Aung San's suggestion, the BNA was allowed by Mountbatten to change its name to Patriotic Burmese Forces (PBF) at the end of June. The question of whether and how the PBF might be absorbed into a new Burma Army became one of the issues to be discussed.[102] This was important for Burmans as before the War, colonial Burmese formations had been mostly created from the minority races, and having a major stake in the Army would naturally strengthen the Burman political position.

The tension created by courting the AFO and the newly named PBF was such that Brigadier Prescott, the deputy head of the CAS(B), blamed Force 136 for doing more harm to Burma than he could remember in his 30 years of service in the country. As far as Prescott and his colleagues in CAS(B) could tell, their predictions about boosting nationalist claims to political power had come true. Prescott's opinion was only slightly qualified by his admission that '[t]he old type of civil servant has much to answer for. As things stand at the moment, the sooner we clear out the better'.[103]

The man in charge of *Billet* operations, Major Battersby saw the situation differently. Writing in late 1945, he argued that: 'The Force 136 victory has been complete in a long war of attrition'. He believed that Force 136 had saved CAS(B) from the situation in which the French and Dutch found themselves in their former Southeast Asian empires. Neither the French in Indochina nor the Dutch in the East Indies were able to defeat nationalist revolts after the War. 'It is to be hoped [wrote Battersby] that they appreciate this fact.' Gardiner, as head of BCS, agreed that the:

> biggest success was not the intelligence supplied or enemy killed, but the re-establishment of relations with a potentially dangerous group in Burma whom the CAS would certainly have estranged – if not worse.[104]

These differences between CAS(B) on the one hand, and Mountbatten, Slim and Force 136 on the other, were never resolved.

Conclusions

The wrangling over who was right about how to deal with Aung San, PBF and AFO continued to resonate through the decades after 1945.

In 1959, Professor Hugh Tinker, who had served in XIV Army, published *The Union of Burma*, and in 1983 *Burma, The Struggle for Independence*. These works provoked much ill-feeling amongst Burma's SOE veterans because of the accusation that they had caused the civil war by arming the AFO and BNA on the one hand, and the Karen and Kachin on the other. In 1972, Mountbatten wrote a letter to Mackenzie stating that as far as this policy towards arming the Burmese was concerned, 'I think history shows conclusively that we were right and they were wrong'.[105]

So who was right? Politically, the evidence presented here from both Force 136 intelligence and postwar Burmese sources is that a revolt against the British was planned. It seems likely that this was averted during late March and April, when Force 136 allocated substantial personnel and weapons to *Billet* operations dropped in the area of Thakin Than Tun's headquarters. Battersby believed this to be the reason why the BNA and AFO never turned against the British, despite the knowledge that they had planned to do so in September 1945.

Above all, and this is stressed throughout the documents, the Burmans wanted freedom from any foreign control. In 1945, the third Anglo-Burmese war of 1885–6 was still a living memory, and since that date there had been many challenges to British rule. Force 136 may have averted another war between Burmese and British, but to what extent did SOE's pursuit of military objectives encourage civil war? As Major Rubinstein said in 1989, 'I don't think Force 136 mucked it up. Burma is a very multi-racial country.'[106] Force 136 should be seen as a contingent part of over 60 years of Burmese Nationalist history, and the civil war that started after 1945 owes much to a long history of ethnic violence, compounded by British colonial policy between 1885 and 1948.[107]

Regarding the charge that SOE in Burma worked outside of accepted command structures, no evidence has been found to vindicate this. Rather, what has been shown is that SOE worked within them, but was willing to bypass part of the chain of command in order to ensure their policy was not defeated by CAS(B). Instead of appealing to ALFSEA against the latest order not to arm the BNA and AFO in February 1945, Force 136 went straight to Mountbatten to get it overturned. This does not seem to have been unusual in this theatre when it is considered that P Division was often by-passed by OSS to achieve their aims.

In purely military terms, the race for Rangoon in 1945 was able to benefit from relations with the BNA and AFO that prevented them from being a threat to Allied forces. Slim had worried, understandably, that 10,000 BNA might affect his plans, and so he had supported Force 136 in their war against CAS(B) to bring Burmese Nationalist forces over to the Allied side. The AFO and BNA were then armed, and in some part they contributed to the liberation of Burma from Japanese rule even if this was just by ceasing to actively oppose Slim's forces.

It was claimed that the Jedburgh teams that were deployed on *Billet* operations in the Arakan provided 80 per cent of XV Corps' intelligence, and called in airstrikes which killed over a thousand of the enemy.[108] On the strength of this experience, operation *Billet* was rolled out into central Burma. The admiration for certain officers (Majors Britton and Rubinstein for example) and the success in a significant number of operational areas is apparent throughout the files, and not only from the reports of the Force 136 community. Testimony to the operational utility of Force 136 was provided during the conflict by a letter from the commander of Brigade commander, Brigadier Charles Jerrard, to General Rees, commander 19 Indian Division.

In addition, the Game Book statistics offer an insight into the contribution of *Billet* operations while the Army regrouped between May and August 1945 in anticipation of an invasion of Malaya. Ultimately, Force 136 had gone from almost ceasing to exist in late 1944 to conducting operations which satisfied the Army commander's needs by assisting his reclamation of Rangoon by May 1945. While it is clear that not all parts of the *Billet* operation had significant military success, overall the military contribution of this operation proved worthwhile.

EPILOGUE

A LEGACY? FORCE 136 AND POSTWAR BURMA, 1945-50

The Special Operations Executive was dissolved in January 1946, just months after the last Force 136 teams were 'repatriated' from the Burmese jungle. It might therefore seem logical to end the story of SOE in Burma in the last months of 1945, but that would be to leave the story unfinished. After Burmese independence in 1948 and into the 1950s, the civil affairs argument that had warned against arming Burmese Nationalists persisted, fuelling accusations of a Force 136 'legacy' that shaped Burma's decolonisation process.[1] In addition, press reports during the immediate post-independence years told stories of former Force 136 men returning to Burma to fight with the Karen against the Burmese Government. These stories were taken up in the 1990s after the release of SOE files to the National Archives by the BBC, and an article about 'Renegade SOE' in Burma was written by Richard Aldrich.[2]

At the centre of the controversy for the alleged Force 136 legacy in Burma is the supply of weapons to the Burma National Army (BNA), or Patriotic Burmese Forces (PBF) as they were renamed in June 1945. Many British officials had preferred the name 'Burma Traitor Army' since 1942, so embracing what they considered to be a quisling army from late 1944 was an objectionable policy. It had caused bitter disputes during the War, involving SOE, Mountbatten, the exiled Government of Burma, the Civil Affairs Service, Burma (CAS(B)), General Leese and the Foreign Office in London. Equally distasteful to the same people was the arming of the Anti-Fascist Organisation (AFO), an amalgamation of Burmese Nationalists with a particularly strong communist leadership. This accusation of an 'SOE legacy' based on arming groups who would later fight each other is echoed by similar accusations in, for example, Malaya, Albania and Greece.

The aim of this epilogue is to explore the 'legacy' of Force 136 in Burma, and to discuss the allegations brought against it. To do this, it is divided into three sections:

(1) From victory over Japan to Panglong, 1945–7.
(2) From Panglong to Assassination.
(3) 'Renegade SOE'.

From Victory over Japan to Panglong, 1945–7

After the War, the AFO was more widely known as the Anti-Fascist People's Freedom League (AFPFL). SOE had worked with the AFO since November 1943, and in 1945 had armed and trained them. As such, understanding the postwar legacy of that cooperation demands an understanding of its wartime roots.

These have been dealt with in Chapter Four and Six above, but can be briefly summarised here. In July 1942, Thein Pe and Tin Shwe had arrived in India. These two Burmese Nationalists were members of the Thakin Party, who hoped to enlist British support against the Japanese. Tin Shwe was returned to Burma by SOE in December 1943 to investigate the possibility of using the Burmese underground. Initial contact was positive, so this route was fostered and developed throughout 1944. As Slim advanced XIV Army into Burma after the failed Japanese attack on India of March–June 1944, Aung San and other Nationalist Burmese leaders began to decide that it was time to swap sides.

The accusation made by both Donnison and Tinker is that Force 136 – specifically the head of mission, Colin Mackenzie – informed Burmese Nationalist leaders that they would be supplied arms to assist the final victory in Burma, and that if they helped Force 136, the returning Burma Government would be unable to ignore their political demands.[3] Mackenzie was accused of having by-passed both the head of CAS(B), Major General Pearce, and the Supreme Allied Commander (SAC),

Admiral Mountbatten. In Donnison's opinion Mackenzie's unilateral assurance had 'far reaching implications for the future'.

This charge was taken up by Tinker in his work, *The Union of Burma*, published in 1957. In 1972, Tinker's accusations against Force 136 in the *Union of Burma* led to Bickham Sweet-Escott writing to the journal of *International Affairs*.[4] Sweet-Escott claimed that 'the book seriously misrepresents, in the view of many of those concerned, the activities of Force 136'. He argued that Mountbatten was not by-passed, and that General Slim was in the picture. Tinker's reply to Sweet-Escott was published in the same correspondence section of the journal. He defended his position, saying that 'former leaders of Force 136 do not like my interpretation of how they operated'.

When Tinker published his two-volume document compilation charting Burma's path to independence in 1983, he again presented Force 136 as having acted irresponsibly by arming the AFO and BNA, asserting that 'The decision to recognise the AFO, and thereby accept the BNA as a pro-Allied force, was arguably the most important British policy commitment made in Burma's re-conquest and decolonisation.'[5]

As shown in Chapter Six, these decisions were fiercely contested at the time, but Mountbatten had overruled those who opposed SOE's plans. From December 1944, Force 136 teams were parachuted into Burma to work with the AFO and BNA. By March 1945, the BNA had become impatient of waiting for their leaders to assent to an anti-Japanese revolt, and SOE accelerated their insertion of teams in an effort to direct the BNA uprising.

Part of the reason that Force 136 was able to do this was because both Mountbatten and General Slim wanted to secure any military advantage they could in order to seize Rangoon before the monsoon started. Memories of Fifth Column Burmese in 1942 meant Slim wanted nationalist forces either fighting on the Allied side, or at least neutral. Politically, Mountbatten had a pragmatic longer-term vision which included a 'generous and tolerant view' of former Burmese enemies so that Burma could 'resume its place in the Empire on a basis of goodwill'.[6] In other words he offered those who had fought against Britain an opportunity to work their passage home.

After Rangoon was recaptured, there was discussion of Burmese forces continuing the war against Japan beyond Burma's borders. Significantly, the War came to an abrupt end after the two atomic bombs were dropped on Japan on 6 and 9 August 1945. This forced the British into a premature need to politically engage with the BNA/PBF and AFO. It had previously been assumed that a longer period of war would allow more time to reassert British dominance under the guise of military rule. With the War over, however, the focus of Asian nationalism shifted to preventing their other enemy, European colonialism, from re-establishing firm political control. Across a great crescent from India through Burma, French Indochina, and Malaya to Indonesia, nationalist movements prepared to combat a reinstitution of pre-war imperial powers.

What is not made clear by Tinker is why he considered recognition of the BNA and AFO from November 1943 as 'arguably the most important' of British decisions. There are others which seem equally momentous when considering the postwar history of Burma. These range from British indecisiveness to act on the murder charge levelled at Aung San and other civil law cases against quisling Burmese such as Ba Maw, to decisions made because of the bigger problem of the decolonisation of India.[7] For example, the decision was made against deployment of Indian troops, or to slow down demobilisation, to deal with the widespread lawlessness prevalent in Burma during 1945–7. This was at a time when British troops were also being demobilised and sent home. Major General Symes, commander of the South Burma District in 1945, was 'extremely disturbed' because 'there was an indeterminate area between armed dacoity and armed rebellion'. He believed that without the troops to ensure British power, British policy 'was founded on a bluff'.[8] It must have been obvious to Aung San that the power of SEAC demonstrated at the victory parade in Rangoon on 15 June 1945 was no longer available by the end of the year. This may have been one of the influences upon his decision not to allow all his PBF to be absorbed in the new Burma Army, as agreed with Mountbatten and Slim in mid-1945. This way, Aung San retained his own paramilitary force in 1946, the People's Volunteer Organisation (PVO), in order to help secure his political base.[9]

At a time when India was on the brink of national self-determination, it did not seem wise to British officials to use Indian troops to prevent self-determination elsewhere. British experience in Indonesia during 1945–6 demonstrated the risks associated with using Indian troops against nationalist movements. Additionally, the British were aware, due to intelligence gathered on Operation *Character*, that since about July 1945 the BNA had been spreading propaganda that the British were going to reclaim Burma for the Empire using Indian troops.[10]

In October 1945, during a secret meeting in Rangoon at which Aung San was present, Burmese Nationalists discussed starting a press attack against the conduct of Indian and African troops to help ensure that the British maintained their decision not to use Indian troops in Burma.[11] While not wanting to play into Burmese Nationalist hands, it was India that was Attlee's bigger concern: after all, until 1937 Burma had been merely a province of India. India's independence was important to the extent that any decisions that needed to be made about Burma were shelved if it was thought that it might endanger precarious negotiations with Indian Nationalists. This meant sending Indian troops home.

While there were some who wanted to be free of European dominance, there were others who had concerns about colonial withdrawal. In many of the colonies of the European empires, there were those for whom their position was – or seemed – dependent upon collaboration with the occupying power.[12] In Burma, the Hill Peoples worried about their position if the British withdrew. In particular, the Karen, who had remained pro-British throughout the Japanese occupation, did not want to be left under the control of a Burman majority. In 1942 during the first Burma campaign, Aung San was accused of having murdered a Karen headman, and the Burma Independence Army had committed war crimes at Papun and Myaungmya.[13] These atrocities had not been forgotten, so the Karen armed by Force 136 refused to give up their weapons.

The Karen wanted an autonomous state within the British Commonwealth.[14] This would give them protection from an independent Burman-dominated government. One of the important disputes at the centre of SOE 'legacy' is the question of whether or not political assurances were made to the Karen in return for fighting the Japanese. There is testimony to the effect that such promises were made. Firstly, the May 1945 'White Paper On Burma Policy' is often referred to as an official statement of intent, in which it was written:

> The administration of the Scheduled Areas, that is the Shan States and the tribal areas in the mountainous fringes of the country, inhabited by peoples differing in language, social customs and degree of political development from the Burmans inhabiting the

central areas, would remain for the time being a responsibility of His Majesty's Government until such time as their inhabitants signify their desire for some suitable form of amalgamation of their territories with Burma proper.[15]

This paper was issued after Force 136 had been deployed in strength to raise the Karen. It therefore seems to have officially endorsed what Force 136 officers had apparently been telling the Karen since their arrival in Karenni in February and March 1945:

> We were ordered to tell the Karen chiefs that if they would fight and die for us and get rid of the Japanese we guaranteed their independence. They just told me a bloody big lie. They wanted the Karens to come in and they promised them everything, because they knew that what the Karens wanted above everything was to be free of the Burmese.
>
> Captain Alex Campbell (Force 136, Operation *Character/ Walrus*)
>
> The Karens said that they were prepared to put up with all their sacrifice and would continue to fight for the British as loyally as ever; but what was going to happen to them after the war was over?
>
> I was in no position to answer the Karens, so I referred the question to the headquarters of Force 136 in Calcutta, who referred it, in their turn, to Mountbatten.
>
> The reply was clear as daylight – that under no circumstances would the Karens be handed over to the Burmese after the war.
>
> Colonel Ronald Kaulback (Force 136 and CAS(B) officer on Operation *Spiers*)[16]

A former member of the First Aid Nursing Yeomanry serving in India as a cipher clerk corroborated these claims by Force 136 officers. When interviewed in 2011, she was adamant that such a promise was given and called Prime Minister Clement Attlee 'a shit' for not keeping the promise made by Force 136 and the wartime coalition government.[17] Apart from the White Paper of May 1945, the research for this work has not found any official documents which explicitly promised the Karen the protection they were told they would receive.[18] The Karen case seems analogous to other 'promises' that Britain has apparently given, such as to the Arabs during the Great War, and assurances made to Cretans by SOE that the Allies would liberate the island.[19]

Between the election in August 1945 and August 1946, the new Labour Government continued the British policy of courting Aung San, treating the Burmans as 'favoured allies and not as enemies'.[20] The Karen became increasingly nervous that wartime assurances were not going to be met: 'They were told that the Burma White Paper promised a separate hill state under the British', but the Labour Government wanted to maintain influence with the Burmese, and supporting the Karen would destroy the relationship.[21] In an effort to gain reassurance and publicity, in August 1946 a delegation of four Karen went to London calling themselves the 'Karen Goodwill Mission'. They hoped to 'persuade the British Government and public that the Karen had a legitimate claim to an autonomous state within the Commonwealth.'[22]

Aung San was expected in London by the end of the year to discuss Burmese independence. Having chosen Aung San as the future for Burma, the Karen delegation was given the cold shoulder. The British Government 'did not wish to get entangled with Karen political demands which might prove embarrassing and would prefer that the object of this mission to the UK should be of a private nature to thank HMG for its assistance'.[23] This was a bitter pill to swallow after loyally serving the British for close to 100 years. It also sat heavily in the stomach of many of the men of Force 136, the Chindits and XIV Army who had served with the Karen and come to hold them in such high regard.

The Karen delegation returned to Burma empty-handed, but there still remained some hope that the British would protect them from being politically subsumed within a Burman state. To this end, on 12 September 1946, the United Karenni Independent States' Council was formed and passed resolutions aimed at attaining autonomy. The resolutions also hoped to encourage disparate Karen groups to unite, for example by allowing freedom of speech and worship if a Karen state was attained.[24] The resolutions were passed to the colonial Government for endorsement.

The British were undecided as to how to react, and stalled. A tour of Karenni to investigate was aborted because of motor transport problems. Reaction was then prolonged on 'the Prime Minister's orders', possibly because of his forthcoming meeting with Aung San in January 1947.[25] In the meantime, the Karen had sent out invitations for a New Year gathering on 23 December 1946. In a letter to the Governor from H.N.C. Stevenson, now Director of the Frontier Areas Commission, the true purpose of this gathering was speculated about. Under the cover of a party, it was suspected that important political meetings would be held. More intriguingly, the letter reveals that the British were aware of how Aung San was manipulating the press for his own political ends:

> It is clear that the Hon'able U Aung San proposes to use the weapon of 'The New Times of Burma' to disseminate information concerning the Frontier Areas which may influence H.M.G. and public opinion elsewhere into believing that the people of the frontier areas are only too anxious to join Burma forthwith.[26]

The British finally reacted to the resolutions of the United Karenni Independent States' Council in early January 1947, when it was stated that the United Karenni Council was unconstitutional and that its resolutions were defective.[27] This response came at about the same time as the Attlee-Aung San Agreement was signed in London, which promised Burmese independence within a year. The policy of the Labour Government had taken shape, and that was to support national unity for independent Burma.

The context in which Attlee supported Aung San was one of postwar lawlessness. In the first quarter of 1947 alone, there were 773 reported murders and 5,743 cases of dacoity. In May 1947 a train was held up near Pegu by 200 armed dacoits and about 27 tonnes of food was stolen.[28] With insufficient troops left in Burma due to demobilisation and the policy of not using Indian troops against nationalist protest, the colonial Government was hard pushed to restore order, thereby not allowing reconstruction to gather any momentum. According to a contemporary observer, Reverend George Appleton, the Burmans' preoccupation with politics meant that there was a 'reluctance to do consistent hard work' which 'made reconstruction still more slow'.[29]

In Appleton's opinion, the military governance of Burma had ended too soon in October 1945, which meant that supply of essential commodities to Burma switched from the Army's responsibility to London's. Mountbatten had advised on the dangers of transferring power too early, but had been overruled.[30] However, Ashton has argued that it is precisely for this reason that the Attlee–Aung San Agreement was signed in January 1947.[31] Such was the need for an end to the political deadlock between the British and the AFPFL, the interpretation is that the British Government sought a quick fix. The result was the promise to the AFPFL in January 1947 that they would have independence by 1948.

From Panglong to Assassination

The Panglong Conference of February 1947 was convened to discuss Burma's now imminent independence from the British Empire. All the ethnic groups in Burma were invited in order to decide what an independent Burma would look like. Further meetings were held in Rangoon in March, and in Maymyo in April 1947. The resulting Panglong Agreement is still nostalgically referred to in the press in modern times.[32] When released from house arrest in 2010, Aung San Su Kyi said that there should be another Panglong Conference.[33] She hoped that a return to the spirit of the 1947 meetings would be a positive step towards solving the ethnic conflict that continues in Burma. Contemporary writers such as Matthew Walton agree:

> The Panglong Conference is the event that came closest to embodying ethnic unity in Burma, and it remains a compelling image of the possibility of ethnic unity. But calls for a return to the 'spirit of Panglong' will remain ineffective unless the event and its consequences are understood.[34]

The Panglong Conference in February 1947 is regarded as the point to which Burma now needs to return because of a perceived national unity, but evidence of national unity was missing at the time of Panglong. In February 1947, at the first meeting, Mon, Arakanese, Wa, Naga and Karens were absent.[35] While the conference was in session, the Karen Central Organisation changed its name to the Karen National Union, and they protested against the British Government's support of Aung San even as he participated in the Panglong meetings.[36]

The end result, the Panglong Agreement of 12 February 1947 stated that '[f]ull autonomy in internal administration for the Frontier Areas is accepted in principle' and a special Counsellor to the Governor would be appointed to deal with the Frontier Areas.[37] Only Shan, Kachin and Chin were written into the agreement, because the Karen had boycotted the meeting. The Foreign Office position on this was that the Karen had missed their chance to act constitutionally.[38] For many Burma veterans, however, this amounted to a deepening of the Karen issue, which had begun with betrayal of the Karen by the British Government in 1946.

These veterans continued to support the Karen cause into the 1980s.[39] One such veteran, Henry Stonor, targeted Tinker for his opinions as expressed in *Burma: The Struggle for Independence*, where it was thought that Tinker blamed 'the tragedy of Burma upon Force 136 and the Karens'.[40] In 1985, Stonor further argued that Tinker had omitted documents which showed how the Burmans had manipulated the Panglong Conference to achieve their aims.[41] At the February 1947 meeting, according to Stonor, 'The majority of witnesses who favoured a federation of Burma, asked for the Right of Secession.' This issue was taken up at the later Rangoon meeting.

In Rangoon in March, Karen representatives including Saw Marshall Shwin (who had served with Force 136 on Operation *Character*) attended discussions and expressed their desire for an autonomous Karen state. Between Rangoon and the signing of an updated Panglong Agreement in Maymyo in April, Karen demands apparently changed from autonomy to acceptance of incorporation within ministerial Burma. Stonor produced evidence from May 1947 which revealed that the Governor of Burma (Sir Hubert Rance) and the Secretary of State (Lord Pethick-Laurence) were (understandably) astonished at this result: 'The report [of the conference] is surprising' and that 'The Karen attitude is even more puzzling.'[42] Walton agreed, writing that 'The Karen role at Panglong also remains somewhat confusing.'[43] Stonor's explanation was that the Burmans had managed to secure Karen representatives for the meeting in Maymyo that 'would suit them better'. Interestingly, it was another Karen who had served with Operation *Character*, Saw Digay, who was one of these new representatives.

Since Panglong deepened a fracture within the Karen population, it is worth considering what divisions existed in the first place. The Karen consisted of 13 clans, including Red Karen, Sgaw Karen, Pwo and Striped Karen.[44] In addition to clan differences, there were also differences in religion. Christian Karen were favoured by the British over their Buddhist (majority religion) and Animist brethren to the extent that Gravers writes that the British only counted as Karen the Christian Karen in the 1931 census.[45] The Japanese later counted 4.5 million Karen, as opposed to the British count of 1.3 million. Karen leadership was dominated by educated Christians, but within the Christian community there were further divisions between Roman Catholics and Baptists.[46]

In terms of geographical location, the mostly Buddhist Karen lived in the Irrawaddy Delta area, mixed with the Burman population. These divides between clan, religion and geography meant that a homogenous Karen entity was an extremely difficult goal to pursue in the ultimate aim of creating the independent 'Karennistan' that some leaders wanted. At the time of Panglong, how many Karen supported secession from a Union of Burma and how many supported absorption is not known.

Following the Panglong Conference, later in April elections to a Constituent Assembly were held in which the AFPFL won 95.3 per cent of the vote.[47] This is not to say that no frontier peoples got elected. Some Karen such as Mahn Ba Khaing stood on an AFPFL ticket. Karen opposition was led by Saw Ba U Gyi and Tha Hto, who had recommended a boycott of the election.[48]

Such was their distrust of the Burmans that on 29 June 1947 the Governor received a letter from the Shwegyin Karen Association via the Karen National Union. In this letter, ex Force 136 soldier Saw Marshall Shwin wrote that 'Virtual Government by the Burmese over the last few months has not led the Karen to believe in their good faith and honesty'.[49] Furthermore, remembering 'past atrocities' of 1942, he stated that the Karen were unwilling to give up the arms supplied by Force 136 to fight the Japanese. As a result, in July 1947, the KNU formed its military wing, the Karen National Defence Organisation (KNDO), mostly from ex-servicemen.[50]

Regarding the letter from Saw Marshall Shwin, after further communications between Rangoon and London, it was decided that the Governor of Burma should tell Thakin Nu about the letter. This was done in order to ensure that there could be no accusation of the British favouring the Karen or encouraging anti-constitutional behaviour.[51] With the British position clear, the United Karenni Independent States' Council produced a constitution. In an act analogous to Ian Smith's Unilateral Declaration of Independence for Southern Rhodesia 18 years later, the Karen National Union declared themselves independent of both Burma and the British on 4 August 1947.[52]

While the Karen worked on gaining independence, on 19 July 1947 Aung San was assassinated.[53] Gunmen entered the secretariat building and opened fire, killing not only Aung San but six other Executive Council ministers. U Saw, who had attempted to mobilise political opposition to Aung San during the elections in April, was found guilty and hanged for his alleged masterminding of the murders.

Two British officers were also arrested and charged with supplying the arms that were used to kill Aung San.[54] This resulted in a conspiracy theory that the British were behind the assassination. Another theory is that U Saw was framed, the true conspirators being U Nu, Ne Win and Kyaw Nyein. U Nu became the first leader of independent Burma, and Kyaw Nyein was Home Minister. Ne Win was put in charge of the military, and was later responsible for the military coup in 1962.[55] This is not the place to try and resolve the conspiracy surrounding the murder of Aung San; what is important to the story of a Force 136 legacy is the arrest of Major C. Young and Captain David Vivian.

The two officers were put on trial in April 1948. Major Young was acquitted on 10 April 1948. Captain Vivian was found guilty of fraudulently withdrawing 25,600 rounds of ammunition and on another occasion of taking a quantity of Bren guns. The weapons were alleged to have been passed on to the assassins of Aung San and his colleagues.[56] Found guilty on both charges, Vivian was sentenced to five years on both counts. Of his Burmese accomplices, according to the Foreign Office files, four were executed before their trial. Vivian was sent to Insein gaol. The involvement of ex-British military personnel in the murder of Aung San set the precedent for the Government of the Union of Burma to accuse the British of plots against them in subsequent years, especially in relation to the Karen conflict.

'Renegade SOE'

In 1997, the BBC *Timewatch* series aired a programme about the Karen as part of a series entitled 'Forgotten Allies'.[57] The programme began with a Karen interviewee alleging that 'the British bear a great responsibility for the civil war in Burma. The Karen expected a lot from the British in return for dying for them in great numbers during the last war.' Two years later in 1999, Richard Aldrich wrote an article about an SOE legacy in Burma, which he considered to be probably the most

important in Asia.[58] Like Tinker, he focused on the decision to arm the
BNA and the Karen, arguing that wars of insurgency were easy for secret
services to start, but difficult to stop. The legacy of secret service made
territory 'ungovernable', and this legacy had become manifest 'in a dozen
different countries' around the world by 1948–9.[59]

The last section of this epilogue will consider to what extent Force
136 and later ex-Force 136 officers were implicated in the outbreak and
prosecution of the Karen rebellion.

When Burma gained independence on 4 January 1948, there was still
a chance that rebellion might be averted. Section 180 of the Burmese
Constitution allowed for a Karen state 'with a wide measure of local
autonomy' and a Boundary Commission was appointed in April 1948 to
define that state.[60] That was easier said than done though, and the
Commission never finished its job because there was no obvious
boundary for the mixed population. With basic necessities of life such as
kerosene, cloth, cooking oil, salt and rice still scarce, but plenty of
weapons left over from the War, the Karen Hills were ripe for rebellion.

At the centre of the 'Renegade SOE' story is Lieutenant Colonel John
Cromarty Tulloch, previously an area commander on Operation
Character during 1945. When the Karen Goodwill Mission came to
London in 1946, it was Tulloch who looked after them, and also at this
time that 'the delegation appointed Tulloch as their representative with
full powers to negotiate for them'.[61] In February 1948, the first reports
about Tulloch organising subversive activities against the Burma
Government began to arrive in the FO, where Esler Dening was
concerned enough to write in March: 'People who operated behind the
lines during the war tended to be something of a law unto themselves
and it would not be surprising if this characteristic still persists.'[62]

Tulloch was trying to gain support for the Karen cause by lobbying
British business and MPs. Tulloch also used the Cold War threat of
communism to try and win sympathisers, claiming that support for the
Karen would prevent a Communist coup; the carrot of Burma
joining the Commonwealth if the Karen were installed in office was also
dangled. By August 1948, when Tulloch arranged to meet Esler Dening,
Assistant Under Secretary of State, to sound him out about possible
Foreign Office support for the Karen, the Karen National Defence
Organisation (KNDO) had been fighting a Communist insurgency
since July.[63] Despite some reservations about this situation in Burma,

Dening was unequivocal. He told Tulloch that there could be serious consequences for him if he attempted to carry out his plans.[64] By this point, the British Government was worried that Tulloch might embarrass fragile Anglo-Burmese relations, and so the security services began extensive monitoring of Tulloch and his associates.[65]

In September 1948, there was a significant development in the situation. The other key person implicated in the 'plot' by former Force 136 officers to overthrow the Government of the Union of Burma was Alexander Campbell.[66] In 1948, Campbell, now a reporter for the *Daily Mail*, had been in Rangoon since 23 August, ostensibly to cover the Burmese conflict. Before he had left for Burma, Campbell had attended a dinner in a private room at the Savoy Hotel. This dinner was attended by, amongst others, a Karen called 'Oliver', Sir Reginald Dorman-Smith, the *Daily Mail* editor Frank Owen, and Tulloch. Aldrich called this a 'private SOE unit', which was formed specifically as a result of the perceived betrayal of the Karen by the Labour Government.[67] These people were all members of a group that had been formed in early 1947 calling themselves 'The Friends of the Burma Hill People'. Other notable members included former Burma Army commander Lieutenant General Hutton, the former head of SOE Sir Colin Gubbins, Brigadier Fergusson of Chindit fame, and H.N.C. Stevenson.[68]

Shortly after Campbell arrived in Rangoon, Tulloch arrived in Calcutta. It was common practice at this time for aircraft stewards to accept cash for delivering parcels or letters on a 'no questions asked' basis. This was how Campbell and Tulloch had communicated without alerting the Burmese censors to their plans. Unfortunately for the plotters, the steward Campbell had been using, Rowland Symons, decided to steam open one of the letters Campbell entrusted to him.[69] Realising that the contents might prove lucrative, Symons made a certified copy which he gave to the Burmese embassy in Pakistan. As a result, Burmese CID swooped on Campbell's Rangoon hotel room in September 1948 where they found further incriminating evidence. Campbell and another journalist called Jackson were arrested.

The letter that Symons intercepted was addressed to 'Pop', and signed off 'Skunk'. 'Pop' was Tulloch's nickname, and 'Skunk' had been the codename of Campbell's sub-mission on Operation *Character*. The letter had reference to arms shipments that Tulloch was organising, and how the Karen were 'awaiting [Tulloch] and the first consignment of arms and ammo'.[70] This was a major embarrassment for the British Government. The Burmese Government had won a propaganda coup, as this seemed to back their claims that the rebels in Burma had been supported by Britain, claims they had made since the murder of Aung San. There were also accusations of British business backing the Karen rebellion, specifically the Mawchi Mining Company.[71] The British Ambassador to Burma, James Bowker wrote to the Burmese Home Minister on 30 September demanding that Burmese claims be substantiated or else an immediate press release should deny that the British Government was behind the revolt. Kyaw Nyein replied that the 'persistence of these rumours' about Europeans helping the Karen meant that he wanted Bowker to help prove the British Government's assurances about non-involvement. Bowker could start by checking two names, Gamble and Pollard, who were thought to be former Force 136 and in the field with the Karen.[72] Although both these men had served in Burma, neither man had been with Force 136. It was found that Pollard had gone to Nigeria in April 1948, and Lieutenant Colonel Gamble, who had led the Kachin Levies, was eventually traced to Australia (he was Australian).

After this, the British Government increased arms supplies to Burma to help reassure the government of U Nu of their support, but also to ensure that the Communists could not take advantage of the situation in Burma. One Foreign Office official commented in December 1948 that 'it looks as if the scare about British help for the Karens is being deliberately exploited.'[73] The supply of arms alarmed those who supported the Karen, but Bowker recommended that 'the latest Burmese requests for Army and Airforce supplies be met as far as possible and fairly soon, despite the risk that the equipment will be used against the Karens' and that 'we must continue to put our money on the Burmese Gov't'.[74] In Britain, the news that weapons supplied by the British Government might be used to fight the Karen was not well received. Leslie Glass wrote 'I have been stopped on the street by men who fought beside the Karens in the war, who have urged this point on me with tears in their eyes.'[75]

So apart from Tulloch and Campbell, how many ex-Force 136 officers were secretly assisting the Karen in their fight against the Burmese Government? The Burma Government claimed that there were 18 Force 136 men involved, and the Burmese press was continually printing stories about 'white faced persons' that had apparently been seen in the jungle with the Karen.[76] These rumours were strengthened by press reports such as the one about an RAF aircraft that was seen dropping supplies to Karen villages. According to the Foreign Office (FO), the aircraft was flying from Singapore to India carrying equipment for Gurkhas. The crew had to jettison cargo in order to make a landing at Mingaladon, the aerodrome just north of Rangoon.[77]

U Nu suspected all ex Force 136 officers of being potential plotters, and had men such as Frederick Wemyss brought in for interrogation.[78] Wemyss was an Anglo-Burman who had worked on the *Nation* operations to the AFO and BNA, meaning two of the men he had trained were part of the Burman Cabinet in 1948.[79] Since many of the men recruited into SOE had originally worked for business or government in Burma before the War, many went back to their jobs. Wemyss had been a policeman, and had returned to that role. He was not found to have any involvement with Tulloch, but had been mentioned in one of Campbell's letters as someone to contact.[80]

It is true that at least two 'white faced persons' were killed along with the Karen leader Ba U Gyi by the Burmese military in February 1950. One was Captain Vivian, the same man who had been sentenced for his alleged role in the assassination of Aung San. Captain David Vivian had not served with Force 136 though, but a Captain Godfrey Vivian had. Godfrey Vivian had returned to colonial service in Nigeria in late 1945. The *New Times of Burma* described the Captain David Vivian who was shot alongside the Karen leader Ba u Gyi as a 'Renegade British Army Officer', and did not make the link to Force 136. The other man killed with Ba U Gyi was 'Mr Baker'. It is unclear who Baker was; however, there was a Mr Baker who worked at the British embassy in Rangoon who appears to have left the city by February 1950.[81]

Other names that were alleged to have been involved with the conspiracy are Aubrey Buxton, a 'tall man' called John Bingley, Jack Percival, Oscar Jackson, Major Tyce, Major Gilmour, and Major Lovett-Campbell.[82] Of these, only Lovett-Campbell was formerly Force 136. Major Verney Lovett-Campbell had been involved in *Dilwyn* and *Billet* operations between 1943–5. By 1948 though, when he was accused by the Burmese police of leading Karen in an attack north of Tavoy in southern Burma against government troops, he was in Uganda.[83] The evidence of the FO and KV files suggests that there were just two former Force 136 men involved, which makes the story of 'Renegade SOE' somewhat flimsy. It seems that there was a range of people involved for a variety of reasons.

Conclusions

It would be disingenuous to say that there was no SOE legacy in Burma, but that legacy needs to be carefully placed in the context of a colonial legacy, the natural tendency of some decolonising societies to suffer splits along 'ethnic' lines, which offered convenient opportunities for political mobilisation, and the exigencies of war. SOE was itself an exigency of war, founded to raise secret armies when Britain was under threat. Before the War, the defence of Burma had been the responsibility of Burma Rifles and Burma Frontier Force battalions that mostly consisted of Karen, Kachin, and Chins that the colonial authorities perceived as the more trustworthy and 'martial' of the Burmese races. It was the Japanese invasion that derailed that post-1937 process of gradually increasing the Burman proportion of regular forces.

The Burman-dominated and Japanese-trained BIA was deployed from 1942, and by 1945, now rebranded the BNA, as about 10,000 strong. Elements within it had, however, been ready to turn on the Japanese before Force 136 sent Tin Shwe to make contact in December 1943. Above all, the BNA remained pro-Burman and anti-colonial, ready to fight for independence whoever the enemy was. One such enemy, as the history of the colonial years reveals, was Burma's minorities, but especially the Karen. Communal violence was particularly bad in the Irrawaddy Delta area and Papun in May 1942, where the BIA murdered Karen villagers in the power vacuum left between the British withdrawal and the Japanese arrival.[84] In 1945 the Karen had not forgotten this violence.

During the War and immediately following its end, the younger Burman Nationalists of the pre-war period gained ascendancy over their older contemporaries, ushering in a new era of nationalist challenge. In dealing with this new generation, in a changed world which included new international pressures from the United Nations and the developing Cold War, the new Labour Government remained seized of the problem concerning the Frontier Areas in Burma. The difficulty was to adhere to the May 1945 White Paper which promised that the Frontier Areas would remain under HMG 'until such a time as their inhabitants signify their desire for some suitable form of amalgamation of their territories with Burma proper', and sympathy to the desire of the Burman Nationalists not to divide Burma up into multiple political units.[85] Over a year after the White Paper, there was considerable frustration amongst some Burma officials that HMG was dithering on setting out a clear policy for the Frontier Areas.[86] In the end, maintaining amicable relations with the AFPFL Executive Council took precedent, as demonstrated by the reluctance to have Aung San brought up on murder charge made against him.[87] If official promises had been made to the minorities during the War, they were overtaken by the Labour Government's approach to the realities of the postwar world.[88]

The feeling that loyal allies had been betrayed motivated a cross-section of those who had worked or served in Burma before and during the War to become involved in Burmese politics in the approach to independence and after. Involvement varied from long-range support in Britain to action within Burma, and from peaceful methods to actually fighting with the Karen against the new Government. However, with just two of the supporters of the Karen rebellion conclusively having been found to be former SOE, it is probably more accurate to say that at least this part of the Force 136 legacy is an imagined one.

CONCLUSION

At the start of this book, three main reasons why a comprehensive study of SOE in Burma was needed were proposed. These provided three themes which permeated what followed.

The first reason was the need for further clarification of SOE's military impact upon the war in Burma. This is an area where SOE's contribution has previously been given cursory or unsatisfactory treatment.

The second reason was the need to resolve questions about the political impact of SOE. It has been claimed that SOE Burma worked outside of the normal chain of command, and was thereby able to interfere in Burmese Nationalist politics both during the War and afterwards.

The third reason was the need to address the inadequate or incomplete way in which SOE Burma has been integrated (or in some cases neglected) in general SOE histories. The introduction recognised that while overall judgements about SOE have been made, this has been done with insufficient consideration of SOE work in countries outside Europe. Since SOE was involved in Burma for four years, playing a role in the retreat of 1942 through to assisting the re-conquest of Burma in 1945, and generated complex British-American-Chinese inter-relationships, an important case study has therefore not been satisfactorily integrated into the debate.

In order to address these main themes, several subsidiary questions concerning SOE operations in Burma were posed. The salient ones asked what constraints SOE operated under, what SOE Burma's successes and failures were, and what conclusions could be drawn about command and control and the use of Special Forces.

To return to the first of the core reasons for this study: what was SOE's military impact upon the war in Burma between 1941 and 1945? The book addressed this question by dividing the Burma campaign into four distinct phases: pre-conflict (May–December 1941), the first Burma campaign (December 1941–July 1942), stalemate (August 1942–December 1944), and the second Burma campaign (January–October 1945).

For the pre-conflict phase, Cruickshank's official history argued that Oriental Mission (OM) was constrained by its relationship with civil and military authorities. This study has demonstrated, however, that this blanket judgement did not apply in Burma in the same way as in Malaya and Singapore.

Telegrams informing the civil and military authorities of SOE's Far Eastern Mission (FEM) were sent before Killery arrived in Singapore in May 1941. Over the next seven months, Killery established Special Training School (STS) 101 where European and Eurasian officers were trained in SOE work, but virtually no Asian personnel were enrolled. Part of the reason for the latter was the opposition of the Governor of Singapore and the Commander in Chief (C-in-C) Far East, and later the General Officer (GOC) Malaya, General Percival. The result was that, in Malaya, Asians were only trained after the Japanese invaded on the night of 7–8 December. Some SOE teams were sent behind the lines in January 1942, but they were unable to influence the Malayan campaign.

By contrast, Killery and Governor Dorman-Smith had agreed parameters for SOE work in Burma in August 1941, and once this was overruled by C-in-C Brooke-Popham in Singapore, alternative arrangements were found by the Governor which ensured preparations to use Asian personnel continued in Burma. The personality of Dorman-Smith mattered, for he was willing to facilitate the training of Burmese levies under Stevenson that were officially separate from SOE, but were in fact commanded by officers who had been through STS 101 and had SOE code symbols. As a result, Oriental Mission was able to make a military contribution to the first Burma campaign that has hitherto been down-played or in some works entirely overlooked. Two actions in particular were examined in detail because they add significantly to our understanding of the war in Burma.

The first action was that on the Army's eastern flank, which assisted the overall retreat to India in 1942 by delaying a Japanese hook inland through the Shan states. As Chapter Two showed, Oriental Mission-controlled Karen levies commanded by Captain Boyt, reinforced by an under-equipped company of Karen Burma Rifles commanded by Captain Thompson, were responsible for this rear-guard action. After joining forces on the road just east of Toungoo at the end of March 1942, together they provided the only resistance to the Japanese advance towards Mawchi. Thompson's Distinguished Service Order (DSO) recommendation even claimed that this action 'saved the Chinese and British armies in Burma from encirclement'.[1] While Chapter One noted that recommendations and citations by their nature emphasise individual's achievements, there can be no doubt that a significant delay was imposed upon the Japanese by SOE, not only by direct combat and demolitions, but also by allowing the Chinese 6th Army to concentrate and engage the Japanese further south than they otherwise would have done. It is notable that both Slim and Kirby blamed the Army's hasty withdrawal over the Irrawaddy on the Japanese flanking drive into the Shan states: but without the joint SOE-levy actions that withdrawal might have been forced to occur a week or so earlier. This book therefore shows that even with frugal resources committed to it, SOE acted as a force multiplier by assisting the Army's retreat.

This success of the levies and Burma Rifles (Burifs), commanded by SOE officers, also challenges the assertion in many campaign histories that Burmese personnel were overwhelmingly unreliable in the 1942 campaign. In some accounts, the Burifs units have been vilified for the reverses suffered, yet here Boyt's hastily trained levies with Thompson's understrength and poorly equipped Karen company was able to delay the forward battalion of a Japanese division.

In the second action of 1942, SOE helped to prevent the Japanese from completely occupying north-eastern Burma. By assisting in the destruction of five bridges leading north from Myitkyina, the retention of a forward operating base at Fort Hertz, was possible. This was important for two main reasons.

First of all, having a secure base inside Burma helped facilitate American strategy in Burma. This strategy focused upon supplying Chinese Nationalist forces both to keep them belligerent, and to encourage them to strike towards Japan through China. Vital to American strategy was protection of the air corridor that extended from India across Burma to China. The retention of north-eastern Burma greatly assisted that passage, by preventing the Japanese from basing fighters on the airstrip at Fort Hertz, and by allowing the Americans to install an aerial early warning system there.

Secondly, SOE Burma's 1942 actions in helping to ensure the retention of Fort Hertz had offensive value. From Sumprabum, south of Fort Hertz, tentative military probing of Japanese-occupied Burma began in the 1942–3 period, during which American and British forces elsewhere remained mostly pinned back on the India-Burma border. It was from Fort Hertz that some of the earliest insertions of SOE and OSS officers, by land and by air, were launched in early 1943. In the Oriental Mission's reports of late 1942, these demolitions were noted, yet their importance was not immediately recognised. An important corollary of these missions to the Kachin was that aircrew shot down supplying China could be rescued. In the general campaign histories and Kirby's official history, no mention is made of SOE's role in helping to hold, and then use, the north-east.

Another important aspect of SOE's war in Burma arose from OSS and SOE operations from Fort Hertz which both sought to recruit the Kachin as guerrillas. The case study of SOE's Operation *Dilwyn*, deployed in north-east Burma from February 1943 until the end of the War, also adds another facet to an understanding of what Christopher Thorne called 'Allies of a Kind'. Anglo-American rivalry extended from the men on the ground up to theatre command level, and there were concerns raised over the resulting intelligence that was routed through Fort Hertz to India. Competing strategies, American wariness of British colonialism, and learning the lessons of first operations in the theatre carried out side by side were all causes of tension.

The study of Operations *Spiers* and *Hainton* in Chapter Four, furthermore, presented colonial conflict between Britain and Chinese Nationalist forces that also impacted upon SOE operations. Both *Spiers* and *Hainton* were unable to fulfil their mission directives, and instead became embroiled in political intrigue and territorial disputes. In these circumstances, it was difficult for the British to consider the Chinese in the same way as the Americans did, which added further strain to Anglo-American relations.

This book also reappraised the years 1942 until December 1944, a previously neglected period of SOE's history in Burma. Other accounts have not dwelt at length on this period, with Cruickshank arguing that during this time SOE struggled to find a role because there was very little to sabotage as tasked by London. He further argued that SOE was pushed into an intelligence role. It has been shown that, on the contrary, Mackenzie and his Burma section staff had a clearer idea of what they needed to do and what they could accomplish given their limited resources. The priority was not intelligence but the building up of infrastructure, and the evolution and maturation of SOE. From this vital period came the capacity to supply, train and direct secret armies in occupied Burma. Critical to this was re-establishing relationships with Karen and Kachin, and convincing them that the British would liberate them from the Japanese. The exploratory operations of this period were focused upon this task of building networks and recruiting guerrillas, with intelligence as a by-product rather than an explicit objective. It was a fortunate coincidence that SOE's development achieved readiness just as Slim planned an overland reclamation of Burma in late 1944.

Finally, this book re-evaluated operations in support of the advancing Allied army from December 1944 until beyond the Japanese surrender in August 1945. During this period, SOE was able to exploit its training schemes, new airlift capacity, and exploratory operations, to raise and maintain substantial guerrilla forces in the field, and so exert significant effect on the second Burma campaign.

Two major SOE operations in particular contributed to the second Burma campaign in 1945. These were operations *Billet* and *Character*. While general military histories such as Anthony Beevor's *The Second World War* still pay little or no attention to SOE's military impact, specialist SOE and intelligence works have acknowledged SOE's role in respect of these two operations.[2] Richard Aldrich argued that, in these operations, SOE carried out 'its most spectacularly successful military operations of the war'. Cruickshank has also claimed that 'by common consent its [SOE's] guerrillas had played a significant part in the Allied victory in Burma'.[3] These conclusions were, however, reached by providing a general overview of the Far East, rather than by conducting a more comprehensive analysis of how SOE in Burma was able to achieve military impact.

This gap has been filled by providing the detail of SOE Burma's evolution, and what SOE did in the second Burma campaign. Where existing work has exemplified SOE Burma's military impact through the stark casualty statistics found in SOE's Game Book, this work has demonstrated the substantial difference between SOE operations in 1942 and 1945. By December 1944, not only the theatre commander, Admiral Mountbatten, but General Slim, the Army commander, supported SOE operations. This meant that from January 1945, SOE was deployed specifically to support Slim's offensive against Rangoon. It is in this context that SOE can be judged as having been 'spectacularly successful', as Aldrich has argued, and able to record a combined total of 16,122 Japanese for 58 Allied dead in operations *Character* and *Billet*. This roughly equates, in British terms, to the Japanese loss of a division for half a company.

Of course, gaining the support of generals and being deployed in support of an advancing army are not the only prerequisites for military success, as Chapters Five and Six showed. Operation *Character* would never have been as successful without the Karen, who joined SOE in their thousands, and the experience and personality of the officers and non-commissioned officers (NCOs) who led them. Similarly, the experienced Jedburgh personnel from Europe, deployed on Operation *Billet*, were able to loosely direct Burmese Nationalist forces, so that both these operations were able to inflict serious casualties upon the retreating Japanese. In combination, these two operations helped propel XIV Army's drive towards Rangoon, so that that city was able to be liberated by an unopposed seaborne assault as the monsoon began. In military terms then, it has been shown that in Burma SOE recorded disproportionate returns for the resources invested in it during all three phases of the war against Japan. This was despite their impact being diminished during the retreat phase because of issues relating to command and control.

Even during the period of stalemate between mid-1942 and mid-1944, SOE was able to make some contribution to the war effort by inserting small numbers of officers, who then provided information from within Burma. This was, furthermore, but a by-product of exploratory operations which were mainly focused upon establishing and improving contact with indigenous forces. These achievements occurred within the context of a build-up of capacity for more meaningful and large-scale operations. Once the critical supporting infrastructure, including relationships with other agencies and the military, was in place, an appreciable contribution to the victory in Burma was made in 1945. This military success has been down-played by Slim, for example, who wrote that Special Forces 'did not give, militarily, a worthwhile return for the resources', and has been overshadowed in postwar years by the political price that critics have argued were a consequence of SOE's handling of the Burmese.[4]

Critics of SOE generally have focused their arguments upon political legacies which they allege SOE bequeathed to the territories in which it worked. This was the second major question addressed: how accurate are the accusations that SOE in Burma acted autonomously and helped create the conditions for postwar political strife? Similar to European countries such as Greece, Burma slipped into a civil war shortly after independence in January 1948, and the resulting ethnic tensions have endured into the twenty-first century. These criticisms arose immediately during and after the War. Regarding the minorities, arming the Kachin and Karen had been a relatively easy decision as on the whole they had not supported the Japanese, and had fought on the Allied side. The extent to which these groups were encouraged by officially sanctioned promises of postwar independence from the Burman population is unclear, but certainly promises were made by sympathetic SOE officers. The Kachin and Karen then became factions in the civil war that started in 1948.

Criticism of arming Nationalist Burmans centred around Frank Donnison's claim in his 1956 work that SOE made politically loaded decisions without 'prior reference' to the appropriate authorities. Donnison claimed that Colin Mackenzie had assured the Burman Nationalist, Thein Pe, that if the BNA/AFO helped liberate Burma then they could not be ignored after the War.[5]

It is argued here that SOE did not 'go rogue' or make promises beyond its remit. Contrary to Donnison's claim (later re-stated by Tinker), Mountbatten, Dorman-Smith and Slim were all well informed by late 1944 of SOE's overtures towards Burmese Nationalists. Evidence was also presented of extensive dialogue between SOE in India and Mountbatten on the one hand, and the Government and Chiefs of Staff (COS) in London on the other. This does not preclude Mountbatten and Mackenzie from having had to respond to fast and fluid circumstance by making some decisions as 'men on the spot', but this is true of senior command anywhere.[6] Thus it is argued that Burma's colonial history and Burma's wider inclusion in the world war must bear a larger burden of responsibility for the political problems Burma has faced since 1945.

This is not to rule out an SOE influence, but that impact must be understood in the wider context of war and decolonisation in the Far East.

In addition to the arguments about SOE's wartime political legacy, accusations were made by the Government of Burma from 1948, and by historians since, that SOE officers had a significant involvement in Karen opposition to the Union of Burma. The British Government's eventual statement on Burma, promulgated in a White Paper in May 1945, is important to the debate because it reassured minority groups that they would not be arbitrarily placed under the control of an independent Burman-dominated Government. This was consistent with what some SOE officers had promised their recruits, particularly amongst the Karen. Attlee's Government very quickly signposted that the assurances of the White Paper would not be fulfilled by backing Aung San, so even before independence in January 1948 the Karen prepared for conflict. Once it started, the Burma Government made repeated accusations of British and especially SOE complicity with the Karen. Far from being an army of ex-SOE officers leading the Karen insurgency, it was found that just two officers were involved, and that after their efforts were uncovered by the Burmese, only Colonel Tulloch of SOE continued to try and assist the Karen cause.

Turning to the final main theme, overall judgements about SOE have generally not taken much, if any, account of the organisation's performance in the Far East. As suggested in the introduction, part of the reason for this is because of a Eurocentric focus. What this book has shown is that concerning the military argument about SOE in World War II, the Burma example adds weight to the side for significant, if varying, military impact. In both Burma campaigns, the evidence presented here demonstrates that far from an 'Exorbitant Cost', or 'a costly and misguided failure', SOE in Burma fulfilled what the organisation was established to do in a way that more than rewarded the limited resources committed: namely to hinder an enemy advance, and later use secret armies to assist the Army in re-conquest and liberation.[7]

Aside from the overall picture of military performance in the War, this case study of Burma offers other evaluations of SOE from which general judgements can be drawn. One such judgement is that governmental machinery needed to provide SOE with clearer guidance and support. The Far Eastern Mission (FEM) was provided with an approved charter for action, but political and military officials in theatre thought it ran contrary to the Foreign Office's policy of non-provocation of Japan. Clear direction from London should have been given to those who obstructed SOE so that preparation for war could occur. The Burma example has shown that as late as September 1944 the Foreign Office was still unable or unwilling to give clear direction in the case of Operations *Spiers* and *Hainton*, which resulted in these operations being withdrawn.

Far from working outside the boundaries of accepted command and control, SOE needed to work within them in order to receive not only practical direction from governmental authority, but to be in a position to outmanoeuvre more stubborn resistance to SOE work, such as that presented in Burma by Civil Affairs officers. Most notably, these officers almost prevented deployment of multiple teams due to support the offensive against Rangoon in February 1945. Only decisive and forceful leadership of Mountbatten, backed by the support of Slim, ensured these operations went ahead.

In Burma, like in many other enemy-occupied countries into which SOE operated, there was an overwhelming sense of urgency to get men on the ground. As Bailey has shown in his work on Italy, this often had catastrophic results, and it is cases such as these which have contributed to SOE being charged with launching operations which were nothing more than 'irrelevant and pointless acts of bravado'.[8] In some European cases there was a reckless loss of lives, but in Burma, where resources including personnel were in short supply, more caution was exercised; the overriding factor in Burmese failures was operational immaturity and bad luck. The overall judgement about Burma Country Section's operations that emerges from this study is, therefore, that success was often contingent upon the organisation having established its supporting infrastructure, and effective relationships with other agencies within its theatre of operations.

When the FEM was dispatched to the Far East in 1941, those tasked with preparing for the coming war against Japan came up against political opposition which remained in place for the duration of the commitment, albeit in different forms. What did change was the attitude of the military, so that by late 1944 in South East Asia Command (SEAC) there was some confidence that SOE could produce something of value to the war effort. This acceptance by regular military command is one of three overall discernible strands that were imperative to SOE success, not only in Burma but to the organisation generally. The growing confidence in SOE as a tool of war by the military (notably as a result of P Force patrols on the Chindwin front in late 1943 and early 1944) was symbiotic with an increasing allocation of resources to SOE as war economies were mobilised, and the accrual of operational experience gained by SOE personnel during 1942–4. With confidence in their own capability and supporting structures behind them, the military was persuaded that SOE should be integrated into offensive plans such as the invasions of mainland Europe, and Burma and Malaya in the Far East.

This Burma case study has demonstrated that SOE was able to achieve military successes in Burma when integrated with the plans of the regular army, as proponents of SOE have argued for operations in France. That it took time to get there was partly due to the fact that whereas Special Forces are now an accepted part of the armoury of warfare, they were not yet widely regarded as such during World War II.

In summary, in 1942, with little support from the military, the Oriental Mission was able to first delay the advance of the Japanese Army in Burma, and then to deny it territory. This was achieved when the Japanese were at their best and SOE was arguably at their worst. In 1945, when the Japanese were at their worst and SOE was at their best, SOE was able to act as a force multiplier, inflicting significant casualties, providing most of the Army's intelligence, and pinpointing targets for airstrikes. Politically, by working with the BNA and the AFO, SOE ensured that once the Japanese had been defeated, Burmese Nationalists did not start an insurgency against the British as they had planned to do. In the absence of evidence of a greater involvement of ex-SOE officers in the Burmese civil war, this is perhaps the political legacy that SOE should be best remembered for.

NOTES

Introduction   The Special Operations Executive in Burma, 1941–5

1. The aim of the epilogue is to examine the loose ends that existed due to SOE's wartime involvement in Burma. As it is concerned with events after SOE had been officially closed down, it has not been covered in the same archival detail as the 1940–5 period.
2. For a detailed discussion of the formation of SOE, see, for example, M.R.D. Foot, *SOE 1940–1946* (London: Mandarin, 1990), or Mark Seaman, *Special Operations Executive: A New Instrument of War* (London: Routledge, 2006), Chapter One, pp. 7–21.
3. So secret were the 'Aux' Units that they were only represented in the British Remembrance Day Parade in London for the first time in November 2013. See the 'British Resistance Archive', http://www.coleshillhouse.com/march-at-the-cenotaph-campaign.php.
4. Dalton's letter is often quoted. See, for example, Foot, *SOE 1940–1946*, pp. 18–19, or Russell Miller, *Behind the Lines* (London: Pimlico, 2003), pp. 1–2.
5. For details of the FEM, see Richard Gough, *SOE Singapore 1941–42* (London: William Kimber, 1985); Arthur Christie, *Mission Scapula* (Staffordshire: Panda Press, 2004).
6. Gough, *SOE Singapore*, see Chapter Two, pp. 22–35. STS 101's site at the mouth of the Jurong River to the west of Singapore Island was selected after the location chosen by the local military in the Johore Straits proved unsuitable.
7. The most famous member of these left-behind parties is 'Freddy' Spencer Chapman who remained in the Malay jungle until 1944. See F. Spencer Chapman, *The Jungle is Neutral* (London: Chatto & Windus, 1949).
8. The first wave of Japanese planes attacked Hawaii just before 8 am on 7 December 1941. Due to the international dateline, the time in Malaya was just before 1 am on 8 December.

9. 11 December 1941 is the date given by the *History of the SOE Oriental Mission* available at TNA, HS 1/207.

10. For a summary of the Malayan campaign and its historiography, see Karl Hack and Kevin Blackburn, *Did Singapore Have to Fall? Churchill and the Impregnable Fortress* (London: Routledge, 2004).

11. Gough, *SOE Singapore*, pp. 40–1.

12. The National Archives, Kew Gardens, London (hereafter TNA), HS 1/226, 'Notes on Meeting with HE and GOC' (His Excellency, Sir Shenton Thomas, and General Percival), 24 October 1941.

13. Charles Cruickshank, *SOE in the Far East* (Oxford: Oxford University Press, 1986), p. 61, and TNA, HS 1/226, 'Notes on Meeting with HE and GOC', 24 October 1941.

14. TNA, HS 1/202, Memorandum to Sir Frank Nelson from JA Sinclair, 28 June 1941.

15. The Japanese surrendered on 15 August 1945, but SOE teams remained in the field, fighting Japanese who did not believe the war had ended and assisting with the restoration of civil affairs until October 1945.

Literature Review

1. John Keegan, *The Second World War* (London: Pimlico, 1997). See also Max Hastings, *All Hell Let Loose: The World at War 1939–1945* (London: Harper, 2011), p. 406; Norman Davies, *Europe at War 1939–1945: No Simple Victory* (London: Macmillan, 2007), p. 251; Calder Walton, *Empire of Secrets: British Intelligence, the Cold War and the Twilight of Empire* (London: Harper, 2013), p. 58; Jeremy Black, *World War Two: A Military History* (London: Routledge, 2003), pp. 234–5, concedes that SOE made 'a contribution to France and the Balkans', but criticises other operations, such as the assassination of Heydrich.

2. M.R.D. Foot, 'What Use Was SOE?', *The RUSI Journal*, 148, 1 (2003), pp. 76–83. See also Mark Seaman, ed., *Special Operations Executive: A New Instrument of War* (London: Routledge, 2006), pp. 1–6; Ian Dear, *Sabotage and Subversion: The SOE and OSS at War* (London: Cassell, 2002), pp. 16–17; Russell Miller, *Behind the Lines: The Oral History of Special Operations in World War Two* (London: Pimlico, 2002), pp. 268–9.

3. For contemporary criticism, see, for example, 'War Cabinet: India Committee I (45) 15th Meeting' reproduced in Hugh Tinker, *Burma, The Struggle for Independence*, Vol. 1 (London: HMSO, 1983), p. 202. See also Nigel West, *Secret War* (London: Hodder, 1992), particularly pp. 248–9.

4. Frank Owen, *The Campaign in Burma* (London: HMSO, 1946). Humphrey Frank Owen, Liberal MP 1929–31 and journalist, had been editor of *SEAC*, the newspaper created for XIV Army; Louis Allen, *Burma, The Longest War 1941–1945* (London: Phoenix, 1998); Jon Latimer, *Burma, The Forgotten War* (London: John Murray, 2004); Roy Conyers Nesbit, *The Battle for Burma* (Barnsley: Pen & Sword, 2009).

5. Field Marshal William Slim, *Defeat into Victory* (London: Cassell, 1956), p. 499.

6. In the immediate aftermath of the Japanese victories in mid-1942, the perception was that the Oriental Mission had failed to make any meaningful contribution to the campaign, meaning that SOE's India Mission had to fight for its survival, see TNA HS 1/201, 'General Report, SOE Mission India', August 1942. In late 1944 and early 1945 too, SOE was under pressure to justify its existence on the Burma front, see Chapter Six.

7. John Keegan, *The Second World War* (London: Arrow, 1990), p. 484.

8. See Black, *World War Two*, p. 235. Codenamed Operation *Anthropoid*, Heydrich was killed in Prague in 1942 by SOE-trained Czech agents.

9. West, *Secret War*, pp. 246–54.

10. Foot, 'What Use Was SOE?', pp. 76–83.

11. General Eisenhower, quoted in David Stafford, *Secret Agent: Britain's Wartime Secret Service* (London: BBC, 2002), p. 252.

12. Quoted in Peter Wilkinson and Joan Bright Astley, *Gubbins and SOE* (Barnsley: Pen & Sword, 2010), p. i.

13. Stafford, *Secret Agent*, p. 252.

14. William Mackenzie, *The Secret History of SOE* (London: St Ermin's Press, 2002), p. 745.

15. Bailey, *Target Italy*, pp. 276–8. Examples include securing ball-bearings from Sweden and acquiring foreign currencies.

16. See also Brian Lett, *SOE's Mastermind* (Barnsley: Pen & Sword, 2016). The French historian Henri Michel, however, was more modest about SOE's military impact, writing that the Resistance was 'only a bonus' which 'had it been wisely used, it could have . . . hastened victory.' Henri Michel, *The Shadow War: Resistance in Europe 1939–45* (London: History Book Club, 1972), p. 358.

17. Neville Wylie, 'SOE: New Approaches and Perspectives', *Intelligence and National Security*, 20,1 (March 2005), pp. 1–13.

18. Mark Seaman, ed., *Special Operations Executive: A new Instrument of War* (London: Routledge, 2006).

19. TNA, HS 1/207 and HS 7/111, 'History of SOE Oriental Mission', undated. The mission reports for Burma and the overall Burma report are in HS 7/104–HS 7/106.

20. The official histories are: M.R.D. Foot, *SOE In France* (London: Routledge, 2006); *SOE in the Low Countries* (London: St Ermin's Press, 2001); Charles Cruickshank, *SOE in Scandinavia* (Oxford: Oxford University Press, 1986); *SOE in the Far East* (Oxford: Oxford University Press, 1986); David Stafford, *Mission Accomplished: SOE and Italy, 1943 – 1945* (London: The Bodley Head, 2011); Roderick Bailey, *Target: Italy* (London: Faber & Faber, 2014). Two books that contribute to the historiography, but are not 'official' histories; Mackenzie, *The Secret History of SOE*; Foot's *SOE, 1940–1946* (London: Pimlico, 1999).

21. Wylie, 'SOE: New Approaches and Perspectives', p. 3.

22. The latest pairing of Official Histories on SOE in Italy by Roderick Bailey and David Stafford should probably be exempted from Wylie's concern, having been researched far beyond the country section reports. For example, Bailey makes substantial use of American and Italian archives.

23. Wylie, 'SOE: New Approaches and Perspectives', p. 6.

24. A study of OSS and SOE in Thailand was published in 2005: E. Bruce Reynolds, *Thailand's Secret War* (Cambridge: Cambridge University Press, 2005).

25. Cruickshank, *SOE in the Far East*, pp. 61–82. Air Chief Marshal Brooke-Popham, commenting in his 'final dispatch' which has three references provided: CAB 106/40, CAB 106/45, and CAB 120/518. The George Moss evidence is not referenced by either author, but comes from TNA, HS 1/226, Sir George Moss to Sir Charles Hambro, 13 June 1942.

26. Alan Ogden, *Tigers Burning Bright: SOE Heroes in the Far East* (London: Bene Factum, 2013), Chapter Two, pp. 32–62. As the subtitle of the book suggests, the aim of this book was to focus on the individuals involved in SOE, rather than a study of SOE in each Far Eastern country.

27. West, *Secret War*, pp. 173–83.

28. Ian Trenowden, *Operations Most Secret SOE: The Malayan Theatre* (Bodmin: Crecy Books, 1994), p. 213. Cheah Boon Kheng, *Red Star Over Malaya: Resistance and Social Conflict During and After the Japanese Occupation, 1941–1945* (Singapore: Singapore University Press, 2003), p. 59.

29. Aldrich, *Intelligence and the War Against Japan*, p. 332.

30. Gough, *SOE Singapore*, see pp. 11–12, but quotation taken from dust jacket.

31. Ibid., pp. 230–3.

32. Cruickshank, *SOE in the Far East*, p. 249.

33. The reason for this is not obvious, however it could be because Burma received independence much sooner than Malaya.

34. For example, the man in charge of levies in Burma was Henry Noel Cochrane Stevenson, not 'Stephenson'. Mount Stephen Cumming, not 'Cummins' and W.D. Reeve, not 'L.D. Reeve' or 'W.D.R. Eve' were Oriental Mission officers. There was no such thing as North Karen Levies that spoke Chingpaw, they were North Kachin Levies (Chingpaw is a Kachin language), and Captain Arthur Thompson led Karens, not Kachins.

35. Cruickshank, *SOE in the Far East*, p. 69; Ogden, *Tigers Burning Bright*, p. 89; and Slim, *Defeat into Victory*, p. 73.

36. Gough, *SOE Singapore*, p. 203.

37. Cruickshank, *SOE in the Far East*, p. 69.

38. For existing work on the infrastructure of SOE in the Far East, see Cruickshank, *SOE in the Far East*, pp. 11–46.

39. SOE's founding charter is reproduced in West, *Secret War*, pp. 20–1.

40. Cruickshank, *SOE in the Far East*, see conclusion pp. 249–58. For Japanese documents on Burmese Independence and inclusion in the Co-Prosperity

Sphere, see Frank Trager, *Burma: Japanese Military Administration, Selected Documents 1941–45*, translated by Won Zoon Yoon (Philadelphia: University of Pennsylvania Press, 1971), pp. 145–64.

41. Cruickshank, *SOE in the Far East*, p. 251.
42. The OSS was the American equivalent of the British Secret Intelligence Service (SIS) and SOE combined. It later became the CIA.
43. TNA, CAB 101/198, 'Clandestine Organizations in SEAC', undated, p. 5.
44. See Chapter Six, Operation *Billet*.
45. Cruickshank, *SOE in the Far East*, p. 251.
46. Colin Gray, *Modern Strategy* (Oxford: Oxford University Press, 1999), pp. 286–90.
47. Slim, *Defeat into Victory*, p. 546.
48. Lyman, *Slim, Master of War*, p. 212. The first Chindit operation was codenamed *Longcloth*, and was launched in February 1943.
49. Ibid, p. 177.
50. TNA, HS 1/194, *Short Report SOE India Mission*, 13 November 1945.
51. Gray, *Modern Strategy*, p. 290. He does not explain why.
52. Raymond Callahan, *Burma 1942–1945* (London: Davis-Poynter, 1978).
53. See, for example, Christopher Sykes, *Orde Wingate* (London: Collins, 1959); David Rooney, *Wingate and the Chindits: Redressing the Balance* (London: Cassell, 1994); Lyman, *Slim: Master of War*, pp. 177–87 & pp. 210–15; Tony Redding, *War in the Wilderness: The Chindits in Burma 1943–1944* (Stroud: Spellmount, 2011).
54. Cruickshank, *SOE in the Far East*, p. 258.
55. Ibid, p. 252.
56. Slim, *Defeat into Victory*, p. 499.
57. Ian Dear, *Sabotage and Subversion: The SOE and OSS at War* (London: Cassell, 2002), Chapter Sixteen, pp. 197–208; Allen, *Burma: The Longest War*, p. 473.
58. Lyman, *Slim, Master of War*, p. 247. See also p. 253 for more comment on the monsoon; Allen, *Burma: The Longest War*, p. 478 and p. 579. Andrew Selth argued that manpower and a shortage of transport aircraft meant '[s]hould Slim be unable to reach the Burmese capital before the wet season began the British would have to face the prospect of falling back to the nearest reliable supply point, which was on the Indian border.' Andrew Selth, 'Race and Resistance in Burma, 1942–1945, *Modern Asian Studies*, 20, 3 (1986), p. 503. Presumably this would only have been necessary if both the landward and seaborne attempts on Rangoon had failed.
59. Allen, *Burma: The Longest War*, p. 481.
60. See, for example, Latimer, *Burma: The Forgotten War*, pp. 409–10.
61. Neville Wylie, 'Ungentlemanly Warriors or Unreliable Diplomats? Special Operations Executive and 'Irregular Political Activities in Europe', *Intelligence and National Security*, 20, 1 (2005), pp. 98–117.
62. Roderick Bailey, *The Wildest Province: SOE in the Land of the Eagle* (London: Jonathan Cape, 2008), see especially Chapter Nine, pp. 252–84.

63. Advancing with the BIA in 1942, an Indian headman was accused of working with the British to organise resistance. Aung San carried out the execution. See Maurice Collis, *Last and First in Burma* (London: Faber & Faber, 1956), p. 273.

64. One of the chief critics of SOE at the time was Brigadier Prescott, Deputy Chief Civil Affairs Officer, and former Burma Policeman. Postwar, Professor Hugh Tinker, who had served as a regular officer in the Burma campaign, published *The Union of Burma* (Oxford: Oxford University Press, 1959) which is particularly critical of SOE and Mountbatten, see pp. 12–16.

65. F.S.V Donnison, *British Military Administration in the Far East* (London: HMSO, 1956), pp. 347–9.

66. Tinker, *The Union of Burma*, p. 12.

67. Ibid, p. 16.

68. Bickham Sweet-Escott and Hugh Tinker, *International Affairs*, 48, 3 (July 1972), pp. 552–5.

69. See Bickham Sweet-Escott, *Baker Street Irregular* (London: Methuen, 1965).

70. On p. 484 and p. 516 of *Defeat into Victory*, Slim outlined how the Burma National Army was brought on side in 1945. Presumably these are the pages that Sweet-Escott referred Tinker to.

71. Kirby, *The War Against Japan*, Vol. 4, pp. 250–1.

72. Hugh Tinker, *Burma, The Struggle for Independence 1944–1948* (London: HMSO, 1983). Volume 1 covers 1944–6, and Volume 2 1946–8. These two volumes are a collection of documents from the National Archives and the British Library.

73. See, for example, Frank Trager, 'Review', *The Journal of Asian Studies*, 44, 1 (Nov. 1984), pp. 251–2. For criticism of omissions and abridging, see Josef Silverstein, 'The Other Side of Burma's Struggle for Independence', *Pacific Affairs*, 58, 1 (Spring 1985), pp. 98–108.

74. See the epilogue. Briefly, even before the publication of Tinker's work in 1983, veterans were concerned that the historical record would be distorted and were motivated to consider blocking publication.

75. Cruickshank, *SOE in the Far East*, p. 177. Richard Aldrich, *Intelligence and the War against Japan: Britain, America, and the politics of Secret Service* (Cambridge University Press, 2000), p. 3.

76. Ibid, p. 180.

77. Allen, *Burma, The Longest War*, p. 581.

78. Ibid, p. 575.

79. Allen only specifies the Karens, although Burma section did work with other ethnic groups, such as the Kachins.

80. British Library (hereafter BL), H.N.C. Stevenson, *The Hill People of Burma*, Burma Pamphlet No. 6 (London: Longman's Green & Co. Ltd, 1944), p. 3.

81. For critiques of Official Histories, see, for example, Martin Blumenson, 'Can Official History be Honest History', in *Military Affairs* 26, 4 (Winter 1962–3), pp. 153–61; Basil Liddell-Hart, 'Responsibility and Judgement in History Writing', *Military Affairs*, 23, 1 (Spring 1959),

pp. 35–6, or Robin Higham, *The Writing of Official Military Histories* (Greenwood Press, 1999).

82. There had been a Captain Vivian in SOE, but his name was Hugh Godfrey Vivian, and he had been sent back to Nigeria on colonial service after the War's end.

83. TNA, FO 371/83139, translation from *Izvestiya*, 18 August 1950.

84. BL, IOR L/PS/12/1378, 'Activities of Lieutenant Colonel J.C. Tulloch Against the Burma Government'. For more on this controversy, see Richard Aldrich, 'Legacies of Secret Service: Renegade SOE & the Karen Struggle in Burma 1948 – 1950', *Intelligence and National Security*, 14, 4 (1999), pp. 130–48.

85. Transcript of comments from the BBC *Timewatch*, 'Forgotten Allies', aired 7 March 1997. Amongst those quoted are two former SOE officers, Major Alex Campbell and Lieutenant Colonel Ronald Kaulback, as well as Professor Richard Aldrich.

86. See, for example, Andrew Selth, 'Race and Resistance in Burma', p. 505, for comment on the nationalist myth.

87. Maung Maung Pye, *Burma in the Crucible* (Rangoon: Khittaya, 1951), pp. 83–5.

88. U Maung Maung, *Burmese Nationalist Movements* (Edinburgh: Kiscadale, 1989).

89. Ibid, p. 128.

90. Ibid, p. 145.

91. Ibid, p. 93.

92. Maurice Collis, *Last and First in Burma, 1941–1948* (London: Faber, 1956), p. 231.

93. Thakin Nu had remained in Burma throughout the Japanese occupation, holding office under the collaborationist Prime Minister Ba Maw during the War. After Aung San's assassination, Nu became leader of independent Burma.

94. Thakin Nu, *Burma Under the Japanese* (London: Macmillan, 1954), p. 103.

95. This idea of a measure of Japanese culpability for causing inter-racial conflict is picked up by Andrew Selth, 'Race and Resistance in Burma', p. 498.

96. Quoted in Aldrich, *Intelligence and the War Against Japan*, p. 336.

Prologue   Burma, its Geography and its People

1. Thant Myint-U, *The River of Lost Footsteps* (London: Faber & Faber, 2008), p. 42.

2. Julian Thompson, *Forgotten Voices of the Burma Campaign* (St Ives: Ebury Press, 2009), p. vii.

3. The bridge was denied to the enemy at the cost of the British 17 Division, which had two brigades on the wrong side of the river when it was blown.

4. A census was completed in 1941, but in the chaos of retreat in 1942, the data was lost. For a detailed study of the demography of Burma, see Judith Richell, *Disease and Demography in Colonial Burma* (Singapore: NUS Press, 2006).

5. British Library (hereafter BL), H.N.C. Stevenson, *The Hill People of Burma*, Burma Pamphlet No. 6 (London: Longman's Green & Co. Ltd, 1944), p. 3.

6. H.N.C. Stevenson, *The Hill Peoples of Burma: Burma Pamphlets No. 6* (London: Longman's Green & Co. Ltd, 1944), p. 3.

7. Mary Callahan, *Making Enemies: War and State Building in Burma* (Cornell University Press, 2003).

8. Ian Morrison, *Grandfather Longlegs* (London: Faber, 1947), pp. 26–7.

9. Ibid, pp. 186–9.

10. Accounts vary as to whether Aung San killed the Indian headman with a bayonet or unsuccessfully attempted to do so with his sword. See Maurice Collis, *Last and First in Burma* (London: Faber, 1956), p. 273, and John McEnery, *Epilogue in Burma* (Tunbridge Wells: Spellmount, 1990), p. 16 and p. 48.

Chapter 1   The Oriental Mission, October 1940–December 1941

1. The National Archives, hereafter TNA, HS 1/340, Aide Memoir to Sir Gladwyn Jebb, 5 February 1941. Jebb was 'seconded soon after the Second World War broke out to assist Hugh Dalton, who now headed the newly created Ministry of Economic Warfare. There, Jebb's real function as a leading force in Special Operations Executive was disguised under the title of Foreign Policy Adviser.' See http://www.independent.co.uk/news/people/obituaries-lord-gladwyn-1360227.html.

2. MI5 were asked to trace Killery on 10 May 1940 to ascertain his reliability. He was approached to work for SOE on 5 December 1940. Killery had extensive knowledge of the Far East, having been Vice Chairman of Imperial Chemical Industries (ICI) in China from 1923. See Killery's personnel file, TNA, HS 9/839/5.

3. Charles Cruickshank, *SOE in the Far East* (Oxford: Oxford University Press, 1986), p. 61.

4. Ibid, p. 82.

5. Ibid, p. 6.

6. Nigel West, *Secret War: The Story of SOE, Britain's Wartime Sabotage Organisation* (London: Hodder & Stoughton, 1992), p. 176.

7. Calder Walton, *Empire of Secrets: British Intelligence, the Cold War and the Twilight of Empire* (London: Harper, 2013), p. 58.

8. Both Johns ended up joining SOE, and served in Burma. Beamish made three operational parachute jumps. Both wrote an account of their experiences, namely: John Beamish, *Burma Drop* (London: Bestseller Library, 1960); and John Hedley, *Jungle Fighter* (Brighton: Tom Donovan, 1996).

9. TNA, HS 1/207, 'History of the Oriental Mission', p. 44.

10. For the estimate of 29 divisions, see a British appraisal dated 6 May 1941, TNA, HS 1/340, 'Far Eastern Notes'.
11. Burif units were primarily drawn from the Karen, Kachin and Chin peoples.
12. According to Julian Thompson, the British considered the border 'impassable by any invader.' Julian Thompson, *Forgotten Voices of Burma* (London: Ebury Press, 2009), p. vii.
13. Cruickshank, *SOE in the Far East*, pp. 4–5.
14. TNA, CAB 102/653, William Mackenzie, 'Additional Volume on Far East and Australia'. The European volume was published in 2000, but this Far East volume remains unpublished.
15. Cruickshank, *SOE in the Far East*, see the conclusion, pp. 249–58.
16. TNA, HS 1/340, 'Far Eastern Mission', 6 April 1941, pp. 1–2.
17. Para-naval operations consisted of raiding parties delivered by boat along the western seaboard of Burma.
18. TNA, HS 1/340, from AD/Z (Lieutenant Colonel F.T. Davies, one of two deputies to Sir Frank Nelson, the first head of SOE) to 'The CEO' (Gladwyn Jebb), 8 April 1941.
19. 'Aux Units' was the intentionally non-descript name given to the parties of specially trained soldiers who were to operate upon German lines of communication should the Nazis have invaded Britain in 1940.
20. Brian P. Farrell, 'High Command, Irregular Forces, and Defending Malaya, 1941–1942', *Global War Studies*, 8, 2 (2011), pp. 53–4. The same policy of non-provocation had been followed regarding Italy, but had been even more strictly enforced than in the Far East, see Bailey, *Target: Italy*, pp. 22–3.
21. TNA, HS 1/340, Mr Sterndale Bennett to Mr Addis (John Mansfield Addis, at this time Private Secretary to the Permanent Under-Secretary of State, Alexander Cadogan) 13 February 1941.
22. TNA, HS 1/340, note dated 14 February 1941.
23. TNA, HS 1/202 and HS 1/340, War Office to C-in-C Far East, 24 January 1941. Similar telegrams were sent by the Foreign Office to their officials in the Far East, for example, the British consul in Chungking, Sir Archibald Clark Kerr, was sent notification of SOE on 7 January 1941.
24. TNA, HS 1/202, Aide Memoir for Mr Jebb, 5 February 1941.
25. TNA, HS 1/207, 'Responsibility for and Liaison with the Killery Mission', Appendix B, 'Para Military Requirements', 7 May 1941.
26. Many of the documents only refer to individuals by their codename. A.E. Jones was 0.101, and Nixon was D/HX.
27. TNA, HS 9/1105/7, personnel file of Major Francis Nixon.
28. See TNA, HS 1/202 for Nixon's 'Report on the F.E. Mission', 18 April 1942.
29. TNA, HS 1/202, War Office to the C-in-C Far East, 24 January 1941. Interestingly, Cruickshank references WO 193/605 where General Dewing urged the War Office on November 19 1940 to start 'what used to be called MI R activities' in the Far East. This obviously raises a question as to when

Brooke-Popham really found out about SOE; Charles Cruickshank, *SOE in the Far East*, p. 4.

30. TNA, HS 1/340, War Office to C-in-C Far East, 24 January 1941.
31. TNA, HS 1/340, War Office to C-in-C, 21 March 1941.
32. TNA, HS 1/338. Killery met Dorman-Smith and Sir David Monteath (Permanent Under-Secretary of State for Burma and India, 1941–1948) on 25 February 1941.
33. Richard Gough, *SOE Singapore* (London: William Kimber, 1985), p. 28.
34. TNA, HS 1/110, details expenses, such as the $46.60 it cost to get Killery to Singapore. Interestingly, there is no mention of the Cathay Building which is where most other sources locate SOE HQ. The Union Building was on the waterfront at Collyer Quay. Today it is the Fullerton Hotel.
35. TNA, HS 1/338, Major General Dewing, 12 and 27 February 1941.
36. TNA, HS 1/202, 'Report on FEM', Major Nixon, 18 April 1942.
37. He is variously described as being 1) a member of MI(R) (one of the organisations that had amalgamated to form SOE but which continued to exist after July 1940); 2) 'formerly with MI R', 3) '101 STS liaison officer' and 4) 'responsible as GSO (1) for all below the belt operations in the Far East.' TNA, HS 1/202, cipher of 28 January 1941; Cruickshank, *SOE in the Far East*, p. 61; Trenowden, *Operations Most Secret*, p. 78; Gough, *SOE Singapore*, p. 18.
38. Cruickshank, *SOE in the Far East*, p. 61.
39. Gough, *SOE Singapore*, p. 18.
40. London objected to Killery changing the name of the mission. See TNA, HS 7/222, 7–9 November, 1941, p. 1925.
41. TNA, HS 1/340, 'Memorandum: O.M. Organisation in the Far East', to C-in-C Far East from Killery, October 1941, and HS 1/227, report of K/L 6 (Major O'Dwyer) to CD (head of SOE, London) appendix D.
42. TNA, HS 1/207, Killery's final report of 31 July 1942.
43. TNA, HS 1/226, 'Notes on meeting with HE and GOC', 24 October 1941.
44. Cruickshank, *SOE in the Far East*, p. 61. Cruickshank did not supply a date for Percival's discovery, but Percival wrote a memorandum to Killery on 3 October stating his opposition to Special Operations. See TNA HS 1/226.
45. TNA, HS 1/226, 'Notes on Meeting with H.E. and GOC', 24 October 1941.
46. TNA, HS 1/226, memorandum from Percival to Killery, 11 November 1941.
47. TNA, HS 1/226, memorandum from Egerton Mott to Percival, 20 November 1941. Major Egerton Mott went on to become FEM's head in Burma until February 1942 when he was switched to Sumatra. From March 1944 until the end of the War he was head of the Far East section of SOE in London, with the code symbol B/B. See personnel file, TNA, HS 9/1069/6.
48. TNA, HS 1/226, reply from Percival to Egerton Mott, 22 November 1941.
49. TNA, HS 9/464/1, personnel file of Major A.B. O'Dwyer. O'Dwyer was appointed Overseas Liaison Officer on 20 August 1941.
50. TNA, HS 1/202, to Killery from O'Dwyer, 20 November 1941.

51. Becca Kenneison, *The Special Operations Executive in Malaya: Impact and Repercussions, 1941–48*, unpublished PhD Thesis, submitted to University of Essex, September 2016.

52. Gough, *SOE Singapore*, p. 20.

53. For documentation of the row between Sir Josiah Crosby, ambassador to Siam, and Killery, see HS 1/340, or Appendix B and C of O'Dwyer's report, TNA, HS 1/227.

54. TNA, HS 1/202, 'Report on FEM', Major Nixon, 18 April 1942.

55. TNA, HS 1/227, O'Dwyer report, 17 December, 1941.

56. TNA, HS 1/202, O'Dwyer report, 17 December, 1941, and HS 1/207, 'History of SOE O.M.', p. 4.

57. Ban Hah Choon, *Absent History: The Untold Story of Special Branch Operations in Singapore, 1942–1945* (Singapore: Raffles, 2001).

58. TNA, HS 1/226, Killery report, August 1942.

59. A Far East Command was created in November 1940.

60. TNA, WO 106/2646, Linlithgow to Amery, 27 August 1940.

61. TNA, WO 106/2646 'Appointment of C-in-C FE in Relation to the Constitution of Burma', 8 November 1940.

62. Sir Robert Brooke-Popham, Supplement to the London Gazette, 'Operations in the Far East', 22 January 1948, p. 535. http://www.ibiblio.org/hyperwar/UN/UK/LondonGazette/38183.pdf.

63. TNA, WO 106/2646 'Appointment of C-in-C FE in Relation to the Constitution of Burma', 8 November 1940.

64. TNA, WO 106/2630, Provisional War Establishment for Burma Rifles, October 1941. See Kirby, *The War Against Japan*, Vol. 2, p. 11, for Malaya's precedence.

65. The British Library, IOR, M/8/42, Amery to Dorman-Smith, 4 April 1942.

66. TNA, HS 1/207, 'History of SOE OM', p. 4.

67. Ibid, pp. 45–6.

68. TNA, HS 1/27, Killery report, 31 July 1942.

69. TNA, HS 1/207, 'History of SOE OM', p. 46.

70. Ibid, p. 47.

71. TNA, HS 7/225, War Diary, 12–14 January 1942.

72. Angelene Naw, *Aung San and the Struggle for Burmese Independence* (Copenhagen: NIAS, 2001), p. 73.

73. Ibid, p. 66.

74. Kirby, *The War Against Japan*, Vol. 2, p. 10 & pp. 16–18.

75. Maurice Collis, *Last and First in Burma* (London: Faber, 1956), pp. 27–8.

76. TNA, HS 1/27, Major Lindsay to Colin Mackenzie, 7 December 1942.

77. Cruikshank, *SOE in the Far East*, pp. 68–9.

78. TNA, HS 1/111, Oriental Mission Casualties.

79. TNA, HS 1/27, Lindsay to Killery, 24 March 1942.

80. TNA, HS 1/27, note by Major Egerton Mott, unknown month, 1942.

81. On the one hand the records indicate that Burma was divided into these three zones, and on the other that the GOC, General McLeod, 'had restricted O.M. activities to Tenasserim', i.e. the Southern zone. TNA, HS 1/27, Major Lindsay to Colin Mackenzie, 7 December 1942.

82. TNA, HS 1/227, O'Dwyer report, 17 December 1941.

83. TNA, HS 1/27, W.D. Reeve to Colin Mackenzie, 14 December 1942.

84. TNA, HS 1/222, War Diary entry 28–30 November 1941.

85. Collis, *Last and First in Burma*, p. 60.

86. See James Lunt, *Hell of a Licking: The Retreat from Burma* (London: Collins, 1986), especially pp. 38–49. The two British Battalions were the Gloucester's and the King's Own Yorkshire Light Infantry (KOYLI).

87. Lunt, *Hell of a Licking*, p. 62.

88. See. for example, Farrell, 'High Command, Irregular Forces, and Defending Malaya, 1941–1942', pp. 32–65. Freddie Spencer Chapman was an instructor at STS 101, and leader of a left-behind party that went into the Malayan jungle in January 1942. He wrote about his experiences in *The Jungle is Neutral* (London: Chatto & Windus, 1949).

89. Immediately after the War started, the civil authorities in Malaya finally allowed locals to be trained, including Communist Chinese.

90. TNA, HS9/1069/6, personnel file for Egerton Mott.

91. Saul Kelly, 'A Succession of Crises: SOE in the Middle East', *Intelligence & National Security*, SOE special edition 2005, pp. 121–146.

92. TNA, HS9/1069/6, 'MEMORANDUM', Major Egerton Mott, 27 June 1943, p. 2.

93. The only other territory where there was limited fulfilment of the charter was in Hong Kong, under Governors Sir Geoffry Northcote, and from September 1941, Sir Mark Young. Plans for left-behind parties had been initiated in 1939, and the personnel trained at STS 101 in 1941. See Cruickshank, *SOE in the Far East*, pp. 75–6.

Chapter 2   The Oriental Mission and the First Burma Campaign, December 1941–June 1942

1. From Victoria Point, today called Kawthaung, to Imphal in Manipur, India, is approximately 1067 miles.

2. Cruickshank, *SOE in the Far East* (Oxford: Oxford University Press, 1986), p. 69.

3. Field Marshal Slim, *Defeat into Victory* (London: Pan, 1999), p. 73.

4. Cruickshank, *SOE in the Far East*, p. 69. Fort Hertz is in the very north of Burma, near the town of Putao.

5. For more in-depth accounts of the first Burma Campaign, see, for example, Slim, *Defeat into Victory*, pp. 3–121; Louis Allen, Burma: *The Longest War*

(London: Phoenix, 1998), pp. 1–90; James Lunt, *Hell of a Licking* (London: Collins, 1986).

6. TNA, WO 106/2675, The First Burma Campaign, 8 December 1941 to 30 May 1942.
7. Allen, *Burma: The Longest War*, p. 43.
8. Slim, *Defeat into Victory*, p. 14.
9. TNA, WO 106/3695, 'Burma Policy', 7 January–26 March 1942.
10. TNA, HS 1/207, 'History of SOE OM', p. 47.
11. TNA, HS 7/223, War Diary, 16–17 December 1941.
12. TNA, HS 7/226, War Diary, 25–28 January and 29–31 January 1942.
13. Bickham Sweet-Escott, *Baker Street Irregular* (London: Methuen, 1965), pp. 74–5.
14. TNA, HS 7/226, War Diary, 15–17 January 1942.
15. TNA, HS 7/227, War Diary, 12–15 February 1942.
16. TNA, HS 7/228, War Diary 23–25 February 1942.
17. TNA, HS 7/226, War Diary 25–28 January 1942.
18. TNA, HS 7/229, War Diary for March 1942.
19. British Library (hereafter BL), IOR, Neg/15495.
20. BL, ibid, Wavell to Chiefs of the Imperial General Staff (CIGS), 9 April 1942.
21. TNA, HS 7/229, War Diary for March 1942. The file refers to 'London' throughout, presumably meaning SOE headquarters.
22. TNA, HS 1/27, Lindsay to Killery, 24 March 1942, p. 3.
23. TNA, HS 1/340, 'Progress Report', cipher telegram from Maymyo, 3 February 1942.
24. For personnel file of Major Seagrim, see HS 9/1334/7. For the story of Major Seagrim, see Ian Morrison, *Grandfather Longlegs* (London: Faber, 1945).
25. TNA, HS 9/490/4, personnel file of William Edward Evans.
26. TNA, HS 7/226, War Diary, 29–31 January 1942.
27. Ibid, 29–31 January 1942.
28. TNA, HS 1/27, 'Burma Country Section', W.D. Reeve to Colin Mackenzie, 14 December 1942, p. 4.
29. Tun Hla Oung was born in 1902. He attended the Military Academy, Sandhurst, from October 1920 to April 1921. He was described as being 'A very promising Burman officer. Popular. Respected by his men.' In April 1927 he resigned from his commission to join the Burma police. He remained in Burma throughout the Japanese occupation, though apparently he remained loyal to the British. See BL, IOR L/MIL/7/19168; IOR L/MIL/14/72633; IOR M/4/2032.
30. TNA, HS 1/27, 'Burma Country Section', W.D. Reeve to Colin Mackenzie, 14 December 1942, p. 4.
31. TNA, HS 1/27, further report of Major Peter Lindsay, 8 May 1943.
32. Fredrick Fleming Wemyss was born 7 December 1897 in Burma. He served in the Great War 1914–19 before joining the Burma police. See TNA, HS 9/1576/4, personnel file of Major Fredrick Wemyss.

33. TNA, HS 1/27, 'Burma Country Section', Reeve to Mackenzie, 14 December 1942, p. 5.
34. TNA, HS 1/27, Lindsay to Mackenzie, 14 December 1942.
35. Allen, *Burma: The Longest War*, p. 21.
36. TNA, HS 1/27, Lindsay to Killery, 24 March 1942, p. 2. Christopher Bayley and Tim Harper, *Forgotten Armies: Britain's Asian Empire and the War With Japan* (London: Penguin, 2004), pp. 163–4.
37. Bayley and Harper, *Forgotten Armies*, p. 164.
38. Donnison papers, quoted in Bayley and Harper, *Forgotten Armies*, p. 164. Colonel Frank Donnison was a Burmese civil servant at this time, gaining his commission later in the War. After the War he wrote *British Military Administration in the Far East* (HMSO, 1956).
39. TNA, HS 1/27, 'Burma Country Section', Reeve to Mackenzie, 14 December 1942, p. 2.
40. For accusations against the Burifs, see, for example, Major General S Woodburn Kirby, *The War Against Japan, vol. 2, India's Most Dangerous Hour* (Uckfield: Naval and Military Press, 2004) p. 31, and Lunt, *Hell of a Licking*, p. 100 & p. 259. Typically, however, 8th Burif is praised, but this unit was not Burmese, consisting of Sikhs and Punjabis.
41. BL, IOR L/MIL/17/7/49, Sir Reginald Dorman-Smith, 'Report on the Burma Campaign 1941–42', September 1943, p. 95.
42. Stanley Short, *On Burma's Eastern Frontier* (London: Marshall, Morgan & Scott, 1945), p. 137.
43. TNA, HS 1/27, 'O.M. – Burma', p. 27.
44. TNA, HS 1/27, Lindsay to Mackenzie, 14 December 1942, p. 28.
45. TNA, HS 1/27, Lindsay to Mackenzie, 7 December 1942, pp. 5–6.
46. TNA, HS 9/1129/1, personnel file of Alfred Ottaway.
47. BL, IOR, L/MIL/17/7/11–13, Burma Army List 1941.
48. TNA, HS 1/27, Reeve to Mackenzie, 14 December 1941.
49. TNA, Ibid, 14 December 1942. This document specifically says that these plans made were despite the orders of the C-in-C, thereby contradicting the extended report which says the C-in-C allowed these operations in Tenasserim. No date is given for the meeting with Lieutenant Colonel Cotton.
50. TNA, HS 1/227, O'Dwyer to Sir Frank Nelson, 17 December 1941.
51. TNA, HS 1/27, Lindsay to Mackenzie, 14 December 1942, p. 23.
52. TNA, HS 1/27, ibid, p. 24.
53. Ian Morrison, *Grandfather Longlegs* (London: Faber, 1945).
54. BL, IOR, L/MIL/17/7/11–13, Burma Army List 1941, p. 43. In 1923, the 1 Kumaon Rifles became part of the 19 Hyderabad Regiment which is the regiment on Seagrim's citations for the George Cross.
55. Morrison, *Grandfather Longlegs*, pp. 36–9.
56. TNA, HS 9/1334/7, personnel file of Major Hugh Seagrim.
57. TNA, HS 1/27, Lindsay to Mackenzie, 7 December 1942.
58. TNA, HS 9/1334/7, personnel file of Major Hugh Seagrim.

59. TNA, HS 9/1334/7, 'Major H.P. Seagrim, DSO, MBE', by Major Eric Battersby, 3 January 1946.

60. TNA, HS 1/27, Lindsay to Mackenzie, 7 December 1942, p. 7.

61. Richard Aldrich, 'Legacies of Secret Service: Renegade SOE and the Karen Struggle 1948–50', *Journal of Intelligence and National Security*, 14, 4 (1999), p. 136.

62. TNA, HS 1/27, Lindsay to Mackenzie, 14 December 1942, p. 8.

63. TNA, HS 9/1334/7, personnel file of Major Seagrim, quoted by Saw Kan Nyun.

64. TNA, HS 9/1460/6, personnel file for Arthur Leonard Bell Thompson.

65. TNA, HS 1/27 report of Captain H.C. Smith.

66. Brigadier A.C. Curtis, his surname is misspelt 'CURTISS' in Boyt's report. Curtis was in command of 13 Indian Brigade. 13 Brigade formed part of Bruce Scott's 1 Burdiv from July 1941. See S. Woodburn Kirby, *The War Against Japan*, vol. 2, Naval and Military Press, Uckfield, 2004, p. 12.

67. Morrison, *Grandfather Longlegs*, p. 55.

68. TNA, HS 1/27, 'Capt. N.E. Boyt's Diary of Oriental Mission work in Burma 1942', 2 March 1943, p. 1.

69. TNA, HS 1/27, ibid, p. 2.

70. Kirby, *The War Against Japan*, vol. 2, p. 149.

71. TNA, HS 1/27, Lindsay to Mackenzie, 7 December 1942.

72. Kirby, *The War Against Japan*, vol. 2, p. 214.

73. Ibid, p. 157.

74. Slim, *Defeat into Victory*, p. 47.

75. Captain Boyt explained in his report that the two Chinese armies were separated by 112 km (70 miles) of road, with only the Oriental Mission and the Burifs in between. TNA, HS 1/27, Report of Captain Boyt, p. 2.

76. TNA, HS 1/27, 'Diary of Captain Thompson & Report on Movements of Karen Company from Toungoo – Mong Pawn', approximate date November 1942. Also available in TNA, WO 203/5712. Thompson was serving with the 1st Battalion, 20 Burma Rifles (1/20 Burifs). The battalion was part of General Bruce Scott's 1 Burma Division which had arrived in Toungoo on about 22 March 1942.

77. Paletwa is a town in Chin State, western Burma, however, there is a Paletwa Bridge on the Toungoo to Mawchi Road. It crosses the Thaukyaygyat River.

78. TNA, HS 1/27 reports of Captains Boyt, p. 2 and Thompson, p. 3.

79. Kan Choke was born in 1899, and was a career soldier. By 1942 he had served over 20 years and his rank of Subedar Major was the most senior rank achievable short of becoming an honorary Second Lieutenant on an equivalent basis with British officers. See TNA, HS 1/28 and HS 1/31.

80. TNA, HS 1/27, report of Captain Thompson, p. 3.

81. Thompson wrote novels after the War using the pseudonym Francis Clifford. In *A Battle is Fought to be Won* (London: Coronet, 1973), pp. 77–8, he wrote about how two Karens were returned to the main character by the Japanese

with their mouths sewn shut after their penises had been stuffed inside. Regardless of the status of this image, the novel certainly reflects reality to some degree, with Thompson and Kan Choke recognisable as the two main characters.

82. TNA, HS 1/27, Diary of Captain Thompson, p. 3.

83. Clifford, A Battle is Fought to be Won, p. 87. The 'he' is the main character Tony Gilling.

84. TNA, HS 1/27, report of Captain Boyt, p. 3.

85. TNA, HS 1/27, report of Captain Thompson, p. 5.

86. Francis Clifford, Desperate Journey (London: Corgi, 1981).

87. Ibid, p. 9. The citation is also in Thompson's personnel file, TNA, HS 9/1460/6.

88. Slim, Defeat into Victory, p. 73. Slim is perhaps a little unkind here. There was a row about the extent to which Oriental Mission should demolish the wolfram mines at Mawchi. Limited demolitions were decided upon because the Japanese had enough wolfram from other sources. TNA, HS 1/27, Lindsay to Mackenzie, 14 December 1942, p. 25.

89. Gough, SOE Singapore, p. 203.

90. Ibid, p. 202. Gough's source was probably Slim, Defeat into Victory, p. 73. A battalion is the estimate given in Thompson's recommendation for a DSO.

91. TNA, HS 1/27, Lindsay to Mackenzie, 14 December 1942.

92. Citations are, of course, written to try and secure that the person concerned gets decorated.

93. The rather unusual word 'stuffing' is frequently used in the Oriental Mission reports to describe the stiffening of levy units with trained troops and officers; TNA, HS 1/27, Lindsay to Mackenzie, 7 December 1942, p. 14.

94. Cruickshank, SOE in the Far East, p. 69.

95. Kirby, The War Against Japan, Vol. 2, p. 204, and Slim, Defeat into Victory, p. 78.

96. TNA, HS 1/27, Lindsay to Mackenzie, 14 December 1942, 'Sweli Bridge', p. 32.

97. Ibid, p. 39, extract from Lieutenant Tindley's letter of 22 November 1942.

98. See TNA HS 1/27. On 7 December 1941, Lindsay reported favourably of Stevenson to Mackenzie, while noting that he had had a 'bust up' with Generals Bruce Scott and Jackie Smyth. By September 1942, when Killery and Stevenson wrote their reports, both men were highly critical of the other.

99. TNA, HS 1/27, report of Lieutenant Colonel Stevenson, 21 September 1942.

100. TNA, HS1/27, Mackenzie to Far East section, London, 28 September 1942. Jack Barnard, one of the officers who carried out the demolitions, disagreed with Lindsay and Mackenzie, recounting Stevenson as 'a man whose soldierly bearing commanded instant respect . . . a leader of men', see Jack Barnard, The Hump (London: Four Square, 1966), p. 24.

101. Kirby, The War Against Japan, Vol. 2, pp. 206–20.

102. Cruickshank, SOE in the Far East, p. 69.

103. It was from this area that the first Office of Strategic Services (OSS, America's SOE equivalent) missions were launched.
104. Clifford, *Desperate Journey*, p. 185.
105. TNA, HS 1/27, Lindsay to Mackenzie, 14 December 1942, pp. 33–5.
106. Kirby, *War Against Japan*, pp. 177–80.
107. Ibid, Chapters Nine & Ten, pp. 145–85; Slim, *Defeat into Victory*, Chapter Four, pp. 60–88.
108. Kirby, *The War Against Japan*, Vol. 2, p. 103.

Chapter 3   Reorganisation and Early Operations, August 1942–August 1943

1. *Quadrant* was the Allied Conference on strategy held at Quebec, Canada, from 14–24 August 1943.
2. See Raymond Callahan, *Burma 1942–45* (London: Davis-Poynter, 1978).
3. TNA, HS 7/111, 'Historical Narrative May 1942 – August 1945', p. 1.
4. Quoted in Callahan, *Burma 1942–45*, p. 43.
5. See TNA, HS 1/226 for a handwritten note by W.J. Keswick, commenting on a report about the Oriental Mission: It says 'This just [Handwriting unclear] is exactly what I expected. Official opposition was very great. The mission was a sad failure'.
6. Charles Cruickshank, *SOE in the Far East* (Oxford: Oxford University Press, 1986), pp. 249–51.
7. TNA, HS 1/200, notes for Mackenzie, 28 April 1942, p. 1. The letter is not signed but the origin of authorship can be identified as SOE HQ in London from the code symbol AD. AD was George Taylor, and his position was chief assistant to the head of SOE in the UK. See William Mackenzie, *The Secret History of SOE* (London: St Ermines Press, 2002), pp. 75–102.
8. TNA, HS 1/194. Many of the documents relating to the establishment of the India Mission are in this file.
9. J & P Coats was a large, international textiles company specialising in threads. For a history of the company, see http://archiveshub.ac.uk/features/02120302.html.
10. TNA, HS 1/194, Viceroy to Secretary of State for India, June 1941 and Sir David Monteath to Secretary of State, 7 June 1941.
11. Ian Trenowden, *Operations Most Secret* (Bodmin: Crecy Books Ltd, 1994), p. 16.
12. Bickham Sweet-Escott, *Baker Street Irregular* (London: Methuen, 1965), p. 228.
13. Gavin Stewart had worked for Stewart & Lloyds, the iron and steel firm. He was succeeded as second in command of the India Mission by Brigadier Guinness in December 1943. Stewart finished the War with the rank of Lieutenant Colonel, having originally kept civilian status, like Mackenzie.
14. HS 1/194, 'India Mission Objectives', 15 August 1941.

15. Cruikshank, *SOE in the Far East*, p. 83.
16. TNA, HS 1/200, 'Notes for Mackenzie', 28 April 1942, p. 1.
17. Richard Aldrich, *Intelligence and the War Against Japan* (Cambridge University Press, 2000), pp. 159–60.
18. TNA, HS 1/200, 'Notes for Mackenzie', 28 April 1942, p. 1.
19. TNA, HS 1/200, 'India Mission', from George Taylor to Mackenzie, 8 August 1942.
20. TNA, HS 1/200, 'Notes for Mackenzie', 28 April 1942, p. 1. See also Bickham Sweet-Escott, *Baker Street Irregular*, Chapter Three, pp. 70–99, and William Mackenzie, *The Secret History of SOE* (London: St Ermin's Press, 2002), Chapter Eight, pp. 169–90.
21. TNA, HS 1/200, Cipher telegram from George Taylor to Mackenzie, 9 March 1942, and 8 August 1942.
22. Ibid, 9 March 1942.
23. TNA, HS 9/527/4, personnel file for Richard Ellis Forrester.
24. TNA, HS 9/562/6, personnel file for Richie Gardiner.
25. A copy of 'Notes on the establishment and maintenance of SOE missions abroad' was sent to Mackenzie on 29 October 1942. It instructed him that SOE officers should not hold ostentatious parties and that mission leaders should encourage their staff to moan about their wages just like regular service personnel did. See TNA, HS 1/200.
26. Mackenzie, *The Secret History of SOE*, p. 170.
27. Bickham Sweet-Escott, *Baker Street Irregular*, pp. 74–5 specifically, but see also Chapter Three 'Muddle East', pp. 70–99.
28. Cruikshank, *SOE in the Far East*, p. 87.
29. TNA, HS 1/200, Taylor to Mackenzie, 9 March 1942.
30. TNA, HS 1/212, Colin Mackenzie, 'General Report, SOE Mission – India', August 1942.
31. TNA, HS 7/104, Richie Gardiner's Report, Chapter Three, 'Reformation In India June–Dec 1942', 30 December 1945, p. 1.
32. See TNA, HS 7/258–259 for the War Diary.
33. TNA, HS 7/104, Richie Gardiner's Report, Chapter Three, 'Reformation In India June–Dec 1942', 30 December 1945, p. 1. It is not only Asian personnel that are missing from SOE records: there is very little about rank and file soldiers of British/Caucasian origin.
34. Francis Clifford, *Desperate Journey* (London: Corgi, 1981), pp. 184–85. On pp. 17–18 of *Desperate Journey*, Thompson (Clifford was his pseudonym) introduced the Karen that were with him but at the end of the book he only names the two Karens in the main text above as flying out with him. See Chapter Two above (pp. 75–82) for Thompson's action on the retreat.
35. TNA, HS 1/29, Training Card and report for Ba Gyaw. The entry says 'sent to B.R.', but where 'B.R.' was is unknown. Training Cards and reports for Asian personnel are kept in alphabetical order from HS 1/29–HS 1/43.
36. TNA, WO 106/2677, 13 June 1942.

37. The Chindit idea was that 'formations of troops supplied from the air could operate for long periods in the jungle. The troops would be organised into columns, each large enough to inflict a heavy blow to the enemy but small enough to evade action if outnumbered.' See http://www.chindits.info/Longcloth/Main.htm.

38. Clifford, *Desperate Journey*, p. 15 and p. 185.

39. TNA, HS 7/115, 'SOE Training in India'. This report gives two different months for the opening of EWS(I).

40. All SOE facilities were designated a Military Establishment (ME) number. EWS(I) was also known as ME 141.

41. Cruickshank, *SOE in the Far East*, p. 16.

42. TNA, HS 1/9, Report by Lieutenant Colonel Richie Gardiner (BB 282) on experience in the jungle, September 1943.

43. Denis Rigden, *How to be a Spy: The WW2 SOE Training Manuel* (Bury St Edmunds: St Edmundsbury Press, 2004), p. 5.

44. TNA, HS 1/336, 'Report on Scapula Mission' by Major Jim Gavin (Officer Commanding STS 101), written in hospital in Cape Town, December 1942 'from rough notes and memory'. See also Richard Gough, *SOE Singapore* (London: William Kimber, 1985), pp. 224–7.

45. EWS(I)'s first commander was Major Arthur Ord. In Ord's personnel file, he was described as having been 'Commandant and Chief Instructor, Guerilla [sic] Training Unit'. However, unable to win the 'confidence or goodwill' of his instructors and students, Ord was replaced in January 1943 by Lieutenant Colonel Ingham-Clark. See personnel files for Ord, HS 9/1124/8, and Ingham-Clark, HS 9/319/7.

46. EWSC's first commander was Major Le Seeleur. Major Le Seeleur had escaped from Singapore with Major Gavin. He was one of the six SOE men who had been sent to Saugor after arriving in India in March 1942, before instructing at EWS (I). Le Seeleur was replaced by Col. Musgrave in November 1944.

47. It was also designated ME 99.

48. Cruickshank, *SOE in the Far East*, p. 17.

49. TNA, HS 7/104, Richie Gardiner's Report, Chapter Three, 'Reformation In India June–Dec 1942', 30 December 1945, p. 1.

50. TNA, HS 1/30, Training Card for Sunil Datta Gupta, alias Anil Ghosh. This agent had been arrested and detained by the Japanese until March 1945; see TNA, HS 7/104, Gardiner Report, Chapter Four, p. 2. On 13 October 1943, two more Indians were parachuted in as *Mahout II*. One agent was killed on infiltration, and the other, Sudhir Ghosh, was arrested within three days, however the Japanese released him on parole because his 'cover story [was] believed'. The cover story is not elaborated on here. See also HS 1/30.

51. TNA, HS 7/115, 'SOE Training in India', Section B, p. 10.

52. TNA, HS 1/197, Colin Mackenzie to Brigadier Guinness, 12 February 1944.

53. TNA, HS 7/115, 'SOE Training in India', Part A, p. 10.

54. TNA, HS 7/115, 'SOE Training in India, 1942–1945', Section B, p. 4.

55. TNA, HS 7/115, 'SOE Training in India', Section A, pp. 1–9.
56. Ibid, p. 3 and p. 6.
57. British Library (BL), IOR/L/Mil/17/7/49, Sir Reginald Dorman-Smith, 'Report on the Burma Campaign 1941–42', September 1943.
58. There are 113 languages in modern Burma/Myanmar.
59. TNA, HS 7/115, 'SOE Training in India', Section A, p. 3.
60. By multi-interpretational, it is meant that one word can have several meanings, which led to confusion during training. In some Chinese languages, for example, a slight difference in tone when spoken can give a word have a completely different meaning.
61. TNA, HS 7/115, 'SOE Training in India', Section A, p. 8.
62. Ibid, p. 11.
63. Ibid, pp. 3–4. 'Dragons' was the codename given to Communist Chinese by SOE.
64. Ibid, p. 3.
65. BL, IOR Neg 15495, communication to Brigadier R.C. McCoy, 27 June 1942.
66. Ashley Jackson, *The British Empire and the Second World War* (London: Continuum, 2006), p. 377.
67. TNA, HS 7/257, War Diary, July 1942, pp. 8–9.
68. BL, IOR Negative 15495. Troopers to Armindia, 18 June 1942. Reply, C-in-C India to War Office, 11 July 1942. These documents are only available on Microfilm as the file has been missing since 2006.
69. TNA, HS 7/115, 'SOE training in India', Section A, p. 9.
70. TNA, HS 7/115, 'SOE training in India', Section B, p. 3.
71. Ibid, p. 3.
72. Ibid.
73. Ibid. Lieutenant Colonel Bush had previously been chief instructor for paramilitary training for 'A Group' in the UK.
74. TNA, HS 7/114, 'Q' History, March 1942–April 1943, p. 32.
75. For comments on the importance of logistics to strategy, see Colin Gray, *Modern Strategy* (Oxford: OUP, 1999), pp. 31–3.
76. TNA, HS 7/287, 'Miscellaneous War Diary, May 1943–June 1944', June 1943, p. 176. Oddly, the rest of this 'miscellaneous War Diary' does not seem to exist for either the period before or after the dates on this file. The war diaries were compiled in London, collated from reports sent from the Far East.
77. TNA, HS 7/114, 'Q' History, May 1943–April 1944, p. 9. Penciled in on the page is the reason why – 'shortages in the UK, Middle East and the chronic shipping position.'
78. Compton Mackenzie, *Eastern Epic*, Vol. 1 (London: Chatto & Windus, 1951), p. 4.
79. TNA, HS 7/114, 'Q' History, May 1943–April 1944, pp. 4–9. See also a handwritten note in this file.

80. Statistics from Compton Mackenzie, *Eastern Epic*, Vol. 1 (London: Chatto & Windus, 1951), p. 1.
81. TNA, HS 7/257, War Diary, December 1942, p. 118.
82. TNA, HS 7/114, O/L (Mr R.R. de Liesching) to B/B 115 (J.L.Callie), 29 December 1942.
83. TNA, HS 7/257, War Diary, April 1943, p. 236.
84. TNA, HS 7/259, War Diary, July 1943, p. 304.
85. TNA, HS 1/227, 'Second Report on India by D/X', 22 January 1943. 'DX' was Nixon.
86. TNA, HS 7/114, 'Q' History, May 1943–April 1944, p. 12.
87. TNA, HS 9/1105/7, personnel file for Lieutenant Colonel Francis Nixon. Nixon served most of the War as section head for the Arab world and Turkey. Previous to this he had been with the Oriental Mission based in Singapore, see Chapter One.
88. TNA, HS 1/227, 'Manufacture and Supply in India', first report, 19 September 1942, p. 4.
89. TNA, HS, 7/116, 'The Tinning of Ammunition'. In April 1945, Major Press, Inspector General of stores for SOE, found that Neaves & Co. had continued to tin defective ammunition at Jubblepore, somewhere that tinning was taking place outside of the system. This report therefore concluded that Q administration was still unsatisfactory into 1945.
90. TNA, HS 7/259, War Diary, July 1943, pp. 303–4.
91. TNA, HS 1/227, 'Second Report on India by D/X' 22 January 1943, p. 3.
92. TNA, HS 7/114, from London to Mackenzie, 11 August 1943.
93. TNA, HS 7/114, 'Q History', May 1943–April 1944, p. 30.
94. Thomas Moon, *The Deadliest Colonel* (New York: Vantage Press, 1975).
95. See Callahan, *Burma 1942–1945*, pp. 41–2.
96. Richard Aldrich, *'Intelligence and the War Against Japan* (Cambridge University Press, 2000), p. 141.
97. Richard Dunlop, *Behind Japanese Lines* (New York: Rand McNally, 1979), pp. 107–8.
98. In *The OSS in Burma*, Sacquety wrote that the British were ambivalent towards an OSS presence in India. On the one hand, short of supplies to fight in Burma, accepting the OSS might lead to more American aid, and on the other, a fear of undermining British colonial power.
99. Winston Churchill, *The Second World War*, Vol. IV 'The Hinge of Fate' (London: The Reprint Society, 1953), p. 179.
100. The Atlantic charter was agreed in August 1941, when Roosevelt and Churchill first met each other on board HMS *The Prince of Wales*. Eight points were agreed, one of which was that liberated peoples had the right to self-determination after the War.
101. TNA, HS 7/257, War Diary, September 1942, p. 34.
102. Ibid.
103. It is recorded in the SOE Diary, TNA, HS 7/257, p. 61, that the Governor sent Major Richmond as advisor to Eifler. This is contrary to the US documents

consulted by Sacquety in *The OSS in Burma*, see p. 24 and endnotes pp. 240–1. Nazira was chosen because it was isolated, but near the Burma border, a US supply base and a railway.

104. TNA, HS 7/257, SOE War Diary, October 1942, p. 62. London replied that they had no intention of sacking Dorman-Smith.

105. William R. Peers and Dean Brelis, *Behind the Burma Road* (New York: Avon, 1963), p. 55.

106. A Group consisted of Captains Jack Barnard, Patrick Maddox and Oliver (Oscar) Milton, Lieutenants John Beamish, Pat Quinn and Dennis Francis, B.V Aganoor, and Saw Judson, a Karen Signaller from the Burma Navy. Personnel files for these men vary. Maddox's file has been declassified in both the UK (HS 9/974/2) and US. Barnard has no OSS record, but his UK file is HS 9/91/1. Barnard wrote about his retreat from Burma in *The Hump* (London: Four Square, 1966). Milton does not have a personnel file in either country. Quinn is declassified in the US, but not the UK. Beamish's file is available in the UK (HS 9/108/4) and he also produced a memoir, *Burma Drop* (London: Best seller Library, 1960), but has no OSS record.

107. Peers and Brelis, *Behind the Burma Road*, p. 77.

108. See Chapter Two for Ottaway's work with the Oriental Mission. Sacquety discussed B Group in his book, *The OSS in Burma*, but there is no mention of Ottaway and the named leader of B Group is Harry Ballard. A rather thin personnel file which provides no further clues is available for Ottaway, TNA, HS 9/1129/1.

109. TNA, HS 7/257, War Diary, November 1942, pp. 90–1.

110. The Kachin Levies had originally been formed in 1941 under H.N.C. Stevenson and the Oriental Mission, but their control had passed to the Army in July 1942 after the retreat from Burma.

111. Peers and Brelis, *Behind the Burma Road*, p. 84.

112. Ibid, p. 83.

113. TNA, HS 1/195, 'OSS Organisation in India', COS, 8 April 1943.

114. TNA, HS 1/195, India Office to Wavell, 14 May 1943, communicating the results of a meeting held the day before.

115. TNA, HS 1/195, 'US Intelligence Activities in India', extract from COS 22nd meeting, 21 May 1943.

116. Aldrich, *Intelligence and the War Against Japan*, p. 145.

117. TNA, HS 7/258, War Diary, August 1943, p. 382.

118. Callahan, *Burma 1942–1945*, p. 83.

119. TNA, HS 1/227, Report from inspection of the India Mission between 8 January 1944 and 20 April 1944.

120. TNA, 1/227, Captain Howe quoted in report from inspection of the India Mission between 8 January 1944 and 20 April 1944.

121. TNA, HS 7/104, Captain R.E. Forrester, 'Appreciation for SOE Operations in Burma', 26 August 1942. Appendix B of Lieutenant Colonel Gardiner's

Burma report. Gardiner had 17 years' experience in Burma as a Forest Manager for MacGregor & Co.

122. In late 1942, 300 Burmese candidates were canvassed, of which four were chosen, and subsequently 'discarded as unsuitable'. TNA, HS 1/200, Mackenzie to Keswick, 22 November 1942.

123. TNA, HS 7/104, 'Burma History', Lieutenant Colonel Gardiner's Report, Chapter Three, p. 2.

124. TNA, HS 1/194, 'Note on Functions and Operations of Indian Group', 14 July 1943.

125. TNA, HS 1/195, 'Directive for Burma Operations', B/B 100 (Mackenzie) to B/B 107 (Forrester), 8 December 1942. The directive is also reproduced in HS 7/104 as Appendix C to Gardiner's report.

126. See Chapter Two, pp. 73–5 above.

127. Until Mountbatten took command, military operations on both sides stopped for the monsoon, hence the use of the word 'season'. Mountbatten immediately changed this way of thinking, and instituted the doctrine of fighting all year.

128. The offensive in the Arakan in 1942–43 ended in failure at Donbaik, where the Japanese defences proved too formidable even for infantry with tank and air support to penetrate. Ramree Island was not captured until February 1945.

129. TNA, HS 1/195, 'Statement of SOE Case on Examination of the proposals for Coordination of British and American Intelligence Organisations in India', 10 June 1943.

130. TNA, HS 7/104, Gardiner Report, Chapter Four, p. 9.

131. Ibid.

132. TNA, HS 1/44, Operations Diary, Operation *Dilwyn*.

133. TNA, HS 7/104, Gardiner Report, Chapter Four, p. 4.

134. See Richard Overy, *Why the Allies Won* (London: Pimlico, 2006), Chapter Six, pp. 220–254.

135. Sacquety, *The OSS in Burma*, pp. 59–60.

136. TNA, HS 1/194, 'Note on the Functions and Operations of Indian Group', 14 July 1943.

Chapter 4   Getting Behind the Lines: The India Mission in Burma, September 1943–December 1944

1. For the reorganisation and establishment of the mission's early infrastructure, see Chapter Three, pp. 88–119.

2. For early complications with OSS, see Chapter Three, pp. 108–13.

3. Robert Lyman, *Slim, Master of War*, pp. 109–10 & p. 116.

4. Louis Mountbatten, *The Personal Diary of Admiral the Lord Louis Mountbatten*, Philip Ziegler (ed.) (London: Collins, 1998), entry for 6 October 1943, p. 6.

5. Richard Hough, *Mountbatten: Hero of Our Time* (London: Book Club Associates, 1981), pp. 203–4.

6. Robert Lyman, *Slim, Master of War* (London: Robinson, 2004), p. 112.

7. The work on the Chindits is vast. For criticism, see Kirby, *The War Against Japan*, Vol. 2, pp. 309–330; Lyman, *Slim, Master of War*, pp. 110–116. For a proponent, see Rooney, *Wingate and the Chindits*. For accounts by Chindits, see, for example, Michael Calvert, *Chindits: Long Range Penetration* (London: Pan, 1974) or Bernard Fergusson, *Beyond the Chindwin* (London: Fontana, 1971).

8. See Rooney, *Wingate and the Chindits*, p. 99.

9. Ian Lyall Grant, *Burma: The Turning Point* (Chichester: Zampi Press, 1993).

10. Christopher Thorne, *Allies of a Kind* (Oxford: Oxford University Press, 1979).

11. TNA, HS 1/194, 'Note on Functions and Operations of Indian Group', 14 July 1943.

12. TNA HS 1/194, 'Training System in India', George Taylor, chief assistant to the head of SOE in the UK, to Major General Colin Gubbins, deputy director of SOE, 1 September 1943.

13. On 24 September 1943, India Mission warned London that unless submarines were put at the mission's disposal, they might as well 'close down Malaya and Sumatra' country sections. TNA, HS 1/194, 'SOE India Group: Present Organisation and Action', Appendix A, sub-heading 'Transport Facilities', 24 September 1943. Operations into these countries were dependent upon two Dutch submarines, but any SOE operation had to fit into the navy's existing operational sorties.

14. In Europe, RAF squadrons such as 59 Sqn. had converted to Mk. III Hudsons in July 1941.

15. By September 1943 the flight had an advanced base established at Dumdum, Bengal. See Cruickshank, *SOE in the Far East*, pp. 32–8.

16. TNA, HS 1/201 and AIR 23/1950, Squadron Leader Coleman, 'Brief History of Clandestine Air Operations', 12 January 1945.

17. TNA, HS 1/194, 'SOE India Group: Present Organisation and Action', 24 September 1943, Appendix A. George Taylor had already sent a message to the Air Ministry making the case for Liberators; see TNA, HS 1/201, George Taylor to Air Ministry, 'Liberators for SOE India', 11 September 1943.

18. See Terrence O'Brien, *The Moonlight War* (London: Collins, 1987) for an account of this squadron's activities by one of its pilots.

19. TNA, HS 1/201, 'Air Operations', 2 February 1945. These figures are sorties for both SIS and SOE. Despite the threefold increase, the author of this document commented 'You will notice that the total is not great.'

20. TNA, HS 1/201, Coleman, 'Brief History of Clandestine Air Operations'.

21. Troy Saquety, *The OSS in Burma* (University Press of Kansas, 2013), p. 28.

22. Source: Reproduced from TNA, HS 1/194.

23. TNA, HS 1/212, 'Note on SOE Communications' compiled by B/B180 (Anthony Butler), December 1942. This note was based upon the use of the Gambier Parry Mk III and Marconi AD67 sets. See also Cruikshank, *SOE in the Far East*, pp. 39–45.

24. Richard Dunlop, *Behind Japanese Lines* (New York: Rand McNally, 1979), pp. 122–23.

25. TNA, HS 7/117 is an entire file on the SFDC.

26. 'X's were used quite often on WT messages as a priority'. Frank Stratton, formerly SOE Force 133 and Force 136. Email to Richard Duckett, 29 October 2014.

27. TNA, HS 7/115, 'History of SOE training in India, 1942–1945', Section B, pp. 3–9.

28. TNA, HS 1/1, 'Airborne Operation Number 5: *Dilwyn 1*', 12 February 1943.

29. Kumje Tawng was born in 1924 in the Bhamo district of northern Burma. He joined SOE in December 1942. Born in 1912, Shan Lone was the son of a Kachin headman from the Sinlumkaba area. Before joining SOE in late 1942, Lone had been training with Wingate's Chindits; see TNA HS 1/28, p. 68 and p. 70.

30. TNA, HS 1/1, 'Airborne Operation Number 5: *Dilwyn 1*', 12 February 1943.

31. TNA, HS 1/44, Operations Diary, '*Dilwyn* (Originally *Tendon*)'. The bomb racks were used to deploy both equipment containers, and if faulty could prevent men from exiting the aircraft.

32. TNA, HS 1/2, 'Brief Account of my operations for a period of over two years behind enemy lines', Major Shan Lone, 4 May 1945.

33. TNA, HS 1/1, 'Notes for *Dilwyn*' (original copies retained by TNA, no date given on redacted version).

34. The documents have yielded no definite answer for why, but presumably it was because they wanted to have control over forces that would eventually assist their offensive towards Myitkyina.

35. TNA, HS 1/44, War Diary, entry for 1 & 10 July 1944.

36. Peers and Brelis, *Behind the Burma Road*, p. 155.

37. TNA, HS 1/17 and HS 1/8, fortnightly report of Captain Howe, based at Fort Hertz, for period 22 November to 15 December 1943.

38. TNA, HS 7/104, Lieutenant Colonel Gardiner report, 'Burma History', 30 December 1945, p. 5.

39. The northernmost point the Japanese reached in Burma was the Hpunchan Hka River, a few miles north of Sumprabum, by August 1943. See Ian Fellowes-Gordon, *Amiable Assassins* (London: Panther, 1958), p. 14.

40. A 'Dah' is a short sword or machete, then commonly carried by the peoples of Burma, including Kachins, hence *Dahforce*.

41. See HS 1/1 for the operational directive for *Dahforce*. According to Major Kemball's report on *Dilwyn*, HS 7/105, the Kachins were told that troops of the second Chindit operation would stay, p. 4.

    Major Kemball placed the blame upon Wingate. Major Peterson, who was involved in liaison between BCS and the Chindits, blamed Herring, see HS 1/1, 'Notes for why *Dilwyn* did not receive *Dahforce*'. See also, Cruickshank, *SOE in the Far East*, pp. 164–5.

42. The head of BCS at this point was Mount Stephen Cumming.

43. IWM 4879, Papers of Lieutenant Colonel D.C. Herring.
44. TNA, HS 1/1, Mackenzie to C.J.P. Hudson, 11 March 1944.
45. TNA, HS 1/44, War Diary, 19 June 1944.
46. TNA, HS 7/105, Major Kemball's report, p. 2. The operations diary, HS 1/44, contradicts this claim that only Zau June was left. The entry for 3 June 1944 indicates that Station X run by 'Matang' was in the Sinlumkaba area, and that Station 1 under 'Magam' was at Fort Morton with the balance of *Dilwyn* personnel.
47. TNA, HS 1/227, report of Lieutenant Colonel MacDonald, 26 April 1944, p. 9.
48. TNA, HS 1/1, Herring to Cumming, 26 June 1944. It is perhaps worthy of note that by 31 August, Herring regretted turning down an offer of attachment to Det.101, and had heard that SOE and OSS had 'signed an armistice' in order to work together in the Kachin Hills. See HS 1/1, Herring to Gardiner, 31 August 1944.
49. TNA, HS 1/44, War Diary, 16–31 August 1944.
50. TNA, HS 1/1, Boyt to Cumming, 28 August 1944.
51. TNA, HS 1/44, War Diary, 6 September 1944.
52. TNA, HS 1/1, BCS to Meerut, 7 August 1944.
53. TNA, HS 1/1, 'Clandestine Operations in North East Burma', Appendix A to 'Summary of Dealings with Lieutenant Colonel Peers, OSS', 17 July 1944.
54. TNA, HS 1/44, War Diary, 25 September 1944.
55. TNA, HS 1/44, War Diary, 1 October 1944.
56. Major General S. Woodburn Kirby, *The War Against Japan*, Vol. IV (Uckfield: Naval & Military Press, 2004), p. 117.
57. TNA, HS 7/105, Report of Major Kemball, p. 4. Approximate date October 1945.
58. TNA, HS 1/44, War Diary, 6 September 1944.
59. TNA, HS 1/1, Report of Captain June, 7 November 1944.
60. TNA, HS 7/105, Report of Major Kemball, p. 5.
61. TNA, HS 1/3, 'Memorandum', undated. The chief source of the state's wealth was from opium.
62. Spelt Yang Wen *Ping* in TNA files, spelt Yang Wen *Pin* in Paul H. Kratoska (see footnote below).
63. Paul H. Kratoska (ed.), *Southeast Asian Minorities in the Wartime Japanese Empire* (London: Routledge-Curzon, 2002), p. 41.
64. In today's money, 100,000 Rupees is approximately £1,020.00.
65. TNA, HS 1/3, undated and unattributed 'Memorandum'.
66. Kratoska, *Southeast Asian Minorities in the Wartime Japanese Empire*, p. 43. *Sze Ling Kuan* was the title given to a commander of independent forces.
67. TNA, HS 1/3, Report by Lieutenant Colonel Paul Munro-Faure, commander *Spiers*, to BCS, 29 March 1944.
68. TNA, HS 1/3, 'Myosa of Kokang', to Military Attaché, Chungking, from Assistant Military Attaché, Kunming (Colonel Clark), 15 April 1943. A Bren Gun was the standard British Light Machine Gun.

69. HS 1/3, 'Myosa of Kokang', Mackenzie to Director of Military Operations (DMO), 8 June 1943.

70. TNA, HS 1/5, 'Kokang', Mackenzie to George Taylor, 30 October 1943, p. 1. The agent was named as Grimsdale.

71. TNA, HS 1/3, 'Entry into Burma from Yunnan', from ISLD (MI6) to India Mission, 9 July 1943. This document has been redacted.

72. TNA, HS 9/502/5, personnel file for P.H. Munro-Faure.

73. Paul Hector Munro-Faure, 'Guerrilla Training, Maymyo 1941', *Journal of the Royal Asiatic Society*, 31 (1991), pp. 113–48; Munro-Faure, 'Behind the Front Lines in Burma, The Marches of the Salween Border, 1942–1944', *Journal of the Royal Asiatic Society*, 32 (1992), pp. 135–79.

74. TNA, HS 1/5, 'Kokang', Mackenzie to Taylor, 30 October 1943, p. 3.

75. TNA, HS 9/502/5, 'M.L.O (India)', 4 August 1943. MLO is Military Liaison Officer, the title Munro-Faure was given for this posting.

76. Files on *Spiers*: TNA, HS 1/3; HS 1/5. B.L, IOR M/3/1737; M/4/2955.

77. There was evidence of trench mortars having been used in the attack, and the only forces in Kokang with these weapons was the Chinese Army.

78. TNA, HS 7/259, War Diary, November 1943, p. 476.

79. TNA, HS 1/3, 'Operations Chinese/Burma Border', Assistant Military Attaché, Kunming, Colonel Clark, 5 January 1944.

80. TNA, HS 1/3, '*Spiers*', M.S. Cumming, 16 January 1944.

81. TNA, HS 1/3, '*Spiers* Personnel', Munro-Faure to Mackenzie, 16 January 1944.

82. TNA, HS 1/3, To BCS from Munro-Faure, 29 March 1944.

83. TNA, HS 1/5, 'A Short History of SPIERS', p. 2. Undated, but written after October 1944, probably by BCS as a summary for London.

84. Major Barnard and Captain Beamish were amongst the officers sent to *Spiers*.

85. TNA, HS 1/5, Chinese Ministry of Foreign Affairs to British Embassy, 16 August 1944.

86. TNA, HS 1/5, Alexander Cadogan to CD (head of SOE, General Gubbins), 27 July 1944.

87. TNA, HS 1/5, 'A Short History of SPIERS', p. 3.

88. TNA, HS 1/45, War Diary and HS 7/105, report of Major G.E. Pennell. Written after October 1945.

89. TNA, HS 1/45, War Diary, monthly report to 31 July 1944.

90. TNA, HS 1/45, War Diary, 23 September 1944.

91. TNA, HS 7/105, report of Major Pennell. It was not just food supplies that were the problem. There was a shortage of blankets which were needed at 8000 feet on the Burmese side of the border.

92. TNA, HS 1/44, Operations Diary, Operation *Character*, 28 November 1943.

93. TNA, HS 7/104, Gardiner report, p. 10.

94. TNA, HS 9/1104/5, personnel file for Major Jimmy Nimmo.

95. Ian Morrison, *Grandfather Longlegs* (London: Faber & Faber, 1946), p. 124 and p. 127.

96. TNA, HS 1/227, report of Lieutenant Colonel MacDonald, 26 April 1944, p. 5.

97. TNA, HS 1/8, 'Memorandum on Operations in the Rangoon [sic] and Bassein Delta', 18 December 1943.

98. Morrison, *Grandfather Longlegs*, p. 123.

99. See Chapter Two, pp. 60–87.

100. TNA, HS 1/3, 'Operational Instruction for B/B250' (Major C.B. Jones), 23 January 1943.

101. TNA, HS 1/3, 'Chindwin Operations', Peacock to Poles, 18 November 1943.

102. TNA, HS 1/3, 'An Appreciation of the Situation for Establishing a Permanent Forward Base Near the Chindwin River in the Area Manmaw – Intabaun G', Major E.H Peacock, 20 February 1944.

103. TNA, HS 1/3, 'B/B 600 Tour Notes' (Brigadier Guinness), 9 March 1944, p. 1.

104. Ibid, p. 1. 'Burma Traitor Army' was the name given to Aung San's Burma National Army in some quarters.

105. TNA, HS 1/3, '8th Periodic Report, 3 October–25 December 1943'.

106. For an account of the Chin Levies, see Lieutenant Colonel Balfour Oatts, *The Jungle in Arms* (London: New English Library, 1976). The criticism centred around the example he set by having his men laden with equipment while all his possessions, including luxuries, were carried by a pony. See TNA, HS 1/3, 'Report on Chin Hills, Oct–Dec 1943', by Captain C.P.H. Wilson.

107. GSI(K) was the cover name for the India Mission until March 1944 when it became Force 136.

108. TNA, HS 1/198, 'SOE Operations: Burma, Siam, Malaya, Sumatra, October 1942–October 1944', p. 1.

109. TNA, HS 7/104, Lieutenant Colonel Gardiner report, 'Burma History', p. 14.

110. For an account of code breaking in the Far East, see Alan Stripp, *Code Breaker in the Far East* (Oxford: OUP, 1995).

111. TNA, HW1/729, intercepted diplomatic message between the Japanese Ambassador in Bangkok and Foreign Ministry in Tokyo, 25 June 1942.

112. Ba Maw, *Breakthrough in Burma: Memoirs of a Revolution, 1939–1946* (New Haven: Yale University Press, 1968), p. 261.

113. U Maung Maung, *Burmese Nationalist Movements, 1940–1948* (Edinburgh: Kiscadale, 1989), p. 71.

114. Robert Taylor, *Marxism and Resistance in Burma, 1942–1945: Thein Pe Myint's Wartime Traveller* (Ohio University Press, 1984), p. 107.

115. TNA, HS 7/105, 'Report on Operations with the AFO [Anti-Fascist Organisation]', Major Battersby, 20 November 1945, pp. 1–2.

116. TNA, HS 1/45, War Diary entry for *Billet*, 12 February 1944.

117. TNA, HS 1/6, 'Future of Billet in Arakan', Major E. Battersby, 27 July 1944.

118. Taylor, *Marxism and Resistance in Burma*, pp. 250–2; TNA, HS 7/105, Major Battersby report, pp. 6–8.

119. TNA, HS 1/45, War Diary, London Newsletter, 19 January 1945.

120. TNA, HS 7/104, Major Battersby Report, p. 10.

121. *Hound, Camel,* and *Lion* were part of *Manual*; *Donkey* was part of *Nation.*

122. TNA, HS 1/7, 'Billet and Jedburghs', 15 September 1944.

123. Aldrich, *Intelligence and the War Against Japan*, p. 204.

124. TNA, HS 7/104, report of Lieutenant Colonel Gardiner, Chapter Four, p. 16.

Chapter 5   Operation *Character,* November 1944–September 1945

1. See Chapter Two, pp. 75–81 for the exploits of Lt. Gyaw and Captain Thompson in 1942.

2. TNA, HS 1/10, Captain Anderson to Lieutenant Colonel Gardiner, 25 August 1944.

3. Imperial War Museum (IWM), 08/49/1, unpublished memoir of Lieutenant Colonel John Cromarty Tulloch, p. 1.

4. Richard Aldrich, *Intelligence and the War Against Japan* (Cambridge University Press, 2000), p. 336.

5. See the previous chapter for more details about P Force.

6. The second Chindit operation had been launched in March 1944 in the area of Indaw. Indicated on the map above are the Chindit landing sites, codenamed Broadway, Piccadilly and Chowringhee.

7. Lt. Kan Choke had fought with the Oriental Mission in 1942. He had been due to parachute in with Lt. Ba Gyaw in February 1943. Choke was a career soldier of more than 26 years' service. He was over 50 years old in 1944, and blind in one eye.

8. The Kachin Levies had originally been raised by SOE's Oriental Mission and H.N.C. Stevenson of the Burma Frontier Service. They continued independently of SOE in 1943–1945. See, for example, Ian Fellowes-Gordon, *Amiable Assassins* (London: Panther, 1958).

9. TNA, HS 1/10, Gardiner to Force 136 HQ, 1 September 1944. Both Karen officers were secured and Saw Torrey ended up in charge of an operational area in the *Hyena* sub mission.

10. TNA, HS 7/104, Gardiner report, Chapter Four, p. 14.

11. Geraldine Peacock, *The Life of a Jungle Walla, Reminiscences in the life of Lieutenant-Colonel E.M. Peacock* (Ilfracombe: Arthur Stockwell Ltd, 1958), p. 67.

12. Peacock's personnel file, TNA, HS 9/1158/1, has his date of birth as 1898. Peacock's grandson says that he lied about his age to sign up in 1939.

13. TNA, HS 9/1158/1, personnel file for Lieutenant Colonel Edgar Peacock.

14. TNA, HS 9/1198/7, personnel file for Major Eustace Poles.

15. TNA, HS 9/1493/8, personnel file for Major Rupert Guy Turrall. There are two different dates of birth on the documents within this file. 1893 rather than 1899 is a more likely date for Turrall's birth.

16. For more on Mission 101, see Duncan McNab, *Mission 101: The Untold Story of the SOE and the Second World War in Ethiopia* (Gloucester: The History Press, 2012).
17. TNA, HS 9/1493/8, personnel file for Major Rupert Turrall.
18. TNA, HS 9/752/5, personnel file for Lieutenant Colonel H.W. Howell.
19. There is no HS 9 file for Tulloch, but such was his personality that both Seagrim's biographer, Ian Morrison, and Terence O'Brien, the RAF Special Duties pilot who flew Tulloch into the Karen Hills, wrote at length about him in their books. After the War he gained notoriety as a supporter of the Karen against the Union of Burma, see the epilogue of this work. See also Terence O'Brien, *The Moonlight War* (London: Collins, 1987), pp. 242–9; Morrison, *Grandfather Longlegs*, pp. 159–60.
20. MI(R), Military Intelligence (Research), was one of the three existing departments which formed SOE in 1940. See Chapter One.
21. TNA, HS 9/373/8, personnel file for Lieutenant Colonel R.A. Critchley.
22. TNA, HS 1/3, Major Peacock, 'An appreciation of the situation for establishing a permanent force base near the Chindwin River', 20 February 1944.
23. For information on Camp Tweed, see TNA HS 7/115 Training file, HS 7/116 Medical section and HS 7/106 Peacock's report, p. 3. The camp had to be closed down in August 1944 because of the higher than average risk of contracting malaria there.
24. TNA, HS 7/106, report of Lieutenant Colonel Peacock, 3 November 1945, p. 3.
25. TNA, HS 9/1080/2, Lieutenant Colonel G.R. Musgrave personnel file. The file has various correspondences relating to Musgrave's health, and the process by which his medical officers were overruled to ensure his posting to Ceylon. Musgrave's file also reveals that he had previous Burma experience having worked in the forestry business 1931–5.
26. The most likely explanation for the name 'Jedburgh' is that it was randomly generated in the same way as operational codenames.
27. Adapted from G. Loosmore, *The Jedburghs: A Postscript, Preparing for Burma* (Leicester: privately published, date unknown), p. 3.
28. Glynn Loosmore, *The Jeds: A Postscript*, 'Preparing for Burma', p. 1. Sergeant Loosmore was a W/T operator attached to *Character*. Compiling his postscript, he obviously had access to official documents, some of which are available at TNA, such as, for example, Peacock's report.
29. Lieutenant Colonel Musgrave to Colonel George Taylor, Head of Overseas Missions, India, 21 September 1944, reproduced in G. Loosmore, *The Jeds: A Postscript*, Section G, entitled 'Preparing for Burma', pp. 5–7.
30. Colin Mackenzie, 'Organisation of Special Groups', 14 September 1944, reproduced in Loosmore, *The Jeds*, Section G, pp. 3–5.
31. TNA, HS 7/106, report of Lieutenant Colonel Peacock, 3 November 1945, pp. 4–5.

32. TNA, HS 7/115, 'SOE Training in India', Part 1, p. 6.
33. Loosmore, *The Jeds*, Section H, 'Preparing for Burma: 2 The Practice', p. 1
34. O'Brien, *The Moonlight War*, p. 200.
35. TNA, HS 7/106, report of Lieutenant Colonel Peacock, 3 November 1945, p. 4.
36. TNA, HS 7/106, report of Major Campbell, Operation *Walrus – Skunk* (inserted with Tulloch's report).
37. TNA, HS 7/106, report of Lieutenant Colonel J.C. Tulloch, 20 September 1945, p. 1. Belgaum was a long established Army training facility just outside Goa. There is no reference to Belgaum as an SOE facility with an ME number.
38. TNA, HS 7/106, report of Major Denning, *Walrus Red*, p. 1 (inserted with Tulloch's report).
39. See TNA, HS 7/106, for numerous reports of officers sent on Operation *Character*.
40. William Mackenzie, *The Secret History of SOE* (St Ermin's Press: London, 2002), p. 605.
41. TNA HS 7/106, report of Lieutenant Colonel Peacock, 3 November 1945, p. 6.
42. O'Brien, *The Moonlight War*, pp. 246–7.
43. Major Lewis is described as being a big man, and due to a shortage of parachutes he was given the wrong parachute for his weight. TNA HS 7/106, Tulloch Report, Part II, pp. 1–2. See also O'Brien, *The Moonlight War*, pp. 243–44.
44. TNA, HS 7/106, Report of Major Denning, p. 1.
45. TNA, HS 7/106, Report of Captain Barron, *Walrus White*, p. 1.
46. TNA, HS 7/106, and IWM, P463, report of Major Lucas, 28 November 1945, p. 20.
47. TNA, HS 7/106, report of Lieutenant Colonel H.W. Howell, *Hyena HQ*, 24 November 1945, p. 14.
48. TNA, HS 7/106, report of Major Campbell.
49. TNA, HS 7/106, Major Denning, p. 1
50. TNA, HS 7/106, report of Captain J.W. Wilson, 25 August 1945, p. 13.
51. TNA, HS 7/106, Peacock report, p. 1.
52. TNA, HS 7/106, report of Captain Barron, *Hyena White*, 28 November 1945, p. 7.
53. TNA, HS 7/106, report of Major Neville, p. 5.
54. Burma Rifles units (Burifs) had mostly consisted of Karens, Kachins and Chins, with some resident Gurkhas and Burman companies, before the War.
55. Roger Leney, *'Mongoose White' Behind the Japanese Lines in Burma*, 2005. Unpublished memoir kept by family.
56. See TNA, HS 7/106, for the reports of the officers involved.
57. HS 7/106, Peacock, Phase IV, 23 March–23 April, p. 13.
58. Slim, *Defeat into Victory*, p. 499.
59. HS 7/106, Peacock, Phase IV, 23 March–23 April, pp. 13–14.

60. HS 7/106, Lt. Marlam, Report on Mills-Cordtex Ambush, 4 May 1945, Appendix XIIE to Major Turrall's report, 5 May 1945.
61. HS 7/106, Peacock, Part 1, pp. 7–8. A Hawkins grenade was an anti-tank grenade developed by Captain Hawkins in 1940. It consisted of 900 g (2lb) of gelignite which exploded when enough pressure or impact was exerted upon it to break the phials inside. The more widely known Mills bomb (as used in the cordtex trap) was anti-personnel.
62. Slim, *Defeat into Victory*, pp. 499–500.
63. TNA, HS 7/106, report of Lieutenant Colonel Peacock, p. 22.
64. HS 1/27, from Tactical HQ Force 136 to Brigadier Anstey, 27 June 1945.
65. TNA, HS 1/27, ibid. 12 Army was formed in late May to take over Burma operations from 14 Army.
66. Cruickshank, *SOE in the Far East*, p. 189.
67. TNA, HS 7/106, report of Lieutenant Colonel Tulloch, p. 4.
68. TNA, HS 1/10, report of Captain Sell, 11 September 1945, p. 3.
69. TNA, HS 7/106, report of Lieutenant Colonel Peacock, p. 22.
70. TNA, HS 7/106, report of Major Lucas, *Mongoose Blue*, p. 19.
71. TNA, HS 1/11, report of Captain L.W. Clark, *Mongoose Blue*, p. 3.
72. TNA, HS 7/106, report of Captain Ford, *Mongoose Red*, 7 December 1945, p. 8.
73. TNA, HS 7/106, report of Major Lucas, pp. 7–9.
74. TNA, HS 7/106, report of Lieutenant Colonel Tulloch, p. 5.
75. The refugees made it to Toungoo. See IWM, Captain Marchant interview, http://www.iwm.org.uk/collections/item/object/80017158.
76. TNA, HS 7/106, report of Lieutenant Colonel Peacock, pp. 17–18.
77. TNA, HS 7/106, report of Lieutenant Colonel Howell, p. 5.
78. TNA, HS 7/106, report of Lieutenant Colonel Howell, p. 11.
79. Louis Allen, *Burma, the Longest War*, p. 488.
80. TNA, HS 7/106, Tulloch report, p. 6.
81. TNA, HS 7/106, report for *Hyena White*, personnel included Major Saw Torry, Captain Barron, and sergeants Henney and Moore.
82. TNA, HS 7/106, report of Major Milner, *Mongoose White*, 30 December 1945, p. 5.
83. TNA, HS 1/10, extracted from 'The Game Book of Casualties', sent to HQ Force 136 from HQ Group A Force 136, 5 September 1945.
84. HS 7/106, Howell report, p. 7.
85. Adapted from TNA, HS 1/10.
86. TNA, HS 1/11, report of Captain L.W Clark. Clark reported that he made contact with the commander of 4 Division, Chaw Zaw, Patriotic Burmese Forces (PBF) on 18 April.
87. TNA HS 7/106 and IWM P463, report of Major J.P. Lucas, *Mongoose Blue*, p. 6.
88. IWM, P463, Major J.P. Lucas, *Behind the Enemy Lines – A Burma Incident*. Unpublished memoir.
89. TNA HS 7/106, Howell report, pp. 7–9.

90. TNA HS 7/106, report of Major Lucas, pp. 19–20.
91. TNA, HS 7/106, report of Major Milner, p. 3.
92. For many teams the fighting went on beyond the 15 August surrender. Major Turrall went to the Japanese to inform them of the War's end, and nearly lost his life. See Allen, *Burma, The Longest War*, pp. 540–3.
93. TNA, HS 7/106, report of Major Lucas, p. 12.
94. TNA, HS 1/11, notes for a talk by Lieutenant Colonel Drummond, 26 April 1945.
95. Smith Dun, *Memoirs of the Four Foot Colonel*, Data Paper 113, Southeast Asia Program, Department of Asian Studies (New York: Cornell University, 1980), p. 67. The content of this paper was written in 1957. General Smith Dun was a Karen, born in 1906. He was the first Commander-in-Chief of the Union of Burma's armed forces in 1948, a position from which he was relieved in 1949 as the civil war deepened.
96. TNA, CAB 101/198, 'Clandestine Organizations in SEAC', undated, p. 3.

Chapter 6   The *Billet* Operations: *Nation, Manual* and *Grain*, November 1944–September 1945

1. Maung Maung Pye, *Burma in the Crucible* (Rangoon: Khittaya Publishing House, 1951), p. 18. See pp. 17–23 on the formation of the *Dobhama Asiayone*.
2. U Maung Maung, *Burmese Nationalist Movements* (Edinburgh: Kiscadale, 1999), pp. 2–3.
3. Robert Taylor, *Marxism and Resistance in Burma* (Ohio University Press, 1984), pp. 7–13.
4. Colonel Suzuki was head of the *Minami Kikan*, a secret Japanese intelligence group formed to subvert the Burmese against the British.
5. Thakin Thein Pe, *Wartime Traveller*, in Taylor, *Marxism and Resistance in Burma.*, pp. 12–13.
6. Before going to work with SOE, Thein Pe and Tin Shwe worked under Leslie Glass at the Far Eastern Bureau helping to produce propaganda for leaflets, newspapers and radio. See Leslie Glass, *The Changing of the Kings* (London: Peter Owen, 1985), pp. 169–72.
7. Thakin Thein Pe, *Wartime Traveller*, p. 198.
8. See TNA, HS 7/105 for Major Battersby's post-operational report. See HS 9/103/8 for his personnel file, and HS 1/11.
9. These doubts came from former Burma civil personnel working in Force 136.
10. Thein Pe, *Wartime Traveller*, p. 221.
11. The Arakan is the coastal strip of Burma that meets India, running around the Bay of Bengal.
12. The Burma Defence Army (BDA) became the Burma National Army (BNA) in August 1943.

13. As the official historian points out, this is an erroneous application of Arthurian names. Cruikshank, *SOE in the Far East* (Oxford: Oxford University Press, 1986), p. 168.
14. The date 31 March is given by the War Diary, HS1/45. An alternative date of 12 April is offered by Major Battersby in his report, see HS 7/105.
15. The cover name 'Force 136' was put into use from March 1944.
16. See F.S.V Donnison, *British Military Administration in the Far East* (London: HMSO, 1956).
17. TNA, HS 7/105, Battersby report, p. 5.
18. Slim had complained to 11 Army Group on 23 June 1944, and to SACSEA on 28 September. In September he had asked Mountbatten for an expansion of Z Force to 20 patrols. See TNA, CAB 101/198, 'Clandestine Organizations in SEAC', p. 5.
19. See Aldrich *Intelligence and the War Against Japan* (Cambridge University Press, 2000), pp. 220–2; Lieutenant Colonel Cumming to Brigadier General Staff ALFSEA, 2 January 1945, reproduced in Tinker, *Burma The Struggle for Independence* (London: HMSO, 1983), p. 136; TNA, HS 1/230 and HS 1/298.
20. Group A of Force 136 was responsible for Burma, Siam and French Indochina. Group B was responsible for Malaya, Sumatra, and the Dutch East Indies. Group C was responsible for China.
21. The Americans, and the P-Division deputy (Lt. Commander Taylor USNR) in particular, thought that there was a deliberate campaign by SOE 'to break up OSS as an independent organization'. See HS 1/208, Lt. Commander Taylor to Captain Garnons-Williams, 30 August 1944. This nearly 'fatal rift' with the Americans took until January 1945 to be defused.
22. Thein Pe, *Wartime Traveller*, p. 250.
23. TNA, HS 7/105, Battersby report, p. 6.
24. Ibid, p. 7.
25. Major Battersby reproduced correspondence from this period in his post operations report.
26. TNA, HS 7/105, Battersby report, p. 9.
27. The official historian interpreted this same document another way. He took it to mean that CAS(B), not Prescott specifically, should be 'considered hostile'. See Cruikshank, *SOE in the Far East*, p. 178. It should also be noted that Cruickshank presents this quote as originating in March 1945 when it is in Mackenzie's letter dated October 1944. See Battersby report, HS 7/105, p. 9.
28. BL, IOR R/8/13, correspondence between Colin Mackenzie and Sir Reginald Dorman-Smith. Reply to Mackenzie 7 October 1944. See also TNA, HS 7/105, Battersby report, p. 10. In his report, Battersby reproduced the correspondence he received from others such as Dorman-Smith in this instance.
29. See Donnison, *British Military Administration in the Far East*, pp. 33–44 (especially p. 43) for the chain of command for CAS(B), the Governor of Burma, and the military.

30. TNA, HS 7/105, Battersby report, pp. 10–12.

31. Ibid, p. 34.

32. F.S.V Donnison explains how this might have been possible when fitting the new CAS(B) into existing bureaucracy. 'The facts that the officers of the CAS(B) were all substantively civilians, that there was a largely unintelligible working arrangement with the government of Burma dividing responsibility for the administration of Burma, and that the very name of the new Branch suggested something more civilian than military, resulted in a vague but easy assumption that members of the CAS were not really soldiers or really a part of GHQ at all.' See Donnison, *British Military Administration in the Far East*, p. 55.

33. TNA, HS 7/105, Battersby report, p. 12.

34. The letter is reproduced on p. 13 of Battersby's report. The recipient was Lieutenant Colonel Egerton Mott. Egerton Mott had been involved with the Oriental Mission in 1941–2, but by 1944 worked for SOE's Far East section in London.

35. TNA, HS7/105, Battersby report, p. 6.

36. TNA, HS 1/7, '*Billet* and Jedburghs', from HQ A Group to Kandy HQ, Force 136 Operations and Political Warfare, 15 September 1944.

37. Also in India Mission's favour at this meeting was the performance of P Force (see previous chapter) and the fact brought to Slim's attention that most of the intelligence for northern Burma came from SOE (Operation *Dilwyn*), not OSS.

38. TNA, HS 7/104, report of Lieutenant Colonel Gardiner, 'Operations in 1945', see his Chapter Six.

39. The account of this meeting at Barrackpore in TNA, CAB 101/198 does not make reference to the earlier meeting of Cumming and Slim.

40. TNA, HS 1/298, 'Account of meeting held at Barrackpore', 4 January 1945, p. 1.

41. TNA, HS 7/105, Battersby report, p. 19.

42. In his interview, Major Carew tells the story of how he met these two men. Hearing gunshots, Carew decided to investigate. His reasoning for approaching the firing was that if two people were fighting, one side had to be friendly to the British. He found the two Arakanese blind drunk shooting at each other. See IWM, Major Carew interview http://www.iwm.org.uk/collections/item/object/80017197.

43. TNA, HS 7/105, Battersby report, p. 19.

44. TNA, HS 7/105, Major Carew's notes on the meetings, reproduced in Battersby's report, p. 19. HS 1/7 indicates that there was a meeting at Ponnagyun, on the Kaladan River north of Sittwe.

45. TNA, HS 7/105, report of Major Battersby, p. 20.

46. Major Carew interview, http://www.iwm.org.uk/collections/item/object/80017197.

47. TNA, HS 7/105, reproduced in Major Battersby's report, p. 21.

48. In the Irrawaddy Delta there were mixed villages of Karens and Burmans.

49. In Greece, SOE armed both the Royalists and Communists, which then developed into civil war.

50. TNA, HS 1/13, DCCAO Brigadier R.G.B. Prescott to ALFSEA, 'Assistance to Allied Land Forces in Burma by Pro-Allied Burmese Elements', 13 February 1945.

51. Hugh Tinker, *Burma, The Struggle for Independence*, p. 166. This is quoted in a footnote. Tinker does not mention the statement by General Leese.

52. Commander Group A, Force 136 to HQ ALFSEA, 17 February 1945 in Tinker, *Burma, The Struggle for Independence*, pp. 166–7.

53. TNA, HS 1/14, to Kandy from Calcutta, 26 January 1945.

54. Mountbatten to Leese, 27 February 1945, in Tinker, *Burma, The Struggle for Independence*, p. 171.

55. TNA, HS 1/16, B/B100 (Mackenzie) to B/B101 (Gavin Stewart), 28 February 1945.

56. TNA, HS 7/105, Battersby report, p. 6.

57. Ba Maw, *Breakthrough in Burma: Memoirs of a Revolution 1939–1946* (Yale University Press, 1968), p. 366.

58. Thakin Nu, *Burma Under the Japanese* (London: Macmillan, 1954), p. 105.

59. Ba Maw, *Breakthrough in Burma*, pp. 370–1. Ba Maw was referring here to the Indian National Army, led by Subhas Chandra Bose, with whom this plan had been devised. It is not clear if the British knew about the collaboration of the two nationalist armies to prevent a reassertion of colonial power, but certainly the orders given to Force 136 were clear in that the INA were not to be used in Burma.

60. U Maung Maung, *Burmese Nationalist Movements 1940–1948*, p. 114.

61. Ibid. In particular, see chapter five, section sub-headed 'The Underground Organisation', pp. 110–29.

62. TNA, HS 1/298 and HS 7/105, Battersby report, p. 60.

63. TNA, WO 203/2492, Thakin Than Tun to Admiral Mountbatten, 29 May 1945.

64. TNA, HS 1/7, Major Battersby, 'Billet and Jedburghs', 15 September 1944.

65. Collated from TNA, HS 7/105, HS 1/12–HS 1/15.

66. TNA, HS 7/105, Battersby report, p. 29.

67. TNA, HS 7/104, Gardiner report, Chapter Six, *Operations in 1945*, p. 10.

68. The same Major Carew who had commanded *Camel* in Arakan was accompanied by Captain Brown, Sergeant Sharp, Tha Gyaw and a cook called Bagi. See TNA, HS 1/12, 'Operational Instructions for NATION/WEASEL', 16 March 1945.

69. U Maung Maung, *Burmese Nationalist Movements 1940–1948*, pp. 118–20.

70. 27 March is still celebrated in Burma today by the armed forces as *Tatmadaw* Day.

71. The deceased were Captain Peter Vickery, Captain Georges Marchant and Sergeant Peter Colvin. Captains Vickery and Marchant's personnel files are HS 9/1532/5 and HS 9/987/5 respectively. Sergeant Colvin's file is HS 9/338/5.

All had served with the resistance in France. Captain Craster (team *Zebra*) remembered the plane being a ball of fire as he took off for operations that same night. See http://www.iwm.org.uk/collections/item/object/ 80012344207.

72. TNA, HS 1/12, report of Major Carew on Operation *Nation/Weasel*, undated.

73. TNA, HS 7/105, Battersby report, p. 49. Sergeant Gordon Tack recalled this incident when interviewed in 1996. See http://www.iwm.org.uk/collections/ item/object/80016165.

74. TNA, HS 1/12, report of Sergeant Ronald Brierley, 5 September 1945. Brierley also deposited a significant amount of his wartime papers at the Imperial War Museum, see IWM 15095. He was interviewed on 1 August 1988; http://m.iwm.org.uk/collections/item/object/80010094.

75. IWM, Brierley interview, http://www.iwm.org.uk/collections/item/object/ 80010094.

76. TNA, HS 1/12, Brierley report, pp. 4–5.

77. In France, Brierley had been the W/T Sergeant for Team *Daniel*, and Mission *Etoile*.

78. Major Dick Rubinstein interview, http://www.iwm.org.uk/collections/item/ object/80010813.

79. Frank Owen, *The Campaign in Burma* (London: HMSO, 1946), pp. 147–8.

80. Captain Oswin Craster interview, http://www.iwm.org.uk/collections/item/ object/80012344. Interviewed in 1992 at the age of 76, there is much that Craster has forgotten when asked.

81. In contrast to Captain Craster, Major Rubinstein, interviewed in 1989, seems to have had an amazing memory, relating some very precise detail.

82. Sergeant Frederick Bailey, IWM interview, http://www.iwm.org.uk/collecti ons/item/object/80011495. A Piat was an anti-tank weapon fired by infantrymen, which gave the operator a 'hell of a belt in the shoulder'.

83. TNA, HS 1/12, report of Major D.C McCoull, 11 November 1945. *Cow* and *Giraffe* were flown out from Mongoose on 17 June.

84. TNA, HS 1/12, report of Captain Waller, date unknown, but after August 1945. Support from 17 Division was described as 'lamentable'.

85. TNA, HS 1/14, probably written by Captain Livingstone who commanded *Chimp* after Major Rubinstein took over *Reindeer*.

86. Major Rubinstein, IWM interview, http://www.iwm.org.uk/collections/item/ object/80010813.

87. See IWM interviews referenced above, in particular Sergeants Brierley and Bailey, and Major Rubinstein.

88. TNA, HS 1/12, letter from Captain Houseman to Captain J. Waller (*Reindeer*), May 1945.

89. IWM, Sergeant Brierley interview, http://www.iwm.org.uk/collections/item/ object/80010094.

90. TNA, HS 7/105, Battersby report, p. 63.

91. It is not clear if Battersby's figure is for the BNA operating completely independently of SOE or not.
92. TNA, HS 7/104, 'Force 136 REINDEER', from HQ 98 Indian Infantry Brigade to HQ 19 Indian Division, 31 July 1945.
93. Adapted from TNA HS 1/10.
94. TNA, HS 1/12, report of Major Boiteux, 2 August 1945.
95. IWM interview, Major Carew, http://www.iwm.org.uk/collections/item/object/80017197.
96. TNA, HS 1/13, report of Major Clowes, 14 July 1945.
97. TNA, HS 7/105, Battersby report, pp. 53–58.
98. Slim, *Defeat into Victory*, p. 517.
99. A victory parade was held for the same reasons of power and prestige in Malaya on 15 September 1945.
100. TNA, HS 1/16, SACSEA to AMSSO, 29 June 1945.
101. TNA, HS 1/15, Sir Reginald Dorman-Smith to Leo Amery, Secretary of State for Burma, 2 June 1945.
102. TNA, HS 1/16, SACSEA to AMSSO, 29 June 1945.
103. TNA, HS 7/105, quoted in Major Battersby's report, p. 62.
104. TNA, HS 7/104, Gardiner report, Chapter Six, p. 16.
105. IWM, Mountbatten to Mackenzie, 5 September 1972, private papers of Colin Mackenzie (uncatalogued).
106. IWM, Major Dick Rubinstein interview, http://www.iwm.org.uk/collections/item/object/80010813.
107. See Mary Callahan, *Making Enemies: War and State Building in Burma* (New York: Cornell University Press), pp. 36–42.
108. TNA, HS 1/16, 'Notes for Press Conference'. Undated, but the conference was cancelled.

Epilogue   A Legacy? Force 136 and Postwar Burma, 1945–50

1. See especially Hugh Tinker, *The Union of Burma* (Oxford: OUP, 1957), pp. 12–14 and his *Burma: The Struggle for Independence 1944–1948*, vol. 1 (London: HMSO, 1983). See also Frank Donnison, *British Military Administration in the Far East* (London: HMSO, 1956).
2. Foreign Office and Secret Intelligence Services files contain numerous press clippings; see, for example, TNA, FO 371/69513, 'Britons in Burma Rising Plot', *Daily Worker*, 22 December 1948; KV 2/3862, 'Rival Revolts Menace Rangoon', *The Daily Express*, 20 September 1948; BBC *Timewatch*, 'Forgotten Allies', available https://www.youtube.com/watch?v=xTJ3q5yg38Q. Richard Aldrich, 'Legacies of Secret Service': Renegade SOE and the Karen Struggle in Burma, 1948–50', *Intelligence and National Security*, 14, 4 (1999), pp. 130–48.

3. Donnison, *British Military Administration in the Far East 1943–46*, pp. 348–9.

4. Bickham Sweet-Escott, Correspondence, *International Affairs*, 48 (3), July 1972, pp. 552–5. Sweet-Escott wrote about his time with SOE in *Baker Street Irregular* (London: Methuen, 1965). He was sent to the Far East as Colonel, General Staff. His immediate boss was Brigadier John Anstey, to whom he was responsible for 'the coordination of our operations throughout the area' of South East Asia.

5. Tinker, *The Union of Burma*, pp. 12–14, and *Burma: The Struggle for Independence 1944–1948*, vol. 1, pp. xxiv–xxix.

6. 'SACSEA to Headquarters ALFSEA; GHQ India; Government of Burma', 6 December 1944, in Tinker, *Burma: The Struggle for Independence* p. 123.

7. John McEnery, *Epilogue in Burma, 1945–1948* (Tunbridge Wells: Spellmount, 1990). He describes various 'time bombs', of which the decision not to employ Indian troops is just one. See pp. 29–35.

8. McEnery, *Epilogue in Burma, 1945–1948*, p. 35. Dacoity was the act of theft and murder.

9. In Burmese it was known as the *Pyithu Yebaws Tat* (PYT).

10. TNA, HS 7/106, report of Major Lucas, p. 19.

11. British Library, IOR M/4/1455, report by F. Wemyss, Inspector General of Police, Southern Range. This intelligence came from a Burmese informant named Maung Ba Sein.

12. John Darwin, *The End of The British Empire* (Oxford: Blackwell, 1991), see Chapter Five, pp. 85–113.

13. Ian Morrison, *Grandfather Longlegs* (London: Faber & Faber, 1946), pp. 186–9. See also Major Seagrim's personnel file, HS 9/1334/7.

14. TNA, HS 7/104, Lucas report, p19; FO 371/83110, 'The Karens of Burma', F.O. Research Department, 19 January 1950.

15. TNA, CAB 66/65/40, White Paper on Burma Policy, 8 May 1945.

16. BBC *Timewatch*, 'Forgotten Allies', Episode 6, 1997 available on www.youtube.com.

17. Author interview with a former FANY who wished to remain anonymous, Special Forces Club, London, 7 June 2011. A Cipher clerk was responsible for encoding and decoding messages to and from operations, but not the transmission. They were kept strictly separate from those sending and receiving the messages.

18. TNA, CAB 66/65/40, White Paper on Burma Policy, 8 May 1945.

19. See Patrick Leigh Fermor, *Abducting a General* (London: John Murray, 2014).

20. TNA, FO 371/83110, C.F. Grant, 'The Case for the Karens', 4 January 1950. Grant had spent 37 years in the Burma Civil Service.

21. TNA, FO 371/83110, Draft letter to Mr H. Berry MP from the Minister of State, 13 January 1950.

22. Mikael Gravers, 'The Karen Making of a Nation' in *Asian Forms of the Nation*, edited by Stein Tonnesson and Hans Antlov (London: Routledge, 2003), p. 243.

23. BL, IOR M/4/3023, P.G.E. Nash to Sir Gilbert Laithwaite, 12 August 1946, reproduced in Tinker, *Burma, The Struggle for Independence*, pp. 949–50.

24. TNA, FO 643/78, letter to Sir Gilbert Laithwaite, Secretary of State for Burma, from P.G.E. Naah, 15 October 1946.

25. TNA, FO, 643/78, to Governor Sir Reginald Dorman-Smith from H.N.C. Stevenson, 18 December 1946, p. 3.

26. Ibid, p. 4. The *New Times* was regarded as the 'mouthpiece' of the British administration in the frontier areas, so Aung San's control of it was considered important.

27. TNA, FO 643/78, H.N.C. Stevenson, History of the UKIS Council, 18 December 1946.

28. George Appleton, 'Burma Two Years After Liberation', *International Affairs*, 23, 4 (Oct., 1947), p. 513. Appleton first went to Burma in 1927 with the Society for the Propagation of the Gospel (SPG). He escaped to India in 1942, and returned to Burma in 1945 with the civil government.

29. Appleton, 'Burma Two Years After Liberation', p. 511.

30. TNA, CAB 129/3, 'Developments in Burma', Memorandum by the Secretary of State for Burma (Pethick Lawrence), 6 October 1945.

31. S. R. Ashton, 'Burma, Britain, and the Commonwealth, 1946–56', *The Journal of Imperial and Commonwealth History*, 29, 1 (2001), p. 69.

32. See, for example, the *Asian Tribune*, 2010, http://www.asiantribune.com/news/2010/08/20/question-panglong-agreement-union-burma or *The Diplomat*, 2013 http://thediplomat.com/tag/1947-panglong-agreement/.

33. See, for example, http://world.time.com/2012/09/26/charm-offensive-burmas-president-and-opposition-leader-suu-kyi-visit-the-u-s/.

34. Matthew Walton, 'Ethnicity, Conflict, and History in Burma: The Myths of Panglong', *Asian Survey* 48, 6 (Nov/Dec 2008), pp. 889–910.

35. Possibly because these groups did not have the status of living in the Frontier Areas, although this would exclude the Naga.

36. TNA, FO 371/83110, 'The Karens of Burma', FO Research Department, 19 January 1950, pp. 5–6.

37. BL, IOR M/4/2811, The Panglong Agreement.

38. TNA, FO 371/83110, 'The Karens of Burma', p. 6.

39. The desire to help the Karens extended to America. Former OSS Detachment 101 officer Robert Flaherty believed that Tinker's 'claim that Force 136 is to blame for the political woes of the Karens is farcical to say the least', Robert Flaherty to H.A Stonor, 28 March 1982, private correspondence. Bennett family private collection.

40. Henry Stonor to various (un-named but including Tony Bennett), 22 March 1982, private correspondence. Bennett family private collection. Henry Stonor served with the Karens, but not Force 136. His obituary http://www.telegraph.co.uk/news/obituaries/1515119/Henry-Stonor.html.

41. The Burmese writer U Maung Maung shared Stonor's view that Tinker's two volumes excluded many important documents that would challenge the interpretations Tinker presented. See U Maung Maung, *Burmese Nationalist Movements* (Edinburgh: Kiscadale, 1989), p. x. For a defence of Tinker's choice of documents, see S. R. Ashton, 'Burma, Britain, and the Commonwealth, 1946–56', pp. 65–91 & endnote 2, p. 88.

42. Stonor to Saw Maw Reh (President of the Karenni State Revolutionary Council), 6 September 1985, p. 2. Bennett papers.

43. Walton, 'Ethnicity, Conflict, and History in Burma: The Myths of Panglong', p. 901.

44. TNA, FO 371/83110, 'The Karens of Burma', Foreign Office Research Department, 19 January 1950.

45. Gravers, 'The Karen Making of a Nation', p. 248.

46. TNA, FO 371/83110, 'The Karens Of Burma', Foreign Office Research Department, 19 January 1950, pp. 1–3.

47. U Maung Maung, *Burmese Nationalist Movements*, p. 288.

48. TNA, FO 371/83110, 'The Karens of Burma', p. 6.

49. TNA, FO 643/78, Saw Marshall Shwin to Sir Hubert Rance, 29 June 1947.

50. In 1949 the KNDO became the Karen National Liberation Army (KNLA).

51. TNA, FO 643/78, various correspondence between London and Rangoon dated 12 July, 17 July, 1 August, and 8 September 1947.

52. TNA, FO 643/78, hand-written note, 4 August 1947.

53. For the controversy over these events over time, see BBC documentary, *Who Really Killed Aung San*, July 1997. Available https://www.youtube.com/watch?v=N003jRV75kc.

54. TNA, FO 643/101 contains documents about the trials of Vivian and Young.

55. 'Who Really Killed Aung San?', From our Rangoon Correspondent, in *Karen National Union (KNU) Bulletin* Number 4, April 1986, available at http://www.ibiblio.org/obl/docs3/KNUBulletin04.pdf.

56. TNA, FO 643/101, 'Vivian File', 24 December 1948, p. 2. records Vivian as saying 'Someone in England also was interested in seeing him put away and not allowed to talk. If he could tell the facts there would be a big rumpus, espec. between British and Burmese.'

57. BBC *Timewatch*, 'Forgotten Allies', available https://www.youtube.com/watch?v=xTJ3q5yg38Q.

58. Richard Aldrich, 'Legacies of Secret Service', pp. 130–148.

59. See Ed Vulliamy and Helena Smith, 'Athens 1944: Britain's dirty secret', *The Observer*, 30 November 2014 [Online] http://www.theguardian.com/world/2014/nov/30/athens-1944-britains-dirty-secret.

60. TNA, FO 371/83110, 'The Karens of Burma', pp. 6–7.

61. TNA, FO 371/69513, statement by Alex Campbell, undated and untitled copy.

62. TNA, FO 371/69509, Dening to Bowker, 16 March 1948.

63. TNA, FO 371/83110, 'The Case for the Karens', 4 January 1950.

64. TNA, FO 371/69509, Esler Dening minutes, 18 August 1948.
65. TNA, KV 2/3862–69 contain the MI5 files on Tulloch from 1948 until 1952.
66. Major Campbell had served under Tulloch on Operation *Character*.
67. Aldrich, 'Legacies of Secret Service', p. 136.
68. TNA, FO 371/69513, 'Friends of the Burma Hill People', 9 December 1948.
69. Symons was met by Special Branch when he landed in Southampton. In their interrogation report, the police described him as 'a weak and thoroughly despicable character.' TNA, FO 371/69512, Special Branch Report 26 October 1948.
70. TNA, FO 371/69513, Campbell to Tulloch, 9 September 1948.
71. Tulloch contacted the Mawchi Mines for support in May 1949, but been unsuccessful, so it would appear that this claim was unfounded in 1948; See KV 2/3864, 'Extract from Telecheck on Tulloch on 13.4.49'.
72. TNA, FO 643/118, Bowker to Kyaw Nyein, 30 September 1948, and reply, 1 October 1948.
73. TNA, FO 953/286, P. Murray, 8 December 1948.
74. TNA, FO 371/75708, Burma Notes, W.B. Ledridge, 22 February 1949.
75. TNA FO 371/75668, 'Burma', 12 July 1949. Leslie Glass worked in the Burma Civil Service from 1934–47, and then for the Foreign Office. See his memoirs *The Changing of the Kings* (London: Peter Owen, 1985).
76. TNA, FO 371/75730, 'Vernacular Press', 8 July 1949.
77. TNA, FO 371/69509, Bowker to FO, 18 February 1948.
78. TNA, FO 371/69511, Rangoon to FO, 19 October 1948.
79. TNA, FO 643/119, Note, 27 October 1948. Frederick Wemyss' personnel file is HS 9/1576/4.
80. TNA, FO 371/69512, Bowker to FO, 10 November 1948.
81. See TNA, FO 643/101, to 'The British Embassy (Attn: Mr Baker) Rangoon', 16 October 1948.
82. Aubrey Buxton was an advocate for the Karen, see his letter to *The Spectator*, 3 September 1948 http://archive.spectator.co.uk/article/3rd-september-1948/15/letters-to-the-editor; TNA, FO 371/69511 where any suggestion of complicity in plotting with Tulloch was ruled out by Sir Gilbert Laithwaite in a letter to Paul Grey, 5 October 1948. John Bingley was the British Council Representative in Burma, and he had corresponded with U Saw before the latter's execution for the assassination of Aung San. Major Gilmour had served with the Chins, and had returned to the Chin Hills in 1948, see TNA, FO 371/69510, Bowker to FO, 4 October 1948. Jack Percival had been the Sydney Morning Herald's war correspondent, and had been a prisoner of the Japanese for three years in Manila. According to the evidence of Symons, the BOAC steward, Oscar Jackson was working with Major Tyce to ship arms to the Karen from Brisbane. Symonds thought Jackson was smuggling precious stones out of Burma to fund the arms, see TNA, FO 371/69512, Special Branch Report, 26 October 1948.
83. TNA, FO 371/69513, Bowker to FO, 24 December 1948.

84. Morrison, *Grandfather Longlegs*, pp. 186–9.
85. TNA, CAB 66/65/40, White Paper on Burma Policy, 8 May 1945.
86. TNA, FO 643/66, Sir Henry Knight to Lord Pethick-Lawrence, 5 August 1946, reproduced in Tinker, *Burma, The Struggle for Independence*, pp. 932–3.
87. BL, IOR M/4/2602, Minute by Sir Gilbert Laithwaite for Secretary of State for Burma, 5 July 1946, reproduced in ibid, pp. 877–8.
88. It would have been interesting if Churchill had remained Prime Minister, for the course of Burma's path to independence might have been very different. See his response to Attlee's Burma Independence Bill, Hansard, 5 November 1947, http://hansard.millbanksystems.com/commons/1947/nov/05/burma-independence-bill.

Conclusion

1. TNA, HS 9/1460/6, personnel file of Captain Arthur Thompson.
2. Anthony Beevor, *The Second World War* (London: Weidenfeld & Nicolsen, 2012), p. 696, described the Battle of the Breakout in July 1945, attributing 11,000 Japanese losses to 17 Division alone.
3. Richard Aldrich, *Intelligence and the War Against Japan* (Cambridge: Cambridge University Press, 2000), p. 336; Cruickshank, *SOE in the Far East*, p. 252.
4. Field Marshal William Slim, *Defeat into Victory* (London: Cassell, 1956), p. 546.
5. F.S.V Donnison, *British Military Administration in the Far East* (London: HMSO, 1956), p. 348.
6. On matters of high policy, however, this should not be considered a caveat, as the usual tactic was to stall until direction was received from government.
7. Nigel West, *Secret War* (London: Hodder & Stoughton, 1992), p. 173 ('Exorbitant Cost' is a chapter title); John Keegan, *The Second World War* (London: Arrow, 1990), p. 484.
8. Keegan, ibid, pp. 484–5.

BIBLIOGRAPHY

Archives

The National Archives (TNA), London

AIR 20: Air Ministry, and Ministry of Defence: Papers accumulated by the Air Historical Branch.

HS 1: Special Operations Executive: Far East.

HS 7: Special Operations Executive: Histories and War Diaries.

HS 8: Ministry of Economic Warfare, Special Operations Executive and successors: Headquarters: Records.

HS 9: Special Operations Executive: Personnel Files (PF Series).

HW 1: Government Code and Cypher School: Signals Intelligence Passed to the Prime Minister, Messages and Correspondence.

CAB 101: War Cabinet and Cabinet Office: Historical Section: War Histories (Second World War), Military.

CAB 102: War Cabinet and Cabinet Office: Historical Section: War Histories (Second World War), Civil.

CAB 106: War Cabinet and Cabinet Office: Historical Section: Archivist and Librarian Files.

CAB 121: Cabinet Office: Special Secret Information Centre.

FO 371: Foreign Office: Political Departments: General Correspondence from 1906–1966.

FO 643: Burma Office, Burma Secretariat, and Foreign Office, Embassy, Rangoon, Burma: General Correspondence.

KV 2: The Security Service: Personal (PF Series) Files.

PREM 3: Prime Minister's Office: Operational Correspondence and Papers.

PREM 4: Prime Minister's Office: Confidential Correspondence and Papers.

PREM 8: Prime Minister's Office: Correspondence and Papers, 1945–1951.

WO 106: War Office: Directorate of Military Operations and Military Intelligence, and predecessors: Correspondence and Papers.

WO 203: War Office: South East Asia Command: Military Headquarters Papers, Second World War.

WO 208: War Office: Directorate of Military Operations and Intelligence, and Directorate of Military Intelligence; Ministry of Defence, Defence Intelligence Staff.

WO 216: War Office: Office of the Chief of the Imperial General Staff: Papers.

WO 311: War Office: Judge Advocate General's Office, Military Deputy's Department, and War Office, Directorates of Army Legal Services and Personal Services: War Crimes Files.

The British Library (BL)
India Office Library (MSS EUR)

Orr, Cecil Bruce, *A Burma Patchwork*, 1977.
Stevenson, H.N.C., 'The Hill Peoples of Burma', 1944.
Tinker, Hugh Russell, 1941–6.

India Office Records

Records of the Military Department (IOR L/MIL).

Report to the Combined Chiefs of Staff by the Supreme Allied Commander South East Asia 1943–6, Rear-Admiral the Viscount Mountbatten of Burma. Vol. 2 – Appendices and annexures.

The Defence Services List for Burma, January, April and July 1941.

Army in Burma Orders Jan–Mar 1942.

Report on the Burma campaign 1941–2. Sir Reginald Dorman-Smith, GBE, Governor of Burma.

Oung, Tun Hla.

Maung Tun Hla Oung.

1   Political and Secret Department Records (IOR L/PS)
    Lieutenant Colonel J.C. Tulloch: Activities against Burmese Government.
2   War Staff (IOR L/WS)
    War Staff 1942–3.
    War Staff 1942–4.
3   Burma Office Records (IOR M)
    Defence: question of mobilising guerrilla activity behind the lines in Burma, March–April 1942.
    Burma Defence Bureau monthly intelligence summaries, 1941–Mar 1942.
    S.C. Pollard, Burma Frontier Service.
    U Tun Hla Oung, Burma Police.
    Civil Services: L.C. Glass.
    Rebellions in Burma: Disturbances in Pyapon.
    Wish of Karen National Association for expansion of Karen constituencies to Pegu Division.
    Correspondence: fortnightly letters, Defence and External Affairs Dept.
4   India Office Records transferred later through official channels (IOR/R)
    Civil Affairs Service (Burma) Intelligence, 1944–1945.
    Japanese offer of independence to Burma, 28 Jan–11 Feb 1943; Declaration of Burma's independence, 1 August 1943, and effect on future British policy, 3 Aug 194–21 Nov 1944.

5   Official Publications (IOR V)
    Burma Frontier Force: Report on the Administration of the Burma Frontier
    Force, 1937.

The Imperial War Museum (IWM)

Department of Documents

IWM 15095, Papers of Sergeant R. Brierley.
IWM 12840, Papers of Captain D.D. Guthrie.
IWM 4879, Papers of Lieutenant Colonel D. Herring.
Papers of Major J.P. Lucas.
Papers of Colin Mackenzie (un-catalogued).
IWM 12104, Papers of Major R.A. Rubinstein.
IWM, 08/49/1, Lieutenant Colonel J. Cromarty Tulloch, unpublished memoir.
Papers of Lieutenant Colonel J. Smallwood.

Sound Archive

Sergeant Frederick Bailey (Sound Archive interview number 11752).
Captain Robert Barron (Sound Archive interview number 10887).
Major Robert Boiteaux-Burdett (Sound Archive interview number 9851).
Sergeant Ronald Brierley (Sound Archive interview number 10314).
William Brough (Sound Archive interview number 15741).
Sergeant Ken Brown (Sound Archive interview number 16760).
Major Thomas Carew (Sound Archive interview number 18357).
Sergeant Ronald Chatten (Sound Archive interview number 17992).
Captain Oswin Craster (Sound Archive interview number 12612).
Captain Harry Despaigne (Sound Archive interview number 9925).
Sergeant Don Gibbs (Sound Archive interview number 9126).
Sergeant Eric Grinham (Sound Archive interview number 8744).
Captain Duncan Guthrie (Sound Archive interview number 12354).
Major Neville Hogan (Sound Archive interview number 12342).
Captain Harold James (Sound Archive interview number 12438).
Sergeant Robert Loosmore (Sound Archive interview number 17949).
Colin Mackenzie (Sound Archive interview number 9471).
Captain John Marchant (Sound Archive interview number 17326).
Major Jack McFarlane (Sound Archive interview number 9782).
Major Richard Rubinstein (Sound Archive interview number 11037).
Sergeant John Smallwood (Sound Archive interview number 17998).
Sergeant Norman Smith (Sound Archive interview number 17741).
Sergeant Gordon Tack (Sound Archive interview number 16699).
Major Aubrey Trofimov (Sound Archive interview number 11760).

National Archives and Records Administration (NARA),
Maryland, United States

RG 493, Records of the China Burma India Theater.

Papers in Private Hands

Major Eric Battersby (unpublished memoir)
Captain Anthony Bennett
Sergeant Roger Leney (unpublished memoir)
Sergeant Glyn Loosmore

Interviews

Major Ian Abbey
Philip Barnard
Desmond Kelly
Saw Noe
Ian Trenowden
Robert Callow
Anonymous, Special Forces Club

Books, Chapters and Articles

Aldrich, Richard, *Intelligence and the War Against Japan: Britain, America and the politics of Secret Service* (Cambridge: Cambridge University Press, 2000).

———, 'Legacies of Secret Service: Renegade SOE & the Karen Struggle in Burma 1948–1950', *Intelligence and National Security*, 14, 4 (1999), pp. 130–48.

Allen, Louis, *Burma: The Longest War 1942–1945* (London: Phoenix Giant, 1998).

Anglim, Simon, 'MI(R), G(R) and British Covert Operations 1939–1942', *Intelligence and National Security*, 20, 4 (December 2005), pp. 631–53.

Appleton, George, 'Burma Two Years After Liberation', *International Affairs*, 23, 4 (Oct 1947), pp. 510–21.

Ashton, S.R., 'Burma, Britain, and the Commonwealth, 1946–56', *The Journal of Imperial and Commonwealth History*, 29, 1 (2001), pp. 65–91.

Bailey, Roderick, *Forgotten Voices of the Secret War: An Inside History of Special Operations During the Second World War* (London: Ebury Press, 2008).

———, *Target: Italy* (London: Faber, 2014).

———, *The Wildest Province: SOE in the Land of the Eagle* (London: Jonathan Cape, 2008).

Balfour Oatts, Lt. Col., *The Jungle in Arms* (London: New English Library, 1976).

Ban Hah Choon, *Absent History: The Untold Story of Special Branch Operations in Singapore, 1942–1945* (Singapore: Raffles, 2001).

Barnard, Jack, *The Hump* (London: Four Square, 1966).

Bayley, Christopher, and Harper, Tim, *Forgotten Armies: Britain's Asian Empire and the War with Japan* (London: Penguin, 2005).

Beamish, John, *Burma Drop* (London: Bestseller Library, 1960).

Beevor, Anthony, *The Second World War* (London: Weidenfeld & Nicolsen, 2012).

Beevor, Jack, *SOE: Recollections and Reflections 1940–1945* (London: Bodley Head, 1981).

Bidwell, Shelford, 'Wingate and the Official Historians: An Alternative View', *Journal of Contemporary History*, 15, 2 (April 1980), pp. 245–56.

Binney, Marcus, *Secret War Heroes: Men of the Special Operations Executive* (London: Hodder, 2006).

Black, Jeremy, *World War Two: A Military History* (London: Routledge, 2003).

Blumenson, Martin, 'Can Official History be Honest History', *Military Affairs* 26, 4 (Winter 1962–3), pp. 153–61.

Bowen, John, *Undercover in the Jungle* (London: William Kimber, 1978).

Burchett, W.G., *Trek Back From Burma* (Allahbad: Kitabistan, 1942).

Callahan, Mary, *Making Enemies: War and State Building in Burma* (Cornell University Press, 2003).

Callahan, Raymond, *Burma 1942–1945* (London: Davis-Poynter, 1978).

Calvert, Michael, *Chindits: Long Range Penetration* (London: Pan, 1974).

Carew, Keggie, *Dadland* (London: Chatto & Windus, 2016).

Chapman, F. Spencer, *The Jungle is Neutral* (London: Chatto & Windus, 1949).

Cheah Boon Kheng, *Red Star Over Malaya: Resistance and Social Conflict During and After the Japanese Occupation, 1941–1945* (Singapore: Singapore University Press, 2003).

Christie, Arthur, *Mission Scapula* (Staffordshire: Panda Press, 2004).

Churchill, Winston, *The Second World War, Vol. IV 'The Hinge of Fate'* (London: The Reprint Society, 1953).

Clifford, Francis, *A Battle Is Fought to be Won* (London: Corgi, 1973).

———, Desperate Journey (London: Corgi, 1981).

Collis, Maurice, *Last and First in Burma, 1941–1948* (London: Faber, 1956).

Crosby, M.G.M, *Irregular Soldier* (The Guernsey Press, 1993).

Cruickshank, Charles, *SOE in the Far East* (Oxford: Oxford University Press, 1986).

———, *SOE in Scandinavia* (Oxford: Oxford University Press, 1986).

Darwin, John, *The End of The British Empire* (Oxford: Blackwell, 1991).

Davies, Norman, *Europe at War 1939–1945: No Simple Victory* (London: Macmillan, 2007).

Dear, Ian, *Sabotage and Subversion: Stories from the files of SOE and OSS* (London: Arms & Armour, 1996).

Donnison, F.S.V., *British Military Administration in the Far East, 1943–1946* (London: HMSO, 1956).

Dun, Smith, *Memoirs of a Four-Foot Colonel* (New York: Cornell University, 1980).

Dunlop, Richard, *Behind Japanese Lines: With the OSS in Burma* (New York: Rand McNally & Co., 1979).

Evans, Geoffrey, *The Johnnies* (London: Cassell, 1964).

Farrell, Brian, 'High Command, Irregular Forces, and Defending Malaya, 1941–1942', *Global War Studies*, 8, 2 (2011), pp. 32–65.

Fellowes-Gordon, Ian, *Amiable Assassins* (London: Panther Books, 1958).

Fermor, Patrick Leigh, *Abducting a General* (London: John Murray, 2014).

Foot, M.R.D., *SOE 1940–46* (London: Mandarin, 1990).

———, *SOE In France* (London: Routledge, 2006).

———, *SOE in the Low Countries* (London: St Ermin's Press, 2001).

———, 'Reflections on SOE', *Manchester Library and Philosophical Memoirs and Proceedings*, 1968, pp. 87–96.

———, 'Was SOE Any Good?', *Journal of Contemporary History*, 16, 1 (Part 1, Jan 1981), pp. 167–81.

———, 'What Use Was SOE?', *The RUSI Journal*, 148, 1 (Feb 2003), pp. 76–83.

Furnivall, J.S, 'Twilight in Burma: Reconquest and Crisis', *Pacific Affairs*, 22, 1 (Mar 1949), pp. 3–20.

Glass, Leslie, *The Changing of the Kings: Memories of Burma 1934–1949* (London: Peter Owen, 1985).

Gough, Richard, *SOE Singapore 1941–42* (London: William Kimber, 1985).

Grant, Ian Lyall, *Burma: The Turning point* (Chichester: The Zampi Press, 1993).

Gravers, Mikael, 'The Karen Making of a Nation' in *Asian Forms of the Nation*, edited by Stein Tonnesson and Hans Antlov (London: Routledge, 2003).

Gray, Colin S, *Modern Strategy* (Oxford: Oxford University Press, 1999).

Guthrie, Duncan, *Jungle Diary* (London: Macmillan, 1946).

Hack, Karl & Blackburn, Kevin, *Did Singapore Have to Fall? Churchill and the Impregnable Fortress* (London: Routledge, 2004).

Hamond, Robert, *The Flame of Freedom* (London: Leo Cooper, 1988).

Hastings, Max, *All Hell Let Loose: The World at War 1939–1945* (London: Harper, 2011).

Hedley, John, DSO, *Jungle Fighter* (Brighton: Tom Donovan, 1996).

Hendershot, Clarence, 'Burma's Value to the Japanese', *Far Eastern Survey*, 11, 16 (Aug 1942), pp. 176–8.

————, 'The Liberation of Burma', *The Pacific Historical Review*, 13, 3 (Sept 1944), pp. 271–7.

Higham, Robin, *The Writing of Official Military Histories* (London: Greenwood Press, 1999).

Hilsman, Roger, *American Guerrilla: My War Behind Japanese Lines* (Washington DC: Potomac, 2005).

Hough, Richard, *Mountbatten: Hero of Our Time* (London: Book Club Associates, 1989).

Irwin, Anthony, *Burmese Outpost* (London: Collins, 1945).

Jackson, Ashley, *The British Empire and the Second World War* (London: Continuum, 2006).

Keegan, John, *The Second World War* (London: Pimlico, 1997).

Kelly, Desmond, *Kelly's Burma Campaign* (London: Tiddim Press, 2002).

Kelly, Saul, 'A Succession of Crises: SOE in the Middle East', *Intelligence and National Security*, 20, 1 (March 2005), pp. 121–46.

Kirby, S.W., *The War Against Japan*, Vols. I–IV (London: HMSO, 1959–1969).

Kratoska, Paul (Editor), *Southeast Asian Minorities in the Wartime Japanese Empire* (London: Routledge-Curzon, 2002).

Latimer, Jon, *Burma: The Forgotten War* (London: Murray, 2004).

Lett, Brian, *SOE's Mastermind: An Authorized Biography of Major General Sir Colin Gubbins* (Barnsley: Pen & Sword, 2016).

Lewin, Ronald, *Slim: The Standard Bearer* (Ware: Wordsworth, 1999).

Liddell-Hart, Basil, 'Responsibility and Judgement in History Writing', *Military Affairs*, 23, 1 (Spring 1959), pp. 35–6.

Lunt, James, *A Hell of a Licking: The Retreat From Burma 1941–42* (London: Collins, 1986).

Lyman, Robert, *Slim, Master of War: Burma and the birth of modern warfare* (London: Robinson, 2005).

————, *The Generals: From Defeat to Victory, Leadership in Asia 1941–1945* (London: Constable, 2008).

Mackenzie, Compton, *Eastern Epic, Vol. 1* (London: Chatto & Windus, 1951).

Mackenzie, William, *The Secret History of SOE* (London: St Ermin's Press, 2002).

Maung Maung, Pye, *Burma in the Crucible* (Madras: Diocesan Press, 1951).

Maung Maung, U, *Burmese Nationalist Movements 1940–1948* (Edinburgh: Kiscadale, 1989).

Maw, Ba, *Break-Through in Burma: Memoirs of a Revolution, 1939–1946* (London: Yale University Press, 1968).

McEnery, John H., *Epilogue in Burma 1945–48* (Tunbridge Wells: Spellmount, 1990).

McNab, Duncan, *Mission 101: The Untold Story of the SOE and the Second World War in Ethiopia* (Stroud: The History Press, 2012).

Michel, Henri, *The Shadow War: Resistance in Europe 1939–45* (London: History Book Club, 1972).

Miller, Russell, *Behind the Lines: The Oral History of Special Operations in World War Two* (London: Pimlico, 2003).

Morrison, Ian, *Grandfather Longlegs* (London: Faber, 1947).

Mountbatten, Lord Louis, *Personal Diary Supreme Allied Commander South-East Asia 1943–1946*, edited by Philip Ziegler (London: Collins, 1988).

Munro-Faure, Paul Hector, 'Guerrilla Training, Maymyo 1941', *Journal of the Royal Asiatic Society*, 31 (1991), pp. 113–148.

———, 'Behind the Front Lines in Burma, The Marches of the Salween Border, 1942–1944, *Journal of the Royal Asiatic Society*, 32 (1992), pp. 135–79.

Myint-U, Thant, *The River of Lost Footsteps: A Personal History of Burma* (London: Faber & Faber, 2008).

Naw, Angelene, *Aung San and the Struggle for Burmese Independence* (Copenhagen: NIAS, 2001).

Nesbit, Roy Conyers, *The Battle for Burma* (Barnsley: Pen & Sword, 2009).

Nu, Thakin, *Burma Under the Japanese* (London: Macmillan, 1954).

O'Brien, Terrence, *The Moonlight War: The Story of Clandestine Operations in South-East Asia, 1944–5* (London: Collins, 1987).

Ogden, Alan, *Tigers Burning Bright: SOE Heroes in the Far East* (London: Bene Factum, 2013).

Overy, Richard, *Why the Allies Won* (London: Pimlico, 2006).

Owen, Frank OBE, *The Campaign in Burma*, Arrow Books (Tiptree: Anchor Press, 1957).

Peacock, Geraldine, *The Life of a Jungle Walla: Reminiscences in the life of Lieutenant-Colonel E.M. Peacock* (Ilfracombe: Arthur Stockwell Ltd, 1958).

Peers, William R. and Brelis, Dean, *Behind the Burma Road* (New York: Avon, 1963).

Redding, Tony, *War in the Wilderness: The Chindits in Burma 1943–1944* (Stroud: Spellmount, 2011).

Remme, Tilman, *Britain and Regional Cooperation in South-East Asia, 1945–1949* (London: Routledge, 1995).

Reynolds, E. Bruce, *Thailand's Secret War* (Cambridge: Cambridge University Press, 2005).

Richell, Judith, *Disease and Demography in Colonial Burma* (Singapore: NUS Press, 2006).

Rooney, David, *Wingate and the Chindits: Redressing the Balance* (London: Cassell, 2000).

Saquety, Troy, *The OSS in Burma* (Kansas: University Press of Kansas, 2013).

Seaman, Mark, 'A Glass Half Full: Some Thoughts on the Evolution of the Study of SOE', *Intelligence and National Security*, 20, 1 (March 2005), pp. 27–43.

————, *Special Operations Executive: A New Instrument of War* (London: Routledge, 2006).

Selth, Andrew, 'Race and Resistance in Burma, 1942 – 1945', *Modern Asian Studies*, 20, 3 (1986), pp. 483–507.

Short, Stanley, *On Burma's Eastern Frontier*, Marshall (London: Morgan & Scott Ltd, 1945).

Silverstein, Josef, 'The Other Side of Burma's Struggle for Independence', *Pacific Affairs*, 58, 1 (Spring 1985), pp. 98–108.

Slim, Field Marshal Sir William, *Defeat into Victory* (London: Pan, 1989).

Stafford, David, *Britain and European Resistance 1940–1945: A Survey of the Special Operations Executive* (London: Macmillan, 1980).

————, *Churchill and Secret Service* (London: Abacus, 2000).

————, *Mission Accomplished: SOE and Italy, 1943–1945* (London: The Bodley Head, 2011).

————, *Secret Agent: Britain's Wartime Secret Service* (London: BBC, 2002).

Steinbeck, John, *The Moon Is Down* (London: Penguin, 2000).

Stilwell, Joseph, *The Stilwell Papers* (London: Macdonald & Co., 1949).

Sweet-Escott, Bickham, *Baker Street Irregular* (London: Methuen & Co., 1965).

————, 'Correspondence', *International Affairs*, 48, 3 (1972), pp. 552–5.

Sykes, Christopher, *Orde Wingate* (London: Collins, 1959).

Tamayama, Kazuo, & Nunneley, John, *Tales By Japanese Soldiers of the Burma Campaign 1942–1945* (London: Cassell, 2000).

Taylor, C.G. *The Forgotten Ones of South East Asia Command and Force 136* (Ilfracombe: Arthur Stockwell, 1989).

Taylor, Robert H, *Marxism and Resistance in Burma 1942–1945* (Ohio: Ohio University Press, 1984).

Thompson, Julian, *The Imperial War Museum Book of the War in Burma 1942–1945* (London: Pan, 2003).

————, *Forgotten Voices of the Burma Campaign* (London: Ebury Press, 2009).

Thorne, Christopher, *Allies of a Kind: The United States, Britain, and the War Against Japan* (Oxford: Oxford University Press, 1979).

Tinker, Hugh, *The Union of Burma* (Oxford: Oxford University Press, 1959).

Tinker, Hugh and Griffin, Andrew, *Burma – The Struggle for Independence, 1944–48*, HMSO, 1983, Vols 1&2.

Trager, Frank, *Burma: Japanese Military Administration, Selected Documents 1941–45*, translated by Won Zoon Yoon (Philadelphia: University of Pennsylvania Press, 1971).

————, 'Review', *The Journal of Asian Studies*, 44, 1 (Nov. 1984), pp. 251–2.

Trenowden, Ian, *Operations Most Secret: SOE the Malayan Theatre* (Bodmin: Crecy Books, 1994).

Verlander, Harry, *My War in SOE: Behind Enemy Lines in France and Burma* (Bromley: Independent Books, 2010).

Walton, Calder, *Empire of Secrets: British Intelligence, the Cold War and the Twilight of Empire* (London: Harper, 2013).

Walton, Matthew, 'Ethnicity, Conflict, and History in Burma: The Myths of Panglong', *Asian Survey* 48, 6 (Nov/Dec 2008), pp. 889–910.

Warren, Alan, *Burma 1942: The Road from Rangoon to Mandalay* (London: Continuum, 2011).

West, Nigel, *Secret War: The Story of SOE, Britain's Wartime Sabotage Organisation* (London: Hodder and Stoughton, 1992).

Wheeler, Mark, 'The SOE Phenomenon', *Journal of Contemporary History*, 16, 3 (Part 2, July 1981), pp. 513–9.

Wilkinson, Peter, and Astley, Joan Bright, *Gubbins and SOE* (Barnsley: Pen & Sword, 2010).

Wylie, Neville, 'SOE: New Approaches and Perspectives', *Intelligence and National Security*, 20, 1 (March 2005), pp. 1–13.

———, 'Ungentlemanly Warriors or Unreliable Diplomats? SOE and Irregular Political Activities in Europe', *Intelligence and National Security*, 20, 1 (March 2005), pp. 98–120.

Websites (last accessed August 2016)

Asian Tribune, 2010. [Online] Available from: http://www.asiantribune.com/news/2010/08/20/question-panglong-agreement-union-burma.

British Resistance March at the Cenotaph. [Online] Available from: http://www.coleshillhouse.com/march-at-the-cenotaph-campaign.php.

Burma 1942, Clayton Newell, US Army Center of Military History, January 1995 [Online]. http://www.history.army.mil/brochures/burma42/burma42.htm.

Burma Independence Bill, Hansard, 5 November 1947. [Online] Available at http://hansard.millbanksystems.com/commons/1947/nov/05/burma-independence-bill.

Burma Map of Ethnicities. The Rohingya League for Democracy [Online] Available from: http://www.rldb.org/rldb/.

Burma's President and Opposition Leader Suu Kyi Visit the U.S., as Washington Eases Sanctions, Hannah Beech, 26 September 2012. [Online] Available from: http://world.time.com/2012/09/26/charm-offensive-burmas-president-and-opposition-leader-suu-kyi-visit-the-u-s/.

Chindits. [Online] Available from: http://www.chindits.info/Longcloth/Main.htm

The Diplomat, 2013. [Online] Available from: http://thediplomat.com/tag/1947-panglong-agreement/.

Divisional Structure. [Online] Available from: www.mnstartfire.com.

Forgotten Allies, BBC 'Timewatch', 1997. [Online] Available from: http://www.youtube.com/watch?v=MUOUW8Ajjs.

Forgotten Allies. [Online] Available from: www.rainbowends.org/karen/witness.htm.

Imperial War Museum. [Online] Available from: www.iwm.org.uk.

Japanese invasion of Burma. [Online] Available from: www.onwar.com.

Map of Shan States, LnL Mining Co. Ltd. [Online] Available from http://www.lnlmining.com/img/img-35.jpg.

Obituaries: Henry Stonor, 8 April 2006. [Online] Available from: http://www.telegraph.co.uk/news/obituaries/1515119/Henry-Stonor.html.

Obituaries: Lord Gladwyn Jebb, 26 October 1996. [Online] Available from: http://www.independent.co.uk/news/people/obituaries-lord-gladwyn-1360227.html.

Observer, The, Ed Vulliamy and Helena Smith, 'Athens 1944: Britain's dirty secret', The *Observer*, 30 November 2014 [Online] http://www.theguardian.com/world/2014/nov/30/athens-1944-britains-dirty-secret.

Office of Strategic Services. [Online] Available from: https://groups.yahoo.com/neo/groups/osssociety/info.

Operations in the Far East, Sir Robert Brooke-Popham, Supplement to the London Gazette, 22 January 1948, p. 535. [Online] Available from: http://www.ibiblio.org/hyperwar/UN/UK/LondonGazette/38183.pdf.

RAAF personnel serving on attachment in Royal Air Force. [Online] Available from: http://www.awm.gov.au/catalogue/research_centre/pdf/rc09125z008_1.pdf p. 28.

The Reconquest of Burma. [Online] Available from: http://www.ibiblio.org/hyperwar/UN/UK/UK-RAF-III/img/RAF-3-16-5.jpg.

Records of Coats Viyella plc. [Online] Available from: http://archiveshub.ac.uk/features/02120302.html.

Smith, Sir Reginald Dorman (1899–1977), Oxford Dictionary of National Biography, Oxford University Press, 2004. [Online] Available from: www.oxforddnb.com/view/article/58640.

Special Operations Executive. [Online] Available from: www.groups.yahoo.com.

The Spectator, Aubrey Buxton letter, 3 September 1948. [Online] Available from http://archive.spectator.co.uk/article/3rd-september-1948/15/letters-to-the-editor.

'Transportation System 1942–1943', in Charles Romanus and Riley Sunderland, *United States Army in World War II: China-Burma-India Theater* (Location: Dept. of the Army, Office of the Chief of Military History, 1953). [Online] Available from http://www.lib.utexas.edu/maps/historical/india_china_transportation_1942_1943.jpg.

Who Really Killed Aung San? BBC, July 1997. [Online] Available from: https://www.youtube.com/watch?v=N003jRV75kc.

Who Really Killed Aung San? From our Rangoon Correspondent, in *Karen National Union (KNU) Bulletin* Number 4, April 1986. [Online] Available from: http://www.ibiblio.org/obl/docs3/KNUBulletin04.pdf.

INDEX

Plate 1 Sabotage of railway by Major Lucas of Operation *Character, Mongoose Blue* at 20:15 hours on 2 May 1945. Approximately 250 Japanese troops plus four wagons of stores were derailed.
Source: The National Archives, HS 7/107.

Plate 2 Captain Godfrey Vivian, Operation *Character, Otter*, with surrendered Japanese weapons.
Source: The National Archives, HS 7/107.

Plate 3 A Karen levy named 'Maurice', apparently 15 years old. Operation *Character, Mongoose Green* (Major Trofimov).
Source: The National Archives, HS 7/107.

Plate 4 The Toungoo to Mawchi Road, scene of fierce fighting by the Oriental Mission in 1942 and again as Force 136 in 1945.
Source: The National Archives, HS 7/107.

Plate 5   Lt.Col. Peacock with levies of Operation *Character, Otter,* showing off the victim of one of their many ambushes on the Mawchi Road, 1945.
Source: The National Archives, HS 7/107.

Plate 6   A rather macabre photo of the carnage caused by Operation *Character* on the Toungoo to Mawchi Road.
Source: The National Archives, HS 7/107.

Plate 7   Lt.Col. Edgar Peacock with recruits for Operation *Character, Otter.*
Source: The National Archives, HS 7/107.

Plate 8   Japanese officers were attached to some Force 136 teams in order
to help convince other Japanese units that Japan had surrendered and that
the war had been over since 15 August 1945.
Source: The National Archives, HS 7/107.

Plate 9 Major Trofimov of Operation *Character, Mongoose Green* with Karen recruits. The Karen called Trofimov 'Pa-gaw-koe' which means 'Red Haired'. Photograph courtesy of Simon Leney, Sergeant Roger Leney's son.

Plate 10 Lysander on the airstrip at Bolo Auk, Operation *Character, Mongoose White*. Photograph courtesy of Simon Leney.

Plate 11 Lysander at Bolo Auk with unknown Lieutenant and Karen recruits. Photograph courtesy of Simon Leney.

Plate 12 The levies of Operation *Character, Mongoose*, on their own Victory Parade in October 1945 with Major Bourne (front, centre). The Karens called Bourne 'Pa-ma-dai' or 'Mr Tentmaker' 'because wherever he went he asked the Karens to make bamboo huts'. Note 15-year-old Maurice bottom left. Photograph courtesy of Simon Leney.

Plate 13 Major Milner with a mortar platoon, *Mongoose* Victory Parade, October 1945. The Karen called Major Milner 'a gentleman who never swears', and sometimes 'Pa Bren Gun' because of his 'complete mastery over this favourite weapon of his'. Photograph courtesy of Simon Leney.

Plate 14 Lots of Bren Guns on display at the *Mongoose* Victory Parade, October 1945. Photograph courtesy of Simon Leney.

Plate 15 Lysander over the Burmese jungle. Like in Europe, the Lysander did sterling work for SOE in Burma. Photograph courtesy of Simon Leney.

Plate 16 *The Daily Worker*, Wednesday 22 December 1948 'Britons in Burma Rising Plot'. Headlines about the two former Force 136 officers, Tulloch and Campbell, and their alleged postwar support for the Karen against the government of the Union of Burma.
Source: The National Archives, FO 371/69513.

Lightning Source UK Ltd.
Milton Keynes UK
UKHW020636260721
387769UK00007B/187

9 781788 319881